# ART BOOKS

## FROM CRESCENT MOON PUBLISHING

*Leonardo da Vinci*
by James Pearson

*Early Netherlandish Painting*
by Rosalind Mutter

*Piero della Francesca*
by Naomi Haskell

*Giovanni Bellini*
by Julia Davis

*Eric Gill: Nuptials of God*
by Anthony Hoyland

*Minimal Art and Artists In the 1960s and After*
by Laura Garrard

*Postwar Art*
by George Knighton

*Vincent van Gogh: Visionary Landscapes*
by Stuart Morris

*Max Beckmann*
by Stuart Morris

*Egon Schiele: Sex and Death in Purple Stockings*
by D. Simon Eade

*Mark Rothko: The Art of Transcendence*
by Julia Davis

*Jasper Johns*
by L.M. Poole

*Brice Marden*
by Laura Garrard

*Frank Stella: American Abstract Artist*
by James Pearson

# THE EARLIER AND LATER
# WORK OF TITIAN

# THE EARLIER AND LATER
# WORK OF TITIAN

## CLAUDE PHILLIPS

*Keeper of the Wallace Collection*

CRESCENT MOON

First published 1897/ 98. This edition © 2018.

Printed and bound in the U.S.A.
Set in Book Antiqua 10 on 14pt.
Designed by Radiance Graphics.

*British Library Cataloguing in Publication data*

*ISBN-13 9781861716668 (Pbk)*
*ISBN-13 9781861716934 (Hbk)*

CRESCENT MOON PUBLISHING
*P.O. Box 1312, Maidstone, Kent, ME14 5XU*
*Great Britain, www.crmoon.com*

CONTENTS


THE EARLIER WORK OF TITAN

THE LATER WORK OF TITAN

NOTE ON THE TEXT

The text is from *The Earlier Work of Titian* by Claude Phillips, 1897 and *The Earlier Work of Titian* by Claude Phillips, 1898.

Footnotes are in square brackets, thus: [*1]

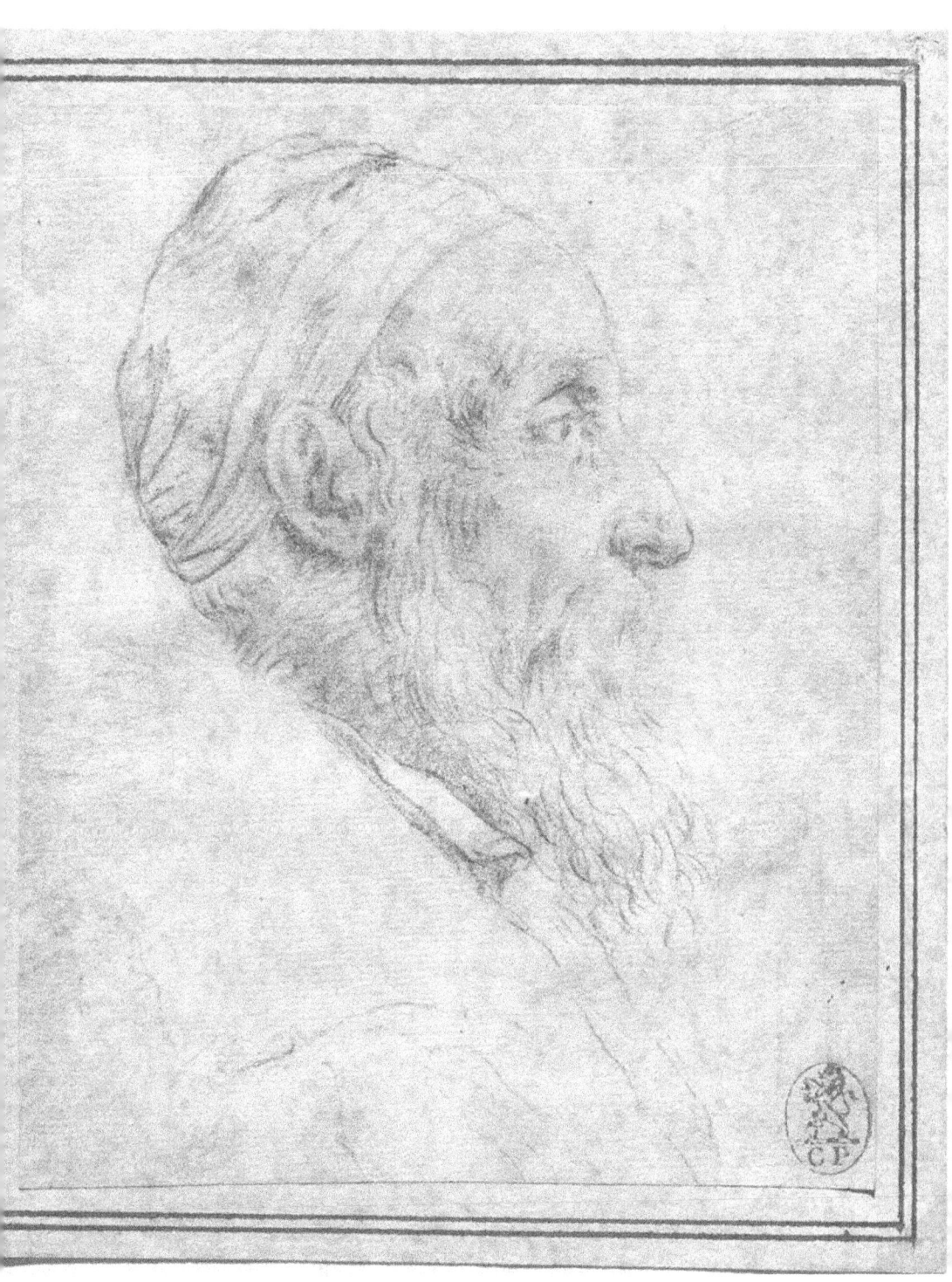

Titian, Self-Portrait

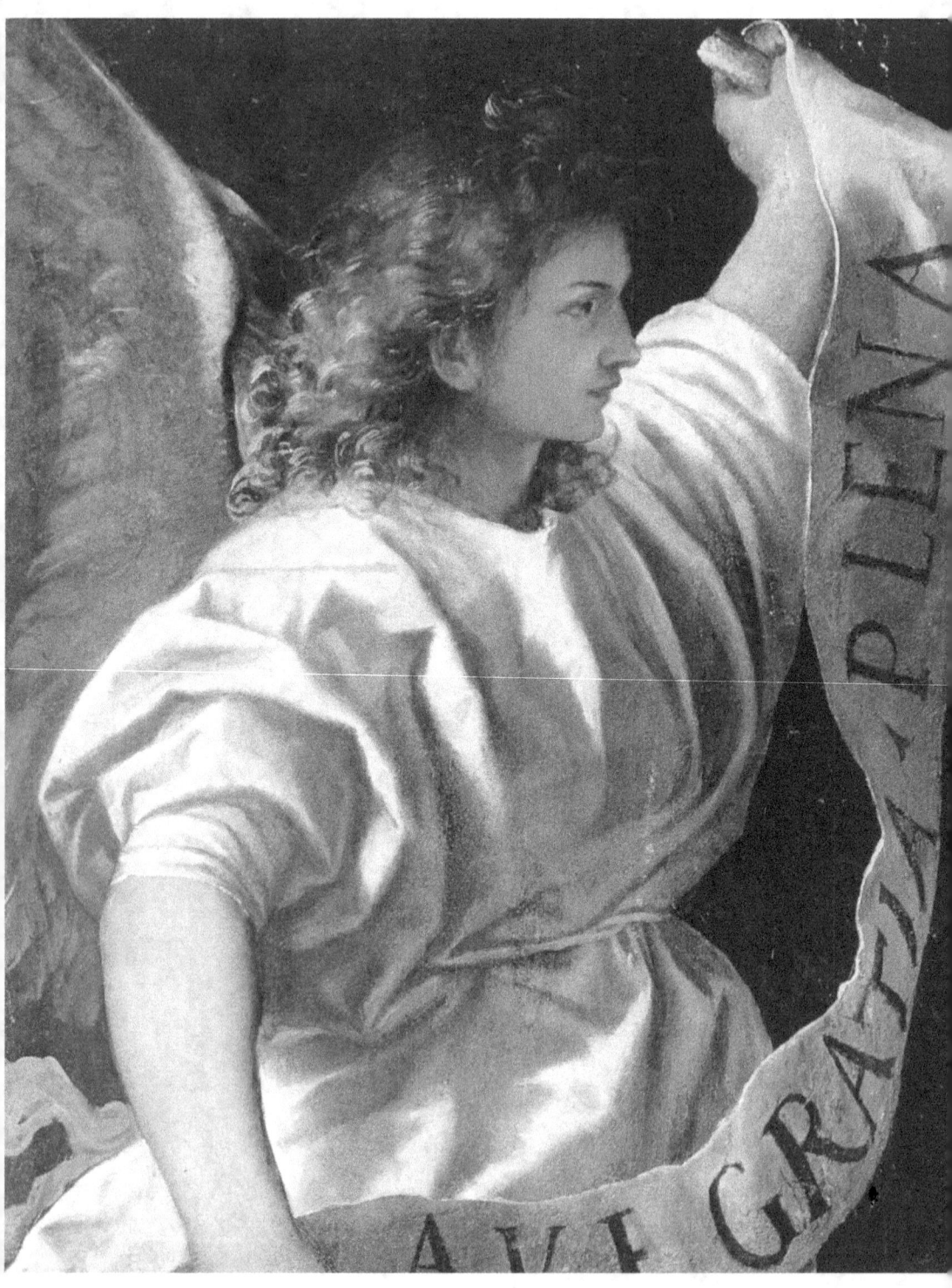

Titian, Annunciation, 1522, detail

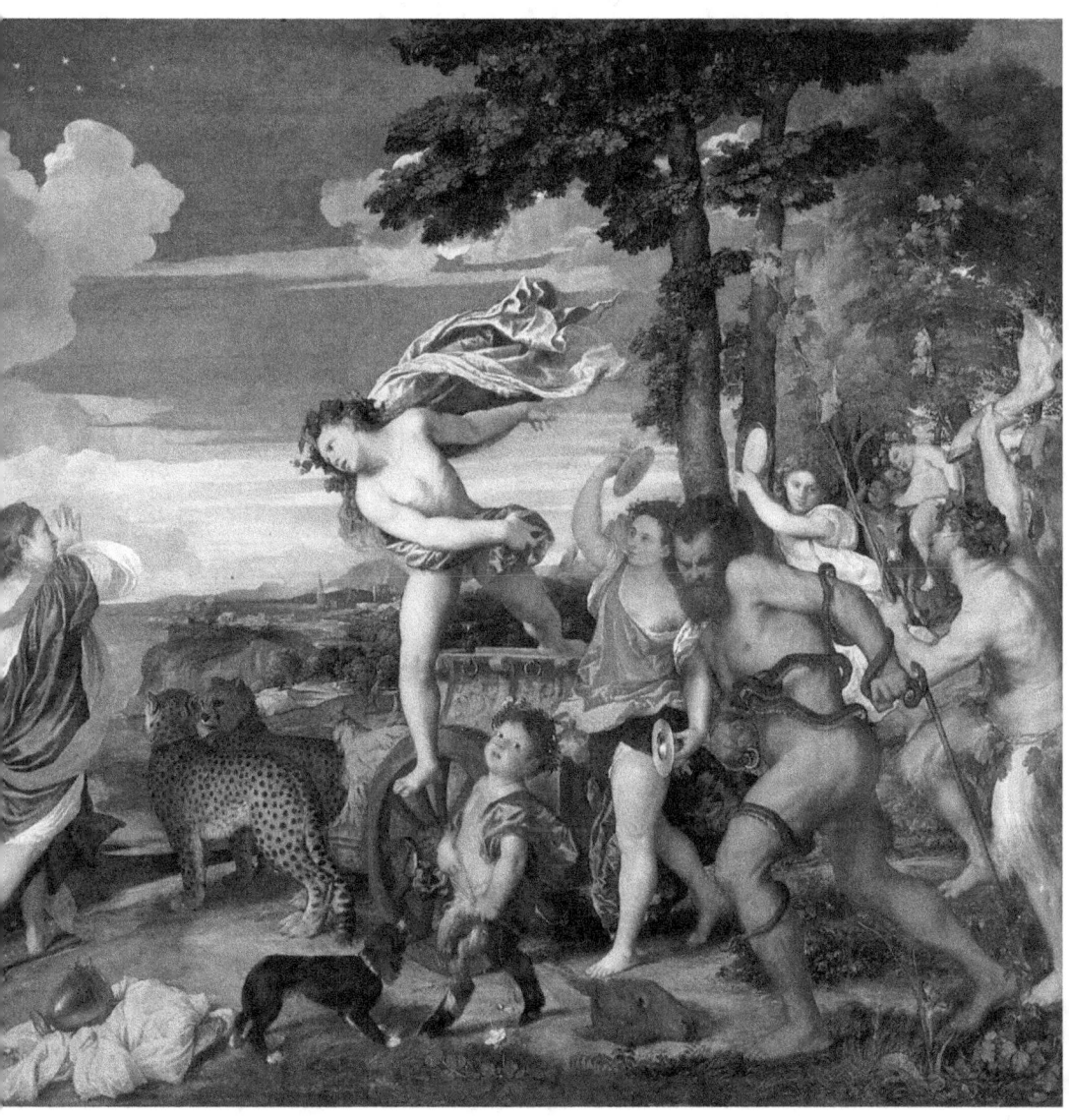

Titian, Bacchus and Ariadne, 1520-23, London

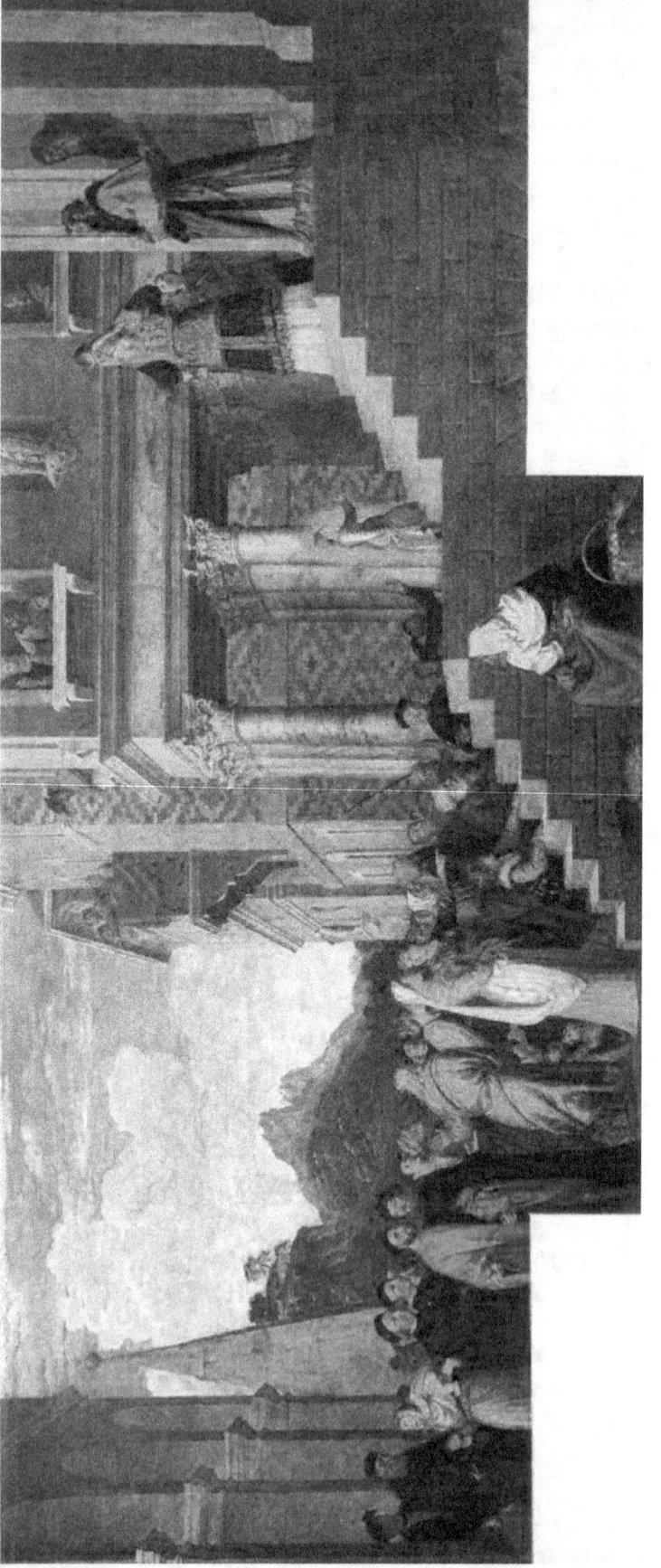

Titian, The Presentation of the Virgin, 1534-38

# INTRODUCTION

There is no greater name in Italian art – therefore no greater in art – than that of Titian. If the Venetian master does not soar as high as Leonardo da Vinci or Michelangelo, those figures so vast, so mysterious, that clouds even now gather round their heads and half-veil them from our view; if he has not the divine suavity, the perfect balance, not less of spirit than of answering hand, that makes Raphael an appearance unique in art, since the palmiest days of Greece; he is wider in scope, more glowing with the life-blood of humanity, more the poet-painter of the world and the world's fairest creatures, than any one of these. Titian is neither the loftiest, the most penetrating, nor the most profoundly moved among the great exponents of sacred art, even of his time and country. Yet is it possible, remembering the *Entombment* of the Louvre, the *Assunta*, the *Madonna di Casa Pesaro*, the *St. Peter Martyr*, to say that he has, take him all in all, been surpassed in this the highest branch of his art? Certainly nowhere else have the pomp and splendour of the painter's achievement at its apogee been so consistently allied to a dignity and simplicity hardly ever overstepping the bounds of nature. The sacred art of no other painter of the full sixteenth century – not even that of Raphael himself – has to an equal degree influenced other painters, and moulded the style of the world, in those great ceremonial altar-pieces in which sacred passion must perforce express itself with an exaggeration that is not necessarily a distortion of truth.

And then as a portraitist – we are dealing, be it remembered, with Italian art only – there must be conceded to him the first place, as a limner both of men and women, though each of us may reserve a corner in his secret heart for some other master. One will remember the disquieting power, the fascination in the true sense of the word, of Leonardo; the majesty, the penetration, the uncompromising realism on occasion, of Raphael; the happy mixture of the Giorgionesque, the Raphaelesque, and later on the Michelangelesque, in Sebastiano del Piombo. Another will yearn for the poetic glamour, gilding realistic truth, of Giorgione; for the intensely pathetic interpretation of Lorenzo Lotto, with its unique combination of the strongest subjective and objective elements, the one serving to poetise and accentuate the other. Yet another will cite the lofty melancholy, the aristocratic charm of the Brescian Moretto, or the marvellous power of the Bergamasque Moroni to present in their natural union, with no indiscretion of over-emphasis, the spiritual and physical elements which go to make up that mystery of mysteries, the human individuality. There is, however, no advocate of any of these great masters who, having vaunted the peculiar perfections in portraiture of his own favourite, will not end – with a sigh perhaps – by according the palm to Titian.

In landscape his pre-eminence is even more absolute and unquestioned. He had great precursors here, but no equal; and until Claude Lorrain long afterwards arose, there appeared no successor capable, like himself, of expressing the quintessence of Nature's most significant beauties without a too slavish adherence to any special set of natural facts. Giovanni Bellini from his earliest Mantegnesque or Paduan days had, unlike his great brother-in-law, unlike the true Squarcionesques, and the Ferrarese who more or less remotely came within the Squarcion-esque influence, the true gift of the landscape-painter. Atmospheric conditions formed invariably an important element of his conceptions; and to see that this is so we need only remember the chilly solemnity of the landscape in the great *Pietà* of the Brera, the ominous sunset in our own *Agony in the Garden* of the National Gallery, the cheerful all-pervading glow of the beautiful little *Sacred Conversation* at the Uffizi, the mysterious illumination of the late *Baptism of Christ* in the Church of S. Corona at Vicenza. To attempt a discussion of the landscape of Giorgione would be to enter upon the most perilous, as well as the most fascinating of subjects – so various is it even in the few well-established examples of his art, so exquisite an instrument of expression always, so complete an exterioration of the complex moods of his personages. Yet even the landscape of Giorgione – judging it from such unassailable works of his riper time as the great altar-piece of Castelfranco, the so-called *Stormy Landscape with the Gipsy and the Soldier*[*1] *in the Giovanelli Palace at Venice, and the so-called Three Philosophers* in the Imperial Gallery at Vienna – has in it still a slight flavour of the ripe archaic just merging into full perfection. It was reserved for Titian to give in his early time the fullest development to the Giorgionesque landscape, as in the *Three Ages* and the *Sacred and Profane Love*. Then all himself, and with hardly a rival in art, he went on to unfold those radiantly beautiful prospects of earth and sky which enframe the figures in the *Worship of Venus*, the *Bacchanal*, and, above all, the *Bacchus and Ariadne*; to give back his impressions of Nature in those rich backgrounds of reposeful beauty which so enhance the finest of the Holy Families and Sacred Conversations. It was the ominous grandeur of the landscape in the *St. Peter Martyr*, even more than the dramatic intensity, the academic amplitude of the figures, that won for the picture its universal fame. The same intimate relation between the landscape and the figures may be said to exist in the late *Jupiter and Antiope (Venere del Pardo)* of the Louvre, with its marked return to Giorgionesque repose and Giorgionesque communion with Nature; in the late *Rape of Europa*, the bold sweep and the rainbow hues of the landscape in which recall the much earlier *Bacchus and Ariadne*. In the exquisite *Shepherd and Nymph* of the Imperial Gallery at

Vienna – a masterpiece in monotone of quite the last period – the sensuousness of the early Giorgionesque time reappears, even more strongly emphasised; yet it is kept in balance, as in the early days, by the imaginative temperament of the poet, by that solemn atmosphere of mystery, above all, which belongs to the final years of Titian's old age.

Thus, though there cannot be claimed for Titian that universality in art and science which the lovers of Leonardo's painting must ever deplore, since it lured him into a thousand side-paths; for the vastness of scope of Michelangelo, or even the all-embracing curiosity of Albrecht Dürer; it must be seen that as a *painter* he covered more ground than any first-rate master of the sixteenth century. While in more than one branch of the painter's art he stood forth supreme and without a rival, in most others he remained second to none, alone in great pictorial decorations of the monumental order yielding the palm to his younger rivals Tintoretto and Paolo Veronese, who showed themselves more practised and more successfully daring in this particular branch.

To find another instance of such supreme mastery of the brush, such parallel activity in all the chief branches of oil-painting, one must go to Antwerp, the great merchant city of the North as Venice was, or had been, the great merchant city of the South. Rubens, who might fairly be styled the Flemish Titian, and who indeed owed much to his Venetian predecessor, though far less than did his own pupil Van Dyck, was during the first forty years of the seventeenth century on the same pinnacle of supremacy that the Cadorine master had occupied for a much longer period during the Renaissance. He, too, was without a rival in the creation of those vast altar-pieces which made the fame of the churches that owned them; he, too, was the finest painter of landscape of his time, as an accessory to the human figure. Moreover, he was a portrait-painter who, in his greatest efforts – those sumptuous and almost truculent *portraits d'apparat* of princes, nobles, and splendid dames – knew no superior, though his contemporaries were Van Dyck, Frans Hals, Rembrandt, and

Velazquez. Rubens folded his Mother Earth and his fellow-man in a more demonstrative, a seemingly closer embrace, drawing from the contact a more exuberant vigour, but taking with him from its very closeness some of the stain of earth. Titian, though he was at least as genuine a realist as his successor, and one less content, indeed, with the mere outsides of things, was penetrated with the spirit of beauty which was everywhere – in the mountain home of his birth as in the radiant home of his adoption, in himself as in his everyday surroundings. His art had ever, even in its most human and least aspiring phases, the divine harmony, the suavity tempering natural truth and passion, that distinguishes Italian art of the great periods from the finest art that is not Italian.

The relation of the two masters – both of them in the first line of the world's painters – was much that of Venice to Antwerp. The apogee of each city in its different way represented the highest point that modern Europe had reached of physical well-being and splendour, of material as distinguished from mental culture. But then Venice was wrapped in the transfiguring atmosphere of the Lagunes, and could see, towering above the rich Venetian plains and the lower slopes of the Friulan mountains, the higher, the more aspiring peaks of the purer region. Reality, with all its warmth and all its truth, in Venetian art was still reality. But it was reality made at once truer, wider, and more suave by the method of presentment. Idealisation, in the narrower sense of the word, could add nothing to the loveliness of such a land, to the stateliness, the splendid sensuousness devoid of the grosser elements of offence, to the genuine naturalness of such a mode of life. Art itself could only add to it the right accent, the right emphasis, the larger scope in truth, the colouring and illumination best suited to give the fullest expression to the beauties of the land, to the force, character, and warm human charm of the people. This is what Titian, supreme among his contemporaries of the greatest Venetian time, did with an incomparable mastery to which, in the vast field which his productions cover, it would be vain to seek for a parallel.

Other Venetians may, in one or the other way, more irresistibly enlist our sympathies, or may shine out for the moment more brilliantly in some special branch of their art; yet, after all, we find ourselves invariably comparing them to Titian, not Titian to them – taking *him* as the standard for the measurement of even his greatest contemporaries and successors. Giorgione was of a finer fibre, and more happily, it may be, combined all the subtlest qualities of the painter and the poet, in his creation of a phase of art the penetrating exquisiteness of which has never in the succeeding centuries lost its hold on the world. But then Titian, saturated with the Giorgionesque, and only less truly the poet-painter than his master and companion, carried the style to a higher pitch of material perfection than its inventor himself had been able to achieve. The gifted but unequal Pordenone, who showed himself so incapable of sustained rivalry with our master in Venice, had moments of a higher sublimity than Titian reached until he came to the extreme limits of old age. That this assertion is not a mere paradox, the great *Madonna del Carmelo* at the Venice Academy and the magnificent *Trinity* in the sacristy of the Cathedral of San Daniele near Udine may be taken to prove. Yet who would venture to compare him on equal terms to the painter of the *Assunta*, the *Entombment* and the *Christ at Emmaus*? Tintoretto, at his best, has lightning flashes of illumination, a Titanic vastness, an inexplicable power of perturbing the spirit and placing it in his own atmosphere, which may cause the imaginative not altogether unreasonably to put him forward as the greater figure in art. All the same, if it were necessary to make a definite choice between the two, who would not uphold the saner and greater art of Titian, even though it might leave us nearer to reality, though it might conceive the supreme tragedies, not less than the happy interludes, of the sacred drama, in the purely human spirit and with the pathos of earth? A not dissimilar comparison might be instituted between the portraits of Lorenzo Lotto and those of our master. No Venetian painter of the golden prime had that peculiar imaginativeness of Lotto, which caused him, while seeking to penetrate into the depths of the human individuality submitted to him, to infuse into it unconsciously much of his own tremulous sensitiveness and charm. In this way no portraits of the sixteenth century provide so fascinating a series of riddles. Yet in deciphering them it is very necessary to take into account the peculiar temperament of the painter himself, as well as the physical and mental characteristics of the sitter and the atmosphere of the time.[*2]

Yet where is the critic bold enough to place even the finest of these exquisite productions on the same level as *Le Jeune Homme au Gant* and *L'Homme en Noir* of the Louvre, the *Ippolito de' Medici*, the *Bella di Tiziano*, the *Aretino* of the Pitti, the *Charles V. at the Battle of Mühlberg* and the full-length *Philip II.* of the Prado Museum at Madrid?

Finally, in the domain of pure colour some will deem that Titian has serious rivals in those Veronese developed into Venetians, the two elder Bonifazi and Paolo Veronese; that is, there will be found lovers of painting who prefer a brilliant mastery over contrasting colours in frank juxtaposition to a palette relatively restricted, used with an art more subtle, if less dazzling than theirs, and resulting in a deeper, graver richness, a more significant beauty, if in a less stimulating gaiety and variety of aspect. No less a critic than Morelli himself pronounced the elder Bonifazio Veronese to be the most brilliant colourist of the Venetian school; and the *Dives and Lazarus* of the Venice Academy, the *Finding of Moses* at the Brera are at hand to give solid support to such an assertion.

In some ways Paolo Veronese may, without exaggeration, be held to be the greatest virtuoso among colourists, the most marvellous executant to be found in the whole range of Italian art. Starting from the cardinal principles in colour of the true Veronese, his precursors – painters such as Domenico and Francesco Morone, Liberale, Girolamo dai Libri, Cavazzola, Antonio Badile, and the rather later Brusasorci – Caliari dared combinations of colour the most trenchant in their brilliancy as well as the subtlest and most unfamiliar. Unlike his predecessors, however, he preserved the stimulating charm while abolishing the abruptness of sheer contrast. This he did mainly by balancing and tempering his dazzling hues with huge architectural masses of a vibrant grey and large depths of cool dark shadow – brown shot through with silver. No other Venetian master could have painted the *Mystic Marriage of St. Catherine* in the church of that name at Venice, the *Allegory on the Victory of Lepanto* in the Palazzo Ducale, or the vast *Nozze di Cana* of the Louvre. All the same, this virtuosity, while it is in one sense a step in advance even of Giorgione, Titian, Palma, and Paris Bordone – constituting as it does more particularly a further development of painting from the purely decorative standpoint – must appear just a little superficial, a little self-conscious, by the side of the nobler, graver, and more profound, if in some ways more limited methods of Titian. With him, as with Giorgione, and, indeed, with Tintoretto, colour was above all an instrument of expression. The main effort was to give a realisation, at once splendid and penetrating in its truth, of the subject presented; and colour in accordance with the true Venetian principle was used not only as the decorative vesture, but as the very body and soul of painting – as what it is, indeed, in Nature.

To put forward Paolo Veronese as merely the dazzling virtuoso would all the same be to show a singular ignorance of the true scope of his art. He can rise as high in dramatic passion and pathos as the greatest of them all, when he is in the vein; but these are precisely the occasions on which he most resolutely subordinates his colour to his subject and makes the most poetic use of chiaroscuro; as in the great altar-piece *The Martyrdom of St. Sebastian* in the church of that name, the too little known *St. Francis receiving the Stigmata* on a ceiling compartment of the Academy of Arts at Vienna, and the wonderful *Crucifixion* which not many years ago was brought down from the sky-line of the Long Gallery in the Louvre, and placed, where it deserves to be, among the masterpieces. And yet in this last piece the colour is not only in a singular degree interpretative of the subject, but at the same time technically astonishing – with certain subtleties of unusual juxtaposition and modulation, delightful to the craftsman, which are hardly seen again until we come to the latter half of the present century. So that here we have the great Veneto-Veronese master escaping altogether from our theory, and showing himself at one and the same time profoundly moving, intensely signific-ant, and admirably decorative in colour. Still what was with him the splendid exception was with Titian, and those who have been grouped with Titian, the guiding rule of art. Though our master remains, take him all in all, the greatest of Venetian colourists, he never condescends to vaunt all that he knows, or to select his subjects as a groundwork for bravura, even the most legitimate. He is the greatest painter of the sixteenth century, just because, being the greatest colourist of the higher order, and in legitimate mastery of the brush second to none, he makes the worthiest use of his unrivalled accomplishment, not merely to call down the applause due to supreme pictorial skill and the victory over self-set difficulties, but, above all, to give the fullest and most legitimate expression to the subjects which he presents, and through them to himself.

# CHAPTER I

*Cadore and Venice – Early Giorgionesque works up to the date of the residence in Padua – New interpretations of Giorgione's and Titian's pictures.*

Tiziano Vecelli was born in or about the year 1477 at Pieve di Cadore, a district of the southern Tyrol then belonging to the Republic of Venice, and still within the Italian frontier. He was the son of Gregorio di Conte Vecelli by his wife Lucia, his father being descended from an ancient family of the name of Guecello (or Vecellio), established in the valley of Cadore. An ancestor, Ser Guecello di Tommasro da Pozzale, had been elected Podesta of Cadore as far back as 1321.[*3] The name Tiziano would appear to have been a traditional one in the family. Among others we find a contemporary Tiziano Vecelli, who is a lawyer of note concerned in the administration of Cadore, keeping up a kind of obsequious friendship with his famous cousin at Venice. The Tizianello who, in 1622, dedicated to the Countess of Arundel an anonymous Life of Titian known as Tizianello's *Anonimo*, and died at Venice in 1650, was Titian's cousin thrice removed.

Gregorio Vecelli was a valiant soldier, distinguished for his bravery in the field and his wisdom in the council of Cadore, but not, it may be assumed, possessed of wealth or, in a poor mountain district like Cadore, endowed with the means of obtaining it. The other offspring of the marriage with Lucia were Francesco, – supposed, though without substantial proof, to have been older than his brother, – Caterina, and Orsa. At the age of nine, according to Dolce in the *Dialogo della Pittura*, or of ten, according to Tizianello's *Anonimo*, Titian was taken from Cadore to Venice, there to enter upon the serious study of painting. Whether he had previously received some slight tuition in the rudiments of the art, or had only shown a natural inclination to become a painter, cannot be ascertained with any precision; nor is the point, indeed, one of any real importance. What is much more vital in our study of the master's life-work is to ascertain how far the scenery of his native Cadore left a permanent impress on his landscape art, and in what way his descent from a family of mountaineers and soldiers, hardy, yet of a certain birth and breeding, contributed to shape his individuality in its development to maturity. It has been almost universally assumed that Titian throughout his career made use of the mountain scenery of Cadore in the backgrounds to his pictures; and yet, if we except the great *Battle of Cadore* itself (now known only in Fontana's print, in a reduced version of part of the composition to be found at the Uffizi, and in a drawing of Rubens at the Albertina), this is only true in a modified sense. Undoubtedly, both in the backgrounds to altar-pieces, Holy Families, and Sacred Conversations, and in the landscape drawings of the type so freely copied and adapted by Domenico Campagnola, we find the jagged, naked peaks of the Dolomites aspiring to the heavens. In the majority of instances, however, the middle distance and foreground to these is not the scenery of the higher Alps, with its abrupt contrasts, its monotonous vesture of fir or pine forests clothing the mountain sides, and its relatively harsh and cold colouring, but the richer vegetation of the Friulan mountains in their lower slopes, or of the beautiful hills bordering upon the overflowing richness of the Venetian plain. Here the painter found greater variety, greater softness in the play of light, and a richness more suitable to the character of Venetian art. All these tracts of country, as well as the more grandiose scenery of his native Cadore itself, he had the amplest opportunities for studying in the course of his many journeyings from Venice to Pieve and back, as well as in his shorter expeditions on the Venetian mainland. How far Titian's Alpine origin, and his early bringing-up among needy mountaineers, may be taken to account for his excessive eagerness to reap all the material advantages of his artistic pre-eminence, for his unresting energy when any post was to be obtained or any payment to be got in, must be a matter for individual appreciation. Josiah Gilbert – quoted by Crowe and Cavalcaselle[*4] – pertinently asks, "Might this mountain man have been something of a 'canny Scot' or a shrewd Swiss?" In the getting, Titian was certainly all this, but in the spending he was large and liberal, inclined to splendour and voluptuousness, even more in the second than in the first half of his career. Vasari relates that Titian was lodged at Venice with his uncle, an "honourable citizen," who, seeing his great inclination for painting, placed him under Giovanni Bellini, in whose style he soon became a proficient. Dolce, apparently better instructed, gives, in his *Dialogo della Pittura*, Zuccato, best known as a mosaic worker, as his first master; next makes him pass into the studio of Gentile Bellini, and thence into that of the *caposcuola* Giovanni Bellini; to take, however, the last and by far the most important step of his early career when he becomes the pupil and partner, or assistant, of Giorgione. Morelli[*5] would prefer to leave Giovanni Bellini altogether out of Titian's artistic descent. However this may be, certain traces of Gentile's influence may be observed in the art of the Cadorine painter, especially in the earlier portraiture, but indeed in the methods of technical execution generally. On the other hand, no extant work of his beginnings suggests the view that he was one of the inner circle of Gian Bellino's pupils – one of the *discipuli*, as some of these were fond of describing themselves. No young artist painting in Venice in the last years of the fifteenth century could, however, entirely withdraw himself from the influence of the veteran master, whether he actually belonged to his following or not. Gian Bellino exercised upon the contemporary art of Venice and the *Veneto* an influence not less strong of its kind than that which radiated from Leonardo over Milan and the adjacent regions during his Milanese period. The latter not only stamped his art on the works of his own special school, but fascinated in the long run the painters of the specifically Milanese group which sprang from Foppa and Borgognone – such men as Ambrogio de' Predis, Bernardino de' Conti, and, indeed, the somewhat later Bernardino Luini himself. To the fashion for the Bellinesque conceptions of a certain class, even Alvise Vivarini, the vigorous head of the opposite school in its latest Quattrocento development, bowed when he painted the Madonnas of the Redentore and S. Giovanni in Bragora at Venice, and that similar one now in the Vienna Gallery. Lorenzo Lotto, whose artistic connection with Alvise Mr. Bernard Berenson was the first to trace, is to a marked extent under the paramount influence of Giovanni Bellini in such works as the altar-piece of S. Cristina near Treviso, the *Madonna and Child with Saints* in the Ellesmere collection, and the *Madonna and Child with St. Peter Martyr* in the Naples Gallery, while in the *Marriage of St. Catherine* at Munich, though it belongs to the early time, he is, both as regards exaggerations of movement and delightful peculiarities of colour, essentially himself. Marco Basaiti, who, up to the date of Alvise's death, was intimately connected with him, and, so far as he could, faithfully reproduced the characteristics of his incisive style, in his later years was transformed into something very like a satellite of Giovanni Bellini. Cima, who in his technical processes belongs rather to the Vivarini than to the Bellini group, is to a great extent overshadowed, though never, as some would have it, absorbed to the point of absolute imitation, by his greater contemporary.

What may legitimately excite surprise in the beginnings both of Giorgione and Titian, so far as they are at present ascertained, is not so much that in their earliest productions they to a certain extent lean on Giovanni Bellini, as that they are so soon themselves. Neither of them is in any extant work seen to stand in the same absolutely dependent relation to the veteran Quattrocentist which Raphael for a time held towards Perugino, which Sebastiano Luciani in his earliest manhood held towards Giorgione. This holds good to a certain extent also of Lorenzo Lotto, who, in the earliest known examples – the so-called *Danaë* of Sir Martin Conway's collection, and the *St. Jerome* of the Louvre – is already emphatically Lotto, though, as his art passes through successive developments, he will still show himself open to more or less enduring influences from the one side and the other. Sebastiano del Piombo, on the other hand, great master as he must undoubtedly be accounted in every successive phase, is never throughout his career out of leading-strings. First, as a boy, he paints the puzzling *Pietà* in the Layard Collection at Venice, which, notwithstanding the authentic inscription, "Bastian Luciani fuit descipulus Johannes Bellinus (*sic*)," is so astonishingly like a Cima that, without this piece of documentary evidence, it would even now pass as such. Next, he becomes the most accomplished exponent of the Giorgionesque manner, save perhaps Titian himself. Then, migrating to Rome, he produces, in a quasi-Raphaelesque style still strongly tinged with the Giorgionesque, that series of superb portraits which, under the name of Sanzio, have acquired a world-wide fame. Finally, surrendering himself body and soul to Michelangelo, and only unconsciously, from the force of early training and association, allowing his Venetian origin to reveal itself, he remains enslaved by the tremendous genius of the Florentine to the very end of his career.

Giorgione and Titian were as nearly as possible of the same age, being both of them born in or about 1477. Lorenzo Lotto's birth is to be placed about the year 1476 – or, as others would have it, 1480. Palma saw the light about 1480, Pordenone in 1483, Sebastiano Luciani in 1485. So that most of the great protagonists of Venetian art during the earlier half of the Cinquecento were born within the short period of eight years – between 1477 and 1485.

In Crowe and Cavalcaselle's *Life and Times of Titian* a revolutionary theory, foreshadowed in their *Painting in North Italy*, was for the first time deliberately put forward and elaborately sustained. They sought to convince the student, as they had convinced themselves, that Palma, issuing from Gian Bellino and Giorgione, strongly influenced and shaped the art of his contemporary Titian, instead of having been influenced by him, as the relative position and age of the two artists would have induced the student to believe. Crowe and Cavalcaselle's theory rested in the main, though not so entirely as Giovanni Morelli appears to have held, on the signature and the early date (1500) to be found on a *Santa Conversazione*, once in the collection of M. Reiset, and now at Chantilly in that of the late Due d'Aumale. This date now proves with the artist's signature to be a forgery, and the picture in question, which, with strong traces still of the Bellinesque mode of conception and the Bellinesque style, shows a larger and more modern technique, can no longer be cited as proving the priority of Palma in the development of the full Renaissance types and the full Renaissance methods of execution. There can be small doubt that this particular theory of the indefatigable critics, to whom the history of Italian art owes so much, will little by little be allowed to die a natural death, if it be not, indeed, already defunct. More and more will the view so forcibly stated by Giovanni Morelli recommend itself, that Palma in many of those elements of his art most distinctively Palmesque leans upon the master of Cadore. The Bergamasque painter was not indeed a personality in art sufficiently strong and individual to dominate a Titian, or to leave upon his style and methods profound and enduring traces. As such, Crowe and Cavalcaselle themselves hesitate to put him forward, though they cling with great persistency to their pet theory of his influence. This exquisite artist, though by no means inventive genius, did, on the other hand, permanently shape the style of Cariani and the two elder Bonifazi; imparting, it may be, also some of his voluptuous charm in the rendering of female loveliness to Paris Bordone, though the latter must, in the main, be looked upon as the artistic offspring of Titian.

It is by no means certain, all the same, that this question of influence imparted and submitted to can with advantage be argued with such absoluteness of statement as has been the rule up to the present time, both on the one side and the other. It should be remembered that we are dealing with three young painters of about the same age, working in the same art-centre, perhaps, even, for a time in the same studio – issuing, at any rate, all three from the flank of Giovanni Bellini. In a situation like this, it is not only the preponderance of age – two or three years at the most, one way or the other – that is to be taken into account, but the preponderance of genius and the magic gift of influence. It is easy to understand how the complete renewal, brought about by Giorgione on the basis of Bellini's teaching and example, operated to revolutionise the art of his own generation. He threw open to art the gates of life in its mysterious complexity, in its fulness of sensuous yearning commingled with spiritual aspiration. Irresistible was the fascination exercised both by his art and his personality over his youthful contemporaries; more and more did the circle of his influence widen, until it might almost be said that the veteran Gian Bellino himself was brought within it. With Barbarelli, at any rate, there could be no question of light received back from painters of his own generation in exchange for that diffused around him; but with Titian and Palma the case was different. The germs of the Giorgionesque fell here in each case upon a fruitful soil, and in each case produced a vigorous plant of the same family, yet with all its Giorgionesque colour of a quite distinctive loveliness. Titian, we shall see, carried the style to its highest point of material development, and made of it in many ways a new thing. Palma, with all his love of beauty in colour and form, in nature as in man, had a less finely attuned artistic temperament than Giorgione, Titian, or Lotto. Morelli has called attention to that element of downright energy in his mountain nature which in a way counteracts the marked sensuousness of his art, save when he interprets the charms of the full-blown Venetian woman. The great Milanese critic attributes this to the Bergamasque origin of the artist, showing itself beneath Venetian training. Is it not possible that a little of this frank unquestioning sensuousness on the one hand, of this *terre à terre* energy on the other, may have been reflected in the early work of Titian, though it be conceded that he influenced far more than he was influenced?[*6] There is undoubtedly in his personal development of the Giorgionesque a superadded element of something much nearer to the everyday world than is to be found in the work of his prototype, and this not easily definable element is peculiar also to Palma's art, in which, indeed, it endures to the end. Thus there is a singular resemblance between the type of his fairly fashioned Eve in the important *Adam and Eve* of his earlier time in the Brunswick Gallery – once, like so many other things, attributed to Giorgione – and the preferred type of youthful female loveliness as it is to be found in Titian's *Three Ages* at Bridgewater House, in his so-called *Sacred and Profane Love (Medea and Venus)* of the Borghese Gallery, in such sacred pieces as the *Madonna and Child with SS. Ulfo and Brigida* at the Prado Gallery of Madrid, and the large *Madonna and Child with four Saints* at Dresden. In both instances we have the Giorgionesque conception stripped of a little of its poetic glamour, but retaining unabashed its splendid sensuousness, which is thus made the more markedly to stand out. We notice, too, in Titian's works belonging to this particular group another characteristic which may be styled Palmesque, if only because Palma indulged in it in a great number of his Sacred Conversations and similar pieces. This is the contrasting of the rich brown skin, the muscular form, of some male saint, or it may be some shepherd of the uplands, with the dazzling fairness, set off with hair of pale or ruddy gold, of a female saint, or a fair Venetian doing duty as a shepherdess or a heroine of antiquity. Are we to look upon such distinguishing characteristics as these – and others that could easily be singled out – as wholly and solely Titianesque of the early time? If so, we ought to assume that what is most distinctively Palmesque in the art of Palma came from the painter of Cadore, who in this case should be taken to have transmitted to his brother in art the Giorgionesque in the less subtle shape into which he had already transmuted it. But should not such an assumption as this, well founded as it may appear in the main, be made with all the allowances which the situation demands?

That, when a group of young and enthusiastic artists, eager to overturn barriers, are found painting more or less together, it is not so easy to unravel the tangle of influences and draw hard-and-fast lines everywhere, one or two modern examples much nearer to our own time may roughly serve to illustrate. Take, for instance, the friendship that developed itself between the youthful Bonington and the youthful Delacroix while they copied together in the galleries of the Louvre: the one communicating to the other something of the stimulating quality, the frankness, and variety of colour which at that moment distinguished the English from the French school; the other contributing to shape, with the fire of his romantic temperament, the art of the young Englishman who was some three years his junior. And with the famous trio of the P.R.B. – Millais, Rossetti, and Mr. Holman Hunt – who is to state *ex cathedra* where influence was received, where transmitted; or whether the first may fairly be held to have been, during the short time of their complete union, the master-hand, the second the poet-soul, the third the conscience of the group? A similar puzzle would await him who should strive to unravel the delicate thread which winds itself round the artistic relation between Frederick Walker and the noted landscapist Mr. J.W. North. Though we at once recognise Walker as the dominant spirit, and see his influence even to-day, more than twenty years after his death, affirmed rather than weakened, there are certain characteristics of the style recognised and imitated as his, of which it would be unsafe to declare that he and not his companion originated them.

In days of artistic upheaval and growth like the last years of the fifteenth century and the first years of the sixteenth, the *milieu* must count for a great deal. It must be remembered that the men who most influence a time, whether in art or letters, are just those who, deeply rooted in it, come forth as its most natural development. Let it not be doubted that when in Giorgione's breast had been lighted the first sparks of the Promethean fire, which, with the soft intensity of its glow, warmed into full-blown perfection the art of Venice, that fire ran like lightning through the veins of all the artistic youth, his contemporaries and juniors, just because their blood was of the stuff to ignite and flame like his own.

The great Giorgionesque movement in Venetian art was not a question merely of school, of standpoint, of methods adopted and developed by a brilliant galaxy of young painters. It was not alone that "they who were excellent confessed, that he (Giorgione) was born to put the breath of life into painted figures, and to imitate the elasticity and colour of flesh, etc."[*7] It was also that the Giorgionesque in conception and style was the outcome of the moment in art and life, just as the Pheidian mode had been the necessary climax of Attic art and Attic life aspiring to reach complete perfection in the fifth century B.C.; just as the Raphaelesque appeared the inevitable outcome of those elements of lofty generalisation, divine harmony, grace clothing strength, which, in Florence and Rome, as elsewhere in Italy, were culminating in the first years of the Cinquecento. This was the moment, too, when – to take one instance only among many – the Ex-Queen of Cyprus, the noble Venetian Caterina Cornaro, held her little court at Asolo, where, in accordance with the spirit of the moment, the chief discourse was ever of love. In that reposeful kingdom, which could in miniature offer to Caterina's courtiers all the pomp and charm without the drawbacks of sovereignty, Pietro Bembo wrote for "Madonna Lucretia Estense Borgia Duchessa illustrissima di Ferrara," and caused to be printed by Aldus Manutius, the leaflets which, under the title *Gli Asolani, ne' quali si ragiona d' amore*,[*8] soon became a famous book in Italy.

The most Bellinesque work of Titian's youth with which we are acquainted is the curious *Man of Sorrows* of the Scuola di S. Rocco at Venice, a work so faded, so injured by restoration that to dogmatise as to its technique would be in the highest degree unsafe. The type approaches, among the numerous versions of the *Pietà* by and ascribed to Giovanni Bellini, most nearly to that in the Palazzo del Commune at Rimini. Seeing that Titian was in 1500 twenty-three years old, and a student of painting of some thirteen years' standing, there may well exist, or at any rate there may well have existed, from his hand things in a yet earlier and more distinctively Quattrocento-style than anything with which we are at present acquainted. This *Man of Sorrows* itself may well be a little earlier than 1500, but on this point it is not easy to form a definite conclusion. Perhaps it is reserved in the future to some student uniting the qualities of patience and keen insight to do for the youthful Titian what Morelli and his school have done for Correggio – that is, to restore to him a series of paintings earlier in date than those which criticism has, up to the present time, been content to accept as showing his first independent steps in art. Everything else that we can at present safely attribute to the youthful Vecelli is deeply coloured with the style and feeling of Giorgione, though never, as is the case with the inferior Giorgionesques, so entirely as to obliterate the strongly marked individuality of the painter himself. The *Virgin and Child* in the Imperial Gallery of Vienna, popularly known as *La Zingarella*, which, by general consent, is accepted as the first in order of date among the works of this class, is still to a certain extent Bellinesque in the mode of conception and arrangement. Yet, in the depth, strength, and richness of the colour-chord, in the atmospheric spaciousness and charm of the landscape back-ground, in the breadth of the draperies, it is already Giorgion-esque. Nay, even here Titian, above all, asserts *himself*, and lays the foundation of his own manner. The type of the divine Bambino differs widely from that adopted by Giorgione in the altar-pieces of Castelfranco and the Prado Museum at Madrid. The virgin is a woman beautified only by youth and intensity of maternal love. Both Giorgione and Titian in their loveliest types of womanhood are sensuous as compared with the Tuscans and Umbrians, or with such painters as Cavazzola of Verona and the suave Milanese, Bernardino Luini. But Giorgione's sensuousness is that which may fitly characterise the goddess, while Titian's is that of the woman, much nearer to the everyday world in which both artists lived.

In the Imperial Gallery of the Hermitage at St. Petersburg is a beautiful *Madonna and Child* in a niche of coloured marble mosaic, which is catalogued as an early Titian under the influence of Giovanni Bellini. Judging only from the reproduction on a large scale done by Messrs. Braun and Co., the writer has ventured to suggest elsewhere[*9] – prefacing his suggestions with the avowal that he is not acquainted with the picture itself – that we may have here, not an early Titian, but that rarer thing an early Giorgione. From the list of the former master's works it must at any rate be struck out, as even the most superficial comparison with, for instance, *La Zingarella* suffices to prove. In the notable display of Venetian art made at the New Gallery in the winter of 1895 were included two pictures (Nos. 1 and 7 in the catalogue) ascribed to the early time of Titian and evidently from the same hand. These were a *Virgin and Child* from the collection, so rich in Venetian works, of Mr. R.H. Benson (formerly among the Burghley House pictures), and a less well-preserved *Virgin and Child with Saints* from the collection of Captain Holford at Dorchester House. The former is ascribed by Crowe and Cavalcaselle to the early time of the master himself.[*10] Both are, in their rich harmony of colour and their general conception, entirely Giorgionesque. They reveal the hand of some at present anonymous Venetian of the second order, standing midway between the young Giorgione and the young Titian – one who, while imitating the types and the landscape of these greater contemporaries of his, replaced their depth and glow by a weaker, a more superficial prettiness, which yet has its own suave charm.

The famous *Christ bearing the Cross* in the Chiesa di S. Rocco at Venice is first, in his Life of the Castelfranco painter, ascribed by Vasari to Giorgione, and then in the subsequent Life of Titian given to that master, but to a period very much too late in his career. The biographer quaintly adds: "This figure, which many have believed to be from the hand of Giorgione, is to-day the most revered object in Venice, and has received more charitable offerings in money than Titian and Giorgione together ever gained in the whole course of their life." This too great popularity of the work as a wonder-working picture is perhaps the cause that it is to-day in a state as unsatisfactory as is the *Man of Sorrows* in the adjacent Scuola. The picture which presents "Christ dragged along by the executioner, with two spectators in the background," resembles most among Giorgione's authentic creations the *Christ bearing the Cross* in the Casa Loschi at Vicenza. The resemblance is not, however, one of colour and technique, since this last – one of the earliest of Giorgiones – still recalls Giovanni Bellini, and perhaps even more strongly Cima; it is one of type and conception. In both renderings of the divine countenance there is – or it may be the writer fancies that there is – underlying that expression of serenity and humiliation accepted which is proper to the subject, a sinister, disquieting look, almost a threat. Crowe and Cavalcaselle have called attention to a certain disproportion in the size of the head, as compared with that of the surrounding actors in the scene. A similar disproportion is to be observed in another early Titian, the *Christ between St. Andrew and St. Catherine* in the Church of SS. Ermagora and Fortunato (commonly called S. Marcuola) at Venice. Here the head of the infant Christ, who stands on a pedestal holding the Orb, between the two saints above mentioned, is strangely out of proportion to the rest. Crowe and Cavalcaselle had refused to accept this picture as a genuine Titian (vol. ii. p. 432), but Morelli restored it to its rightful place among the early works.

Next to these paintings, and certainly several years before the

*Three Ages* and the *Sacred and Profane Love*, the writer is inclined to place the *Bishop of Paphos (Baffo) recommended by Alexander VI. to St. Peter*, once in the collection of Charles I.[*11] and now in the Antwerp Gallery. The main elements of Titian's art may be seen here, in imperfect fusion, as in very few even of his early productions. The not very dignified St. Peter, enthroned on a kind of pedestal adorned with a high relief of classic design, of the type which we shall find again in the *Sacred and Profane Love*, recalls Giovanni Bellini, or rather his immediate followers; the magnificently robed Alexander VI. (Rodrigo Borgia), wearing the triple tiara, gives back the style in portraiture of Gentile Bellini and Carpaccio; while the kneeling Jacopo Pesaro – an ecclesiastic in tonsure and vesture, but none the less a commander of fleets, as the background suggests – is one of the most characteristic portraits of the Giorgionesque school. Its pathos, its intensity, contrast curiously with the less passionate absorption of the same *Baffo* in the renowned *Madonna di Casa Pesaro*, painted twenty-three years later for the family chapel in the great Church of the Frari. It is the first in order of a great series, including the *Ariosto* of Cobham, the *Jeune Homme au Gant*, the *Portrait of a Man* in the Alte Pinakothek of Munich, and perhaps the famous *Concert* of the Pitti, ascribed to Giorgione. Both Crowe and Cavalcaselle and M. Georges Lafenestre[*12] have called attention to the fact that the detested Borgia Pope died on the 18th of August 1503, and that the work cannot well have been executed after that time. He would have been a bold man who should have attempted to introduce the portrait of Alexander VI. into a votive picture painted immediately after his death! How is it possible to assume, as the eminent critics do nevertheless assume, that the *Sacred and Profane Love*, one of the masterpieces of Venetian art, was painted one or two years earlier still, that is, in 1501 or, at the latest, in 1502? Let it be remembered that at that moment Giorgione himself had not fully developed the Giorgionesque. He had not painted his Castelfranco altar-piece, his *Venus*, or his *Three Philosophers (Aeneas, Evander, and Pallas)*. Old Gian Bellino himself had not entered upon that ultimate phase of his art which dates from the great S. Zaccaria altar-piece finished in 1505.[*13]

It is impossible on the present occasion to give any detailed account of the fresco decorations painted by Giorgione and Titian on the facades of the new Fondaco de' Tedeschi, erected to replace that burnt down on the 28th of January 1505. Full particulars will be found in Crowe and Cavalcaselle's often-quoted work. Vasari's many manifest errors and disconcerting transpositions in the biography of Titian do not predispose us to give unlimited credence to his account of the strained relations between Giorgione and our painter, to which this particular business is supposed to have given rise. That they together decorated with a series of frescoes which acquired considerable celebrity the exterior of the Fondaco is all that is known for certain, Titian being apparently employed as the subordinate of his friend and master. Of these frescoes only one figure, doubtfully assigned to Titian, and facing the Grand Canal, has been preserved, in a much-damaged condition – the few fragments that remained of those facing the side canal having been destroyed in 1884.[*14] Vasari shows us a Giorgione angry because he has been complimented by friends on the superior beauty of some work on the "*facciata di verso la Merceria,*" which in reality belongs to Titian, and thereupon implacably cutting short their connection and friendship. This version is confirmed by Dolce, but refuted by the less contemporary authority of Tizianello's *Anonimo*. Of what great painters, standing in the relation of master and pupil, have not such stories been told, and – the worst of it is – told with a certain foundation of truth? Apocryphal is, no doubt, that which has evolved itself from the internal evidence supplied by the *Baptism of Christ* of Verrocchio and Leonardo da Vinci; but a stronger substructure of fact supports the unpleasing anecdotes as to Titian and Tintoretto, as to Watteau and Pater, as to our own Hudson and Reynolds, and, alas! as to very many others. How touching, on the other hand, is that simple entry in Francesco Francia's day-book, made when his chief journeyman, Timoteo

Viti, leaves him: "1495 a di 4 aprile è partito il mio caro Timoteo; chi Dio li dia ogni bene et fortuna!" ("On the 4th day of April 1495 my dear Timoteo left me. May God grant him all happiness and good fortune!")

There is one reason that makes it doubly difficult, relying on developments of style only, to make, even tentatively, a chronological arrangement of Titian's early works. This is that in those painted *poesie* of the earlier Venetian art of which the germs are to be found in Giovanni Bellini and Cima, but the flower is identified with Giorgione, Titian surrendered himself to the overmastering influence of the latter with less reservation of his own individuality than in his sacred works. In the earlier imaginative subjects the vivifying glow of Giorgionesque poetry moulds, colours, and expands the genius of Titian, but so naturally as neither to obliterate nor to constrain it. Indeed, even in the late time of our master – checking an unveiled sensuousness which sometimes approaches dangerously near to a downright sensuality – the influence of the master and companion who vanished half a century before victoriously reasserts itself. It is this *renouveau* of the Giorgionesque in the genius of the aged Titian that gives so exquisite a charm to the *Venere del Pardo*, so strange a pathos to that still later *Nymph and Shepherd*, which was a few years ago brought out of its obscurity and added to the treasures of the Imperial Gallery at Vienna.

The sacred works of the early time are Giorgionesque, too, but with a difference. Here from the very beginning there are to be noted a majestic placidity, a fulness of life, a splendour of representation, very different from the tremulous sweetness, the spirit of aloofness and reserve which informs such creations as the *Madonna of Castelfranco* and the *Madonna with St. Francis and St. Roch* of the Prado Museum. Later on, we have, leaving farther and farther behind the Giorgionesque ideal, the overpowering force and majesty of the *Assunta*, the true passion going hand-in-hand with beauty of the Louvre *Entombment*, the rhetorical passion and scenic magnificence of the *St. Peter Martyr*.

The *Baptism of Christ*, with Zuanne Ram as donor, now in the Gallery of the Capitol at Rome, had been by Crowe and Cavalcaselle taken away from Titian and given to Paris Bordone, but the keen insight of Morelli led him to restore it authoritatively, and once for all, to Titian. Internal evidence is indeed conclusive in this case that the picture must be assigned to a date when Bordone was but a child of tender years.[*15] Here Titian is found treating this great scene in the life of Christ more in the style of a Giorgionesque pastoral than in the solemn hieratic fashion adopted by his great predecessors and contemporaries. The luxuriant landscape is in the main Giorgionesque, save that here and there a naked branch among the leafage – and on one of them the woodpecker – strongly recalls Giovanni Bellini. The same robust, round-limbed young Venetian, with the inexpressive face, does duty here as St. John the Baptist, who in the *Three Ages*, presently to be discussed, appears much more appropriately as the amorous shepherd. The Christ, here shown in the flower of youthful manhood, with luxuriant hair and softly curling beard, will mature later on into the divine *Cristo della Moneta*. The question at once arises here, Did Titian in the type of this figure derive inspiration from Giovanni Bellini's splendid *Baptism of Christ*, finished in 1510 for the Church of S. Corona at Vicenza, but which the younger artist might well have seen a year or two previously, while it was in the course of execution in the workshop of the venerable master? Apart from its fresh naïveté, and its rare pictorial charm, how trivial and merely anecdotic does the conception of Titian appear by the side of that of Bellini, so lofty, so consoling in its serene beauty, in the solemnity of its sunset colour![*16] Alone in the profile portrait of the donor, Zuanne Ram, placed in the picture with an awkwardness attractive in its naïvete, but superbly painted, is Titian already a full-grown master standing alone.

The beautiful *Virgin and Child with SS. Ulfo and Brigida*, placed in the Sala de la Reina Isabel of the Prado, is now at last officially restored to Titian, after having been for years innumerable ascribed to Giorgione, whose style it not more than generally recalls. Here at any rate all the rival wise men are agreed, and it only remains for the student of the old masters, working to-day on the solid substructure provided for him by his predecessors, to wonder how any other attribution could have been accepted. But then the critic of the present day is a little too prone to be wise and scornful *à ban marché*, forgetting that he has been spared three parts of the road, and that he starts for conquest at the high point, to reach which the pioneers of scientific criticism in art have devoted a lifetime of noble toil. It is in this piece especially that we meet with that element in the early art of the Cadorine which Crowe and Cavalcaselle have defined as "Palmesque." The *St. Bridget* and the *St. Ulphus* are both types frequently to be met with in the works of the Bergamasque painter, and it has been more than once remarked that the same beautiful model with hair of wavy gold must have sat to Giorgione, Titian, and Palma. This can only be true, however, in a modified sense, seeing that Giorgione did not, so much as his contemporaries and followers, affect the type of the beautiful Venetian blond, "large, languishing, and lazy." The hair of his women – both the sacred personages and the divinities nominally classic or wholly Venetian – is, as a rule, of a rich chestnut, or at the most dusky fair, and in them the Giorgionesque oval of the face tempers with its spirituality the strength of physical passion that the general physique denotes. The polished surface of this panel at Madrid, the execution, sound and finished without being finicking, the high yellowish lights on the crimson draperies, are all very characteristic of this, the first manner of Vecelli. The green hangings at the back of the picture are such as are very generally associated with the colour-schemes of Palma. An old repetition, with a slight variation in the Bambino, is in the royal collection at Hampton Court, where it long bore – indeed it does so still on the frame – the name of Palma Vecchio.

It will be remembered that Vasari assigns to the *Tobias and the Angel* in the Church of S. Marciliano at Venice the exact date 1507, describing it, moreover, with greater accuracy than he does any other work by Titian. He mentions even "the thicket, in which is a St. John the Baptist kneeling as he prays to heaven, whence comes a splendour of light." The Aretine biographer is followed in this particular by Morelli, usually so eagle-eyed, so little bound by tradition in tracing the beginnings of a great painter. The gifted modern critic places the picture among the quite early works of our master. Notwithstanding this weight of authority, the writer feels bound to dissent from the view just now indicated, and in this instance to follow Crowe and Cavalcaselle, who assign to the *Tobias and the Angel* a place much later on in Titian's long career. The picture, though it hangs high in the little church for which it was painted, will speak for itself to those who interrogate it without *parti pris*. Neither in the figures – the magnificently classic yet living archangel Raphael and the more naïve and realistic Tobias – nor in the rich landscape with St. John the Baptist praying is there anything left of the early Giorgionesque manner. In the sweeping breadth of the execution, the summarising power of the brush, the glow from within of the colour, we have so many evidences of a style in its fullest maturity. It will be safe, therefore, to place the picture well on in Titian's middle period.[*17]

The *Three Ages* in the Bridgewater Gallery and the so-called *Sacred and Profane Love* in the Borghese Gallery represent the apogee of Titian's Giorgionesque style. Glowing through and through with the spirit of the master-poet among Venetian painters, yet falling short a little, it may be, of that subtle charm of his, compounded indefinably of sensuous delight and spiritual yearning, these two masterpieces carry the Giorgionesque technically a pretty wide step farther than the inventor of the style took it. Barbarelli never absolutely threw off the trammels of the Quattrocento, except in his portraits, but retained to the last – not as a drawback, but rather as an added charm – the naïveté, the hardly perceptible hesitation proper to art not absolutely full-fledged.

The *Three Ages*, from its analogies of type and manner with the *Baptism* of the Capitol, would appear to be the earlier of the two imaginative works here grouped together, but to date later than that picture.[*18] The tonality of the picture is of an exquisite silveriness – that of clear, moderate daylight, though this relative paleness may have been somewhat increased by time. It may a little disconcert at first sight those who have known the lovely pastoral only from hot, brown copies, such as the one which, under the name of Giorgione, was formerly in the Dudley House Collection, and now belongs to Sir William Farrer. It is still so difficult to battle with the deeply-rooted notion that there can be no Giorgione, no painting of his school, without the accompaniment of a rich brown sauce! The shepherdess has a robe of fairest crimson, and her flower-crowned locks in tint more nearly approach to the *blond cendré* which distinguishes so many of Palma's *donne* than to the ruddier gold that Titian himself generally affects. The more passionate of the two, she gazes straight into the eyes of her strong-limbed rustic lover, who half-reclining rests his hand upon her shoulder. On the twin reed-pipes, which she still holds in her hands, she has just breathed forth a strain of music, and to it, as it still lingers in their ears, they yield themselves entranced. Here the youth is naked, the maid clothed and adorned – a reversal, this, of Giorgione's *Fête Champêtre* in the Salon Carré of the Louvre, where the women are undraped, and the amorous young cavaliers appear in complete and rich attire. To the right are a group of thoroughly Titianesque amorini – the winged one, dominating the others, being perhaps Amor himself; while in the distance an old man contemplates skulls ranged round him on the ground – obvious reminders of the last stage of all, at which he has so nearly arrived. There is here a wonderful unity between the even, unaccented harmony of the delicate tonality and the mood of the personages – the one aiding the other to express the moment of pause in nature and in love, which in itself is a delight more deep than all that the very whirlwind of passion can give. Near at hand may be pitfalls, the smiling love-god may prove less innocent than he looks, and in the distance Fate may be foreshadowed by the figure of weary Age awaiting Death. Yet this one moment is all the lovers' own, and they profane it not by speech, but stir their happy languor only with faint notes of music borne on the still, warm air.

The *Sacred and Profane Love* of the Borghese Gallery is one of the world's pictures, and beyond doubt the masterpiece of the early or Giorgionesque period. To-day surely no one will be found to gainsay Morelli when he places it at the end of that period, which it so incomparably sums up – not at the beginning, when its perfection would be as incomprehensible as the less absolute achievement displayed in other early pieces which such a classification as this would place after the Borghese picture. The accompanying reproduction obviates all necessity for a detailed description. Titian painted afterwards perhaps more wonderfully still – with a more sweeping vigour of brush, with a higher authority, and a play of light as brilliant and diversified. He never attained to a higher finish and perfection of its kind, or more admirably suited the technical means to the thing to be achieved. He never so completely gave back, coloured with the splendour of his own genius, the rays received from Giorgione. The delicious sunset landscape has all the Giorgionesque elements, with more spaciousness, and lines of a still more suave harmony. The grand Venetian *donna* who sits sumptuously robed, flower-crowned, and even gloved, at the sculptured classic fount is the noblest in her pride of loveliness, as she is one of the first, of the long line of voluptuous beauties who will occupy the greatest brushes of the Cinquecento. The little love-god who, insidiously intervening, paddles in the water of the fountain and troubles its surface, is Titian's very own, owing nothing to any forerunner. The divinely beautiful *Profane Love* – or, as we shall presently see, *Venus* – is the most flawless presentment of female loveliness unveiled that modern art has known up to this date, save only the *Venus* of Giorgione himself (in the Dresden Gallery), to which it can be but little posterior. The radiant freshness of the face, with its glory of half-unbound hair, does not, indeed, equal the sovereign loveliness of the Dresden *Venus* or the disquieting charm of the Giovanelli *Zingarella* (properly Hypsipyle). Its beauty is all on the surface, while theirs stimulates the imagination of the beholder. The body with its strong, supple beauty, its unforced harmony of line and movement, with its golden glow of flesh, set off in the true Giorgionesque fashion by the warm white of the slender, diaphanous drapery, by the splendid crimson mantle with the changing hues and high lights, is, however, the most perfect poem of the human body that Titian ever achieved. Only in the late *Venere del Pardo*, which so closely follows the chief motive of Giorgione's *Venus*, does he approach it in frankness and purity. Far more genuinely classic is it in spirit, because more living and more solidly founded on natural truth, than anything that the Florentine or Roman schools, so much more assiduous in their study of classical antiquity, have brought forth.[*19]

It is impossible to discuss here in detail all the conjectural explanations which have been hazarded with regard to this most popular of all Venetian pictures – least of all that strange one brought forward by Crowe and Cavalcaselle, the *Artless and Sated Love*, for which they have found so little acceptance. But we may no longer wrap ourselves in an atmosphere of dreamy conjecture and show but a languid desire to solve the fascinating problem. Taking as his starting-point the pictures described by Marcantonio Michiel (the *Anonimo* of Jacopo Morelli), in the house of Messer Taddeo Contarini of Venice, as the *Inferno with Aeneas and Anchises* and *Landscape with the Birth of Paris*, Herr Franz Wickhoff[*20] has proceeded, we have seen, to rename, with a daring crowned by a success nothing short of surprising, several of Barbarelli's best known works. The *Three Philosophers* he calls *Aeneas, Evander, and Pallas*, the Giovanelli *Tempest with the Gipsy and the Soldier* he explains anew as *Admetus and Hypsipyle*.[*21] The subject known to us in an early plate of Marcantonio Raimondi, and popularly called, or rather miscalled, the *Dream of Raphael*, is recognised by

Herr Wickhoff as having its root in the art of Giorgione. He identifies the mysterious subject with one cited by Servius, the commentator of Virgil, who relates how, when two maidens were sleeping side by side in the Temple of the Penates at Lavinium (as he puts it), the unchaste one was killed by lightning, while the other remained in peaceful sleep.

Passing over to the Giorgionesque period of Titian, he boldly sets to work on the world-famous *Sacred and Profane Love*, and shows us the Cadorine painter interpreting, at the suggestion of some learned humanist at his elbow, an incident in the Seventh Book of the *Argonautica* of Valerius Flaccus – that wearisome imitation of the similarly named epic of Apollonius Rhodius. Medea – the sumptuously attired dame who does duty as Sacred Love(!) – sits at the fountain in unrestful self-communing, leaning one arm on a mysterious casket, and holding in her right hand a bunch of wonder-working herbs. She will not yield to her new-born love for the Greek enemy Jason, because this love is the most shameful treason to father and people. But to her comes Venus in the form of the sorceress Circe, the sister of Medea's father, irresistibly pleading that she shall go to the alien lover, who waits in the wood. It is the vain resistance of Medea, hopelessly caught in the toils of love, powerless for all her enchantments to resist, it is the subtle persuasion of Venus, seemingly invisible – in Titian's realisation of the legend – to the woman she tempts, that constitute the main theme upon which Titian has built his masterpiece. Moritz Thausing[*22] had already got half-way towards the unravelling of the true subject when he described the Borghese picture as *The Maiden with Venus and Amor at the Well*. The *vraisemblance* of Herr Wickhoff's brilliant interpretation becomes the greater when we reflect that Titian at least twice afterwards borrowed subjects from classical antiquity, taking his *Worship of Venus*, now at Madrid, from the *Erotes* of Philostratus, and our own wonderful *Bacchus and Ariadne* at the National Gallery from the *Epithalamium Pelei et Thetidos* of Catullus. In the future it is quite possible that the Austrian savant may propose new and precise interpretations for the *Three Ages* and for Giorgione's *Concert Champêtre* at the Louvre.

It is no use disguising the fact that, grateful as the true student of Italian art must be for such guidance as is here given, it comes to him at first as a shock that these mysterious creations of the ardent young poet-painters, in the presence of which we have most of us so willingly allowed reason and argument to stand in abeyance, should thus have hard, clear lines drawn, as it were, round their deliciously vague contours. It is their very vagueness and strangeness, the atmosphere of pause and quiet that they bring with them, the way in which they indefinably take possession of the beholder, body and soul, that above and beyond their radiant beauty have made them dear to successive generations. And yet we need not mourn overmuch, or too painfully set to work to revise our whole conception of Venetian idyllic art as matured in the first years of the Cinquecento. True, some humanist of the type of Pietro Bembo, not less amorous than learned and fastidious, must have found for Titian and Giorgione all these fine stories from Virgil, Catullus, Statius, and the lesser luminaries of antique poetry, which luckily for the world they have interpreted in their own fashion. The humanists themselves would no doubt have preferred the more laborious and at the same time more fantastic Florentine fashion of giving plastic form in every particular to their elaborate symbolisms, their artificial conceits, their classic legends. But we may unfeignedly rejoice that the Venetian painters of the golden prime disdained to represent – or it may be unconsciously shrank from representing – the mere dramatic moment, the mere dramatic and historical character of a subject thus furnished to them. Giorgione embodies in such a picture as the *Adrastus and Hypsipyle,* or the *Aeneas and Evander*, not so much what has been related to him of those ancient legends as his own mood when he is brought into contact with them; he transposes his motive from a dramatic into a lyrical atmosphere, and gives it forth anew, transformed into something "rich and strange," coloured for ever with his own inspired yet so warmly human fantasy. Titian, in the *Sacred and Profane Love,* as for identification we must still continue to call it, strives to keep close to the main lines of his story, in this differing from Giorgione. But for all that, his love for the rich beauty of the Venetian country, for the splendour of female loveliness unveiled, for the piquant contrast of female loveliness clothed and sumptuously adorned, has conquered. He has presented the Romanised legend of the fair Colchian sorceress in such a delightfully misleading fashion that it has taken all these centuries to decipher its true import. What Giorgione and Titian in these exquisite idylls – for so we may still dare to call them – have consciously or unconsciously achieved, is the indissoluble union of humanity outwardly quiescent, yet pulsating with an inner life and passion, to the environing nature. It is Nature herself that in these true painted poems mysteriously responds, that interprets to the beholder the moods of man, much as a mighty orchestra – Nature ordered and controlled – may by its undercurrent explain to him who knows how to listen what the very personages of the drama may not proclaim aloud for themselves. And so we may be deeply grateful to Herr Wickhoff for his new interpretations, not less sound and thoroughly worked out than they are on a first acquaintance startling. And yet we need not for all that shatter our old ideals, or force ourselves too persistently to look at Venetian art from another and a more prosaic, because a more precise and literal, standpoint.

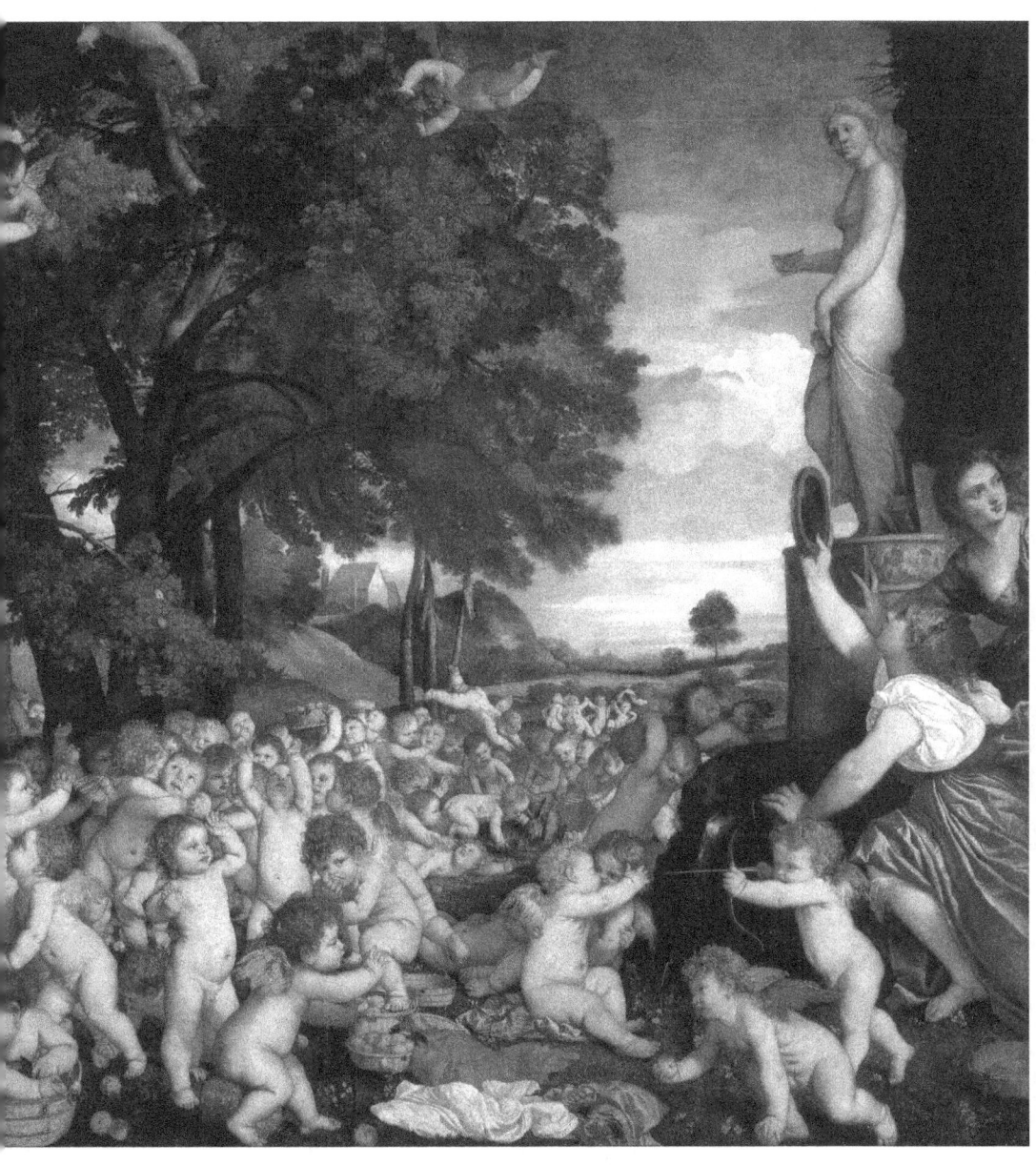

Titian, The Worship of Venus, 1518, Madrid

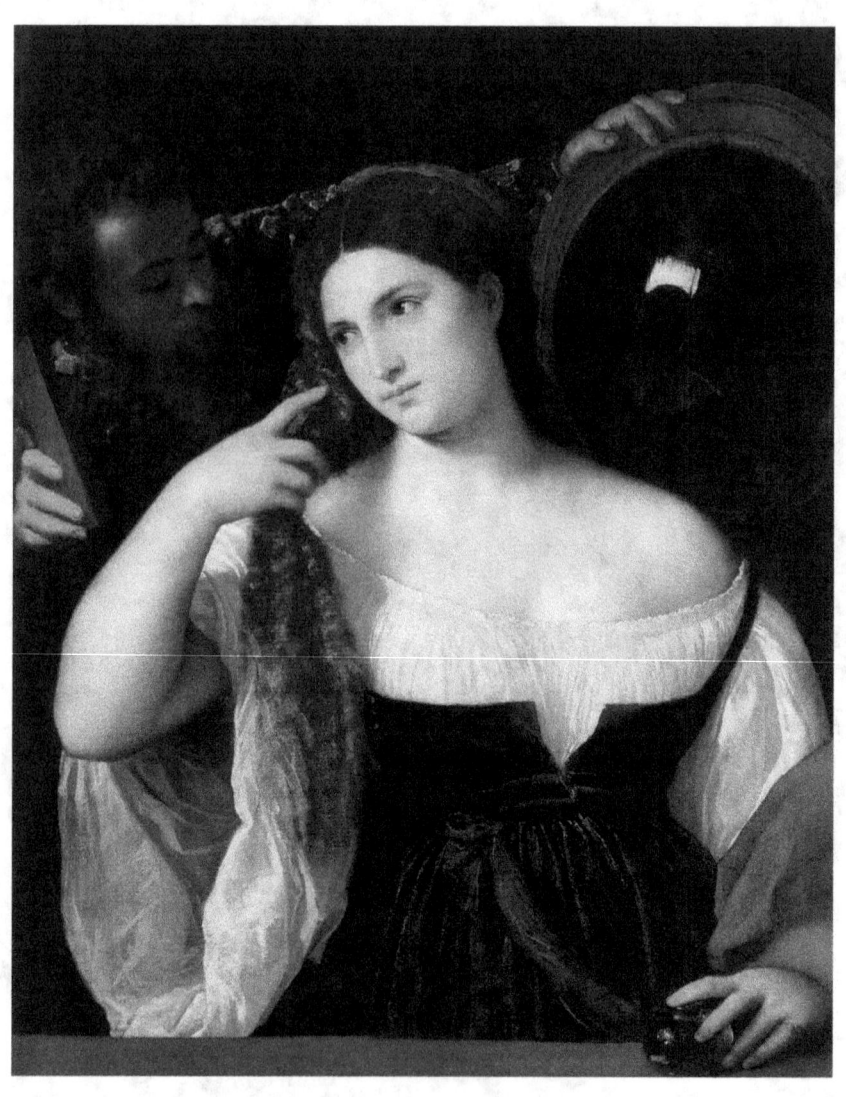

Titian, Woman With a Mirror, 1514, Louvre

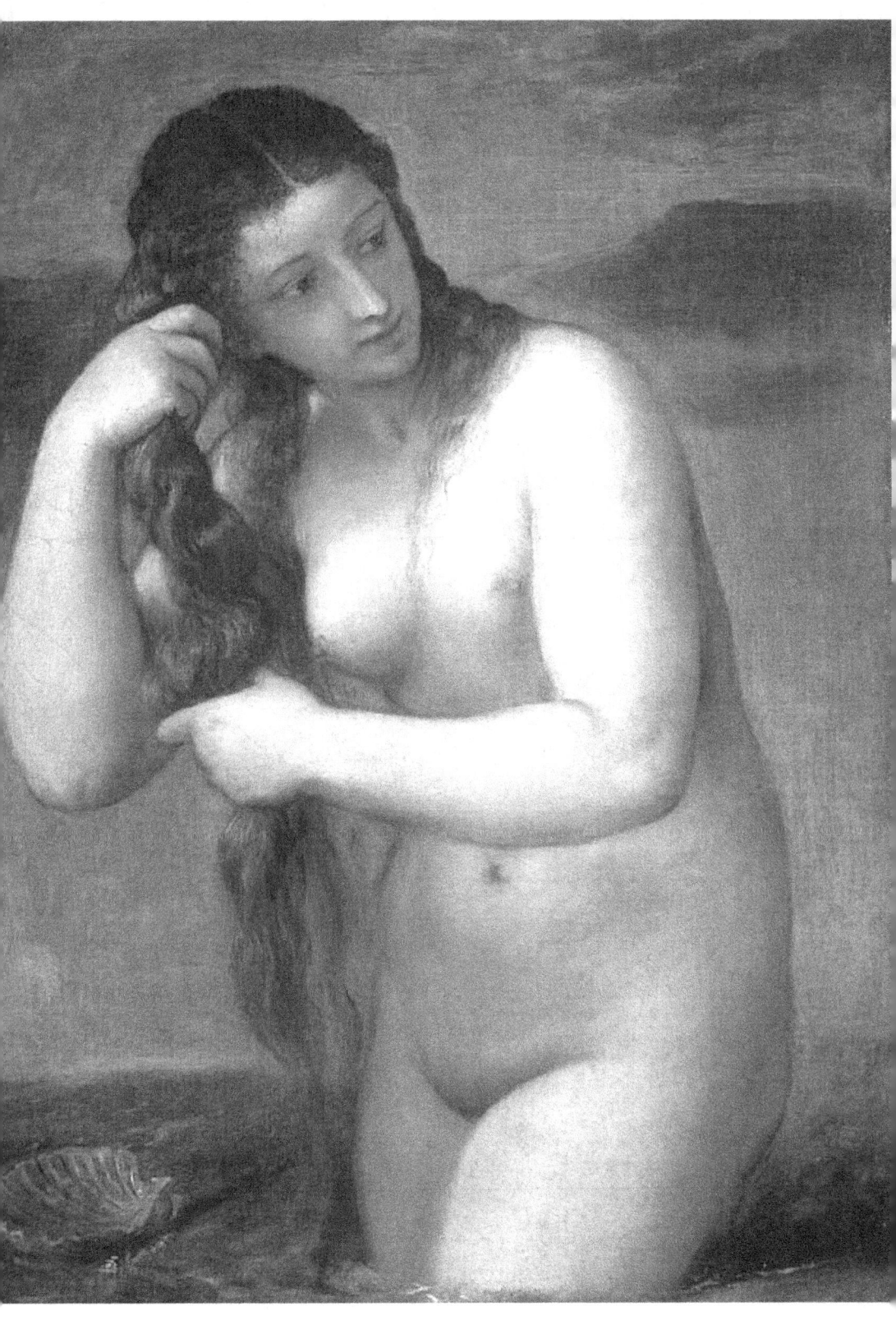

Titian, Venus Rising From the Sea, 1520, Scotland

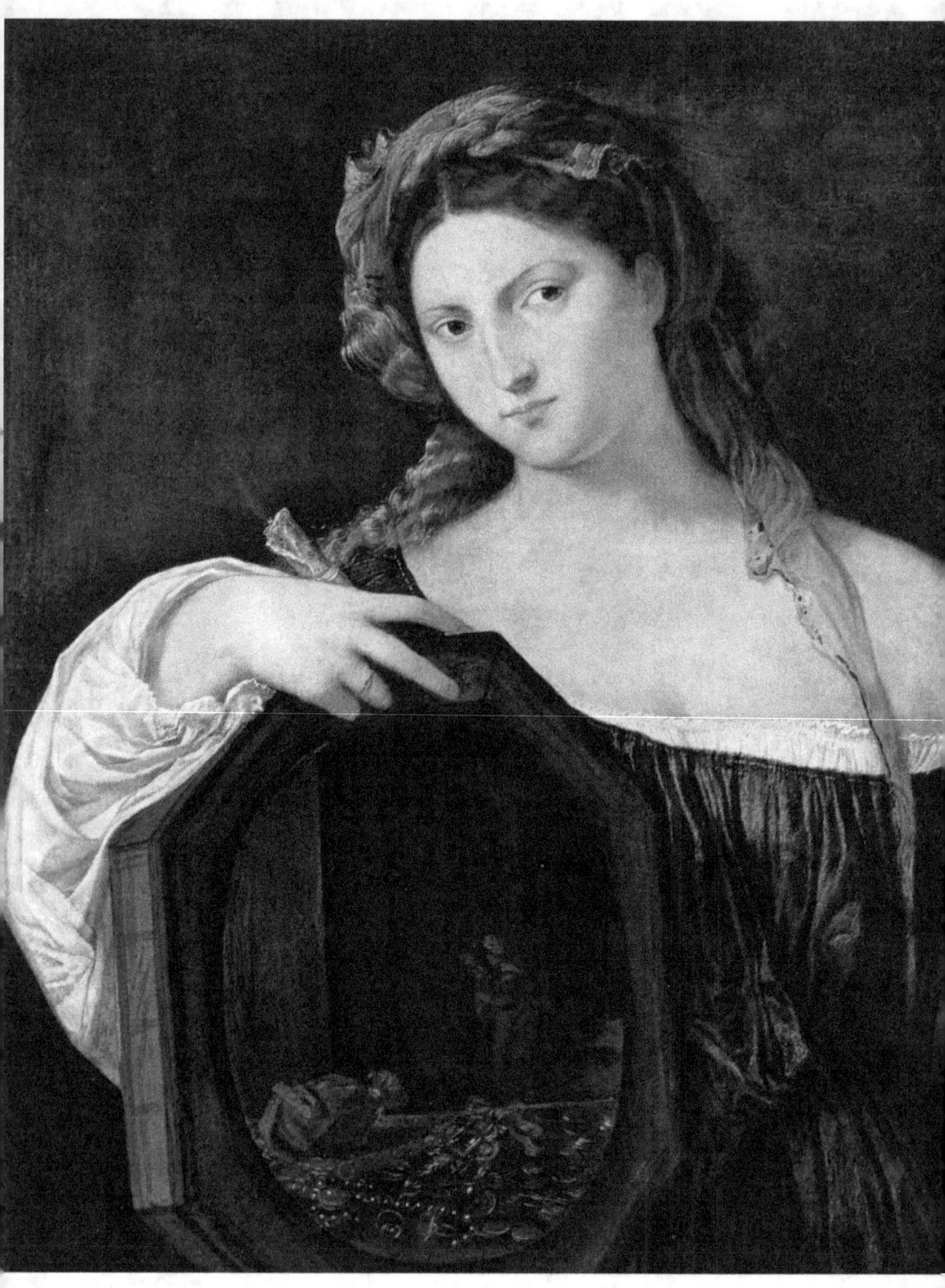

Titian, Vanita, 1511, Alte Pinakothek, München

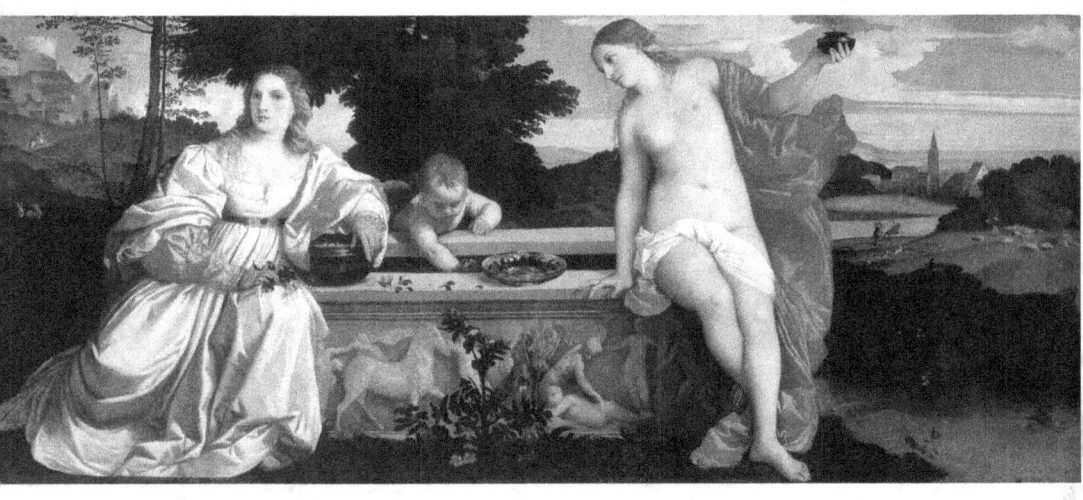

Titian, Sacred and Profane Love, 1514, Villa Borghese

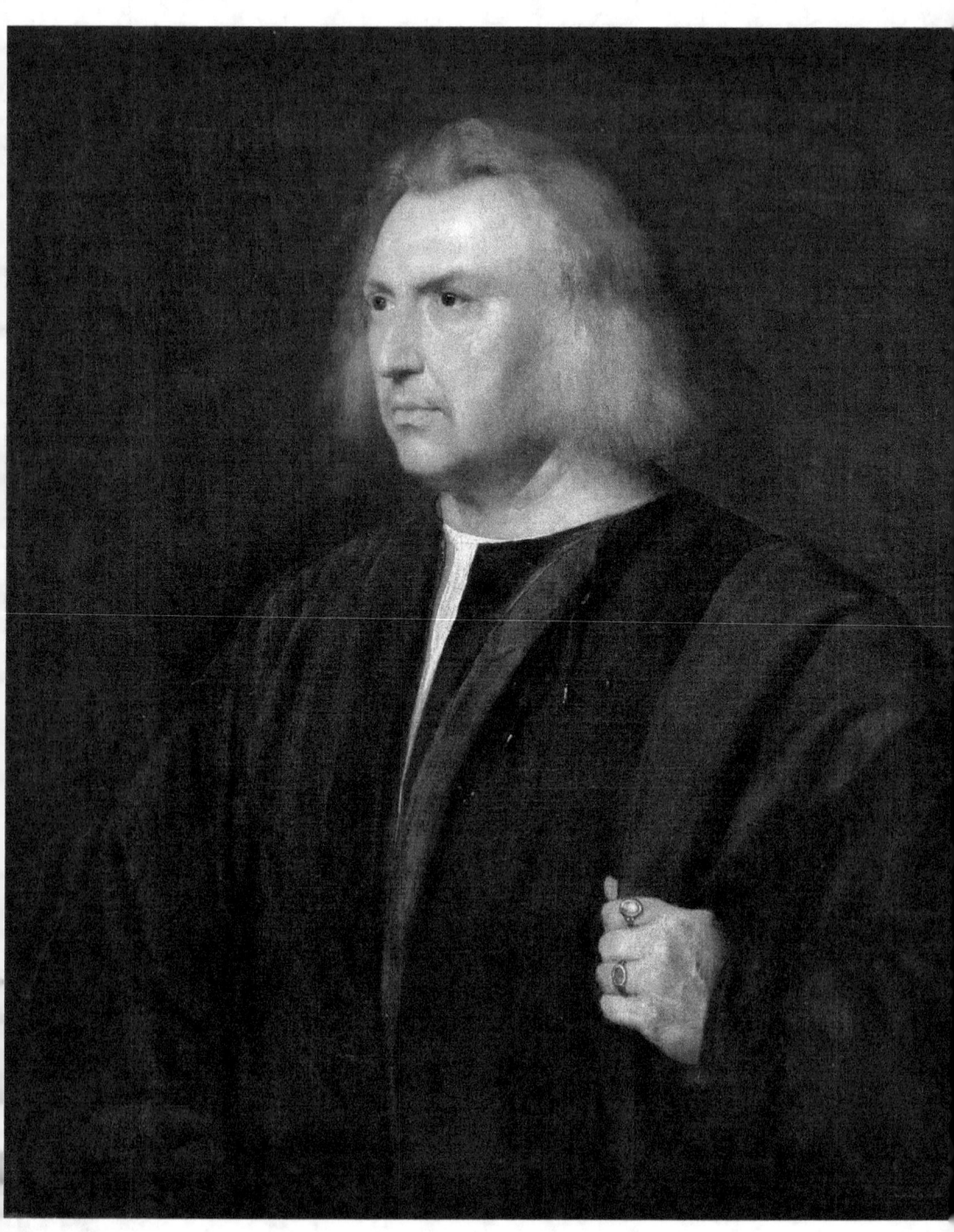

Titian, Gian Giacomo Bartolotti da Parma, 1518, Vienna

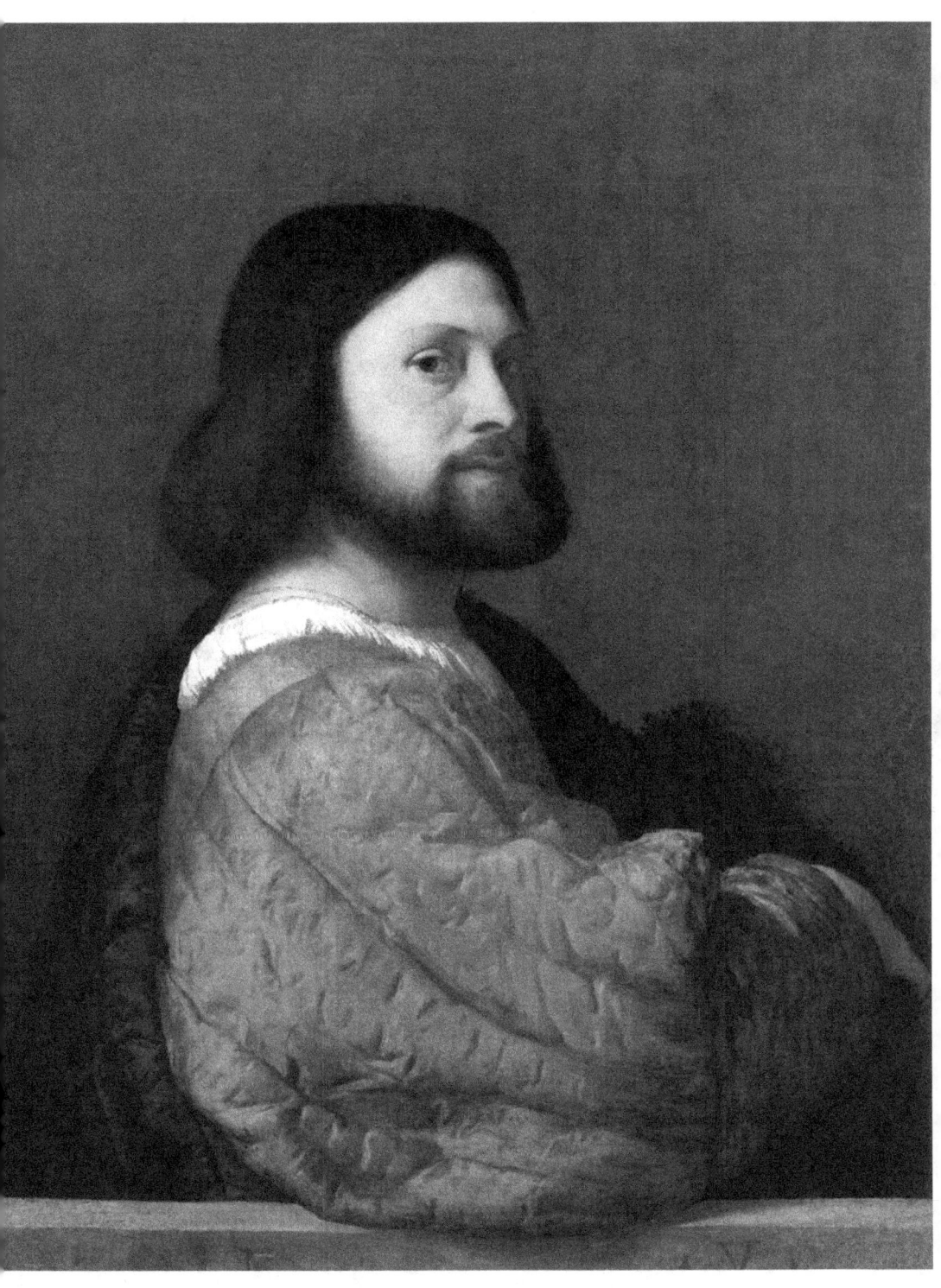

Titian, Man With the Blue Sleeve, 1510-11,
National Gallery, London

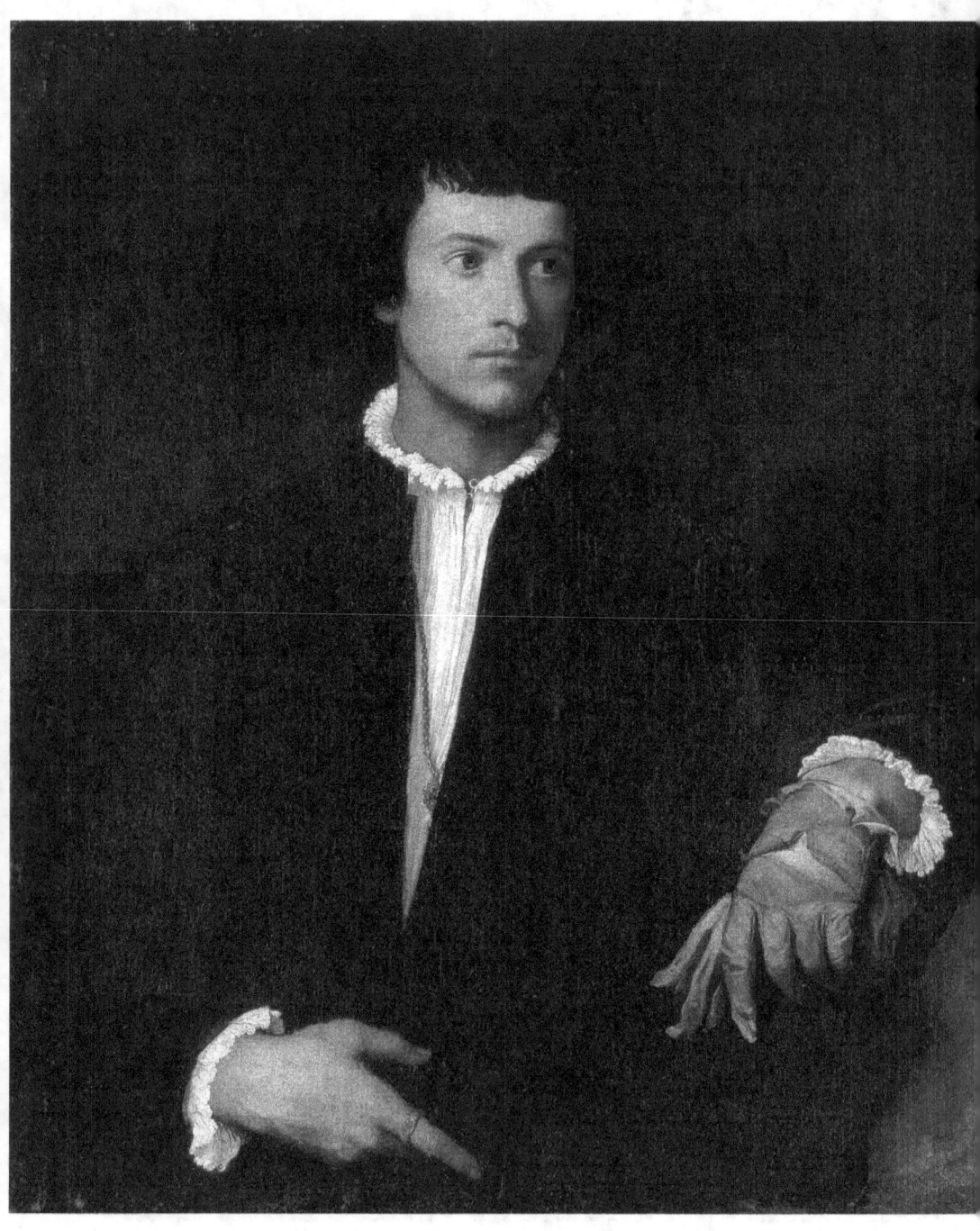

Titian, Man With a Glove, 1520, Louvre

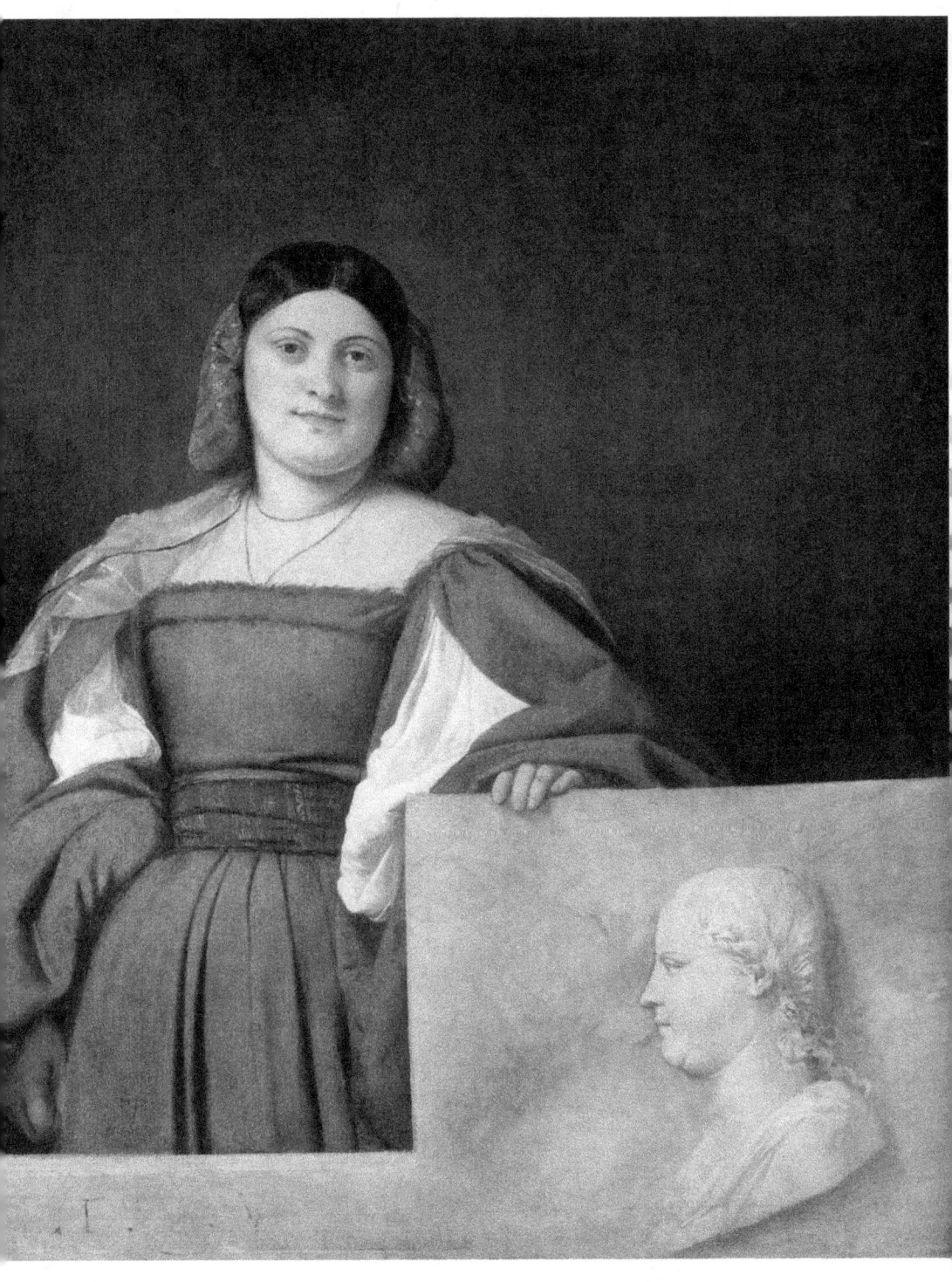

Titian, La Schiavona, 1510,
National Gallery, London

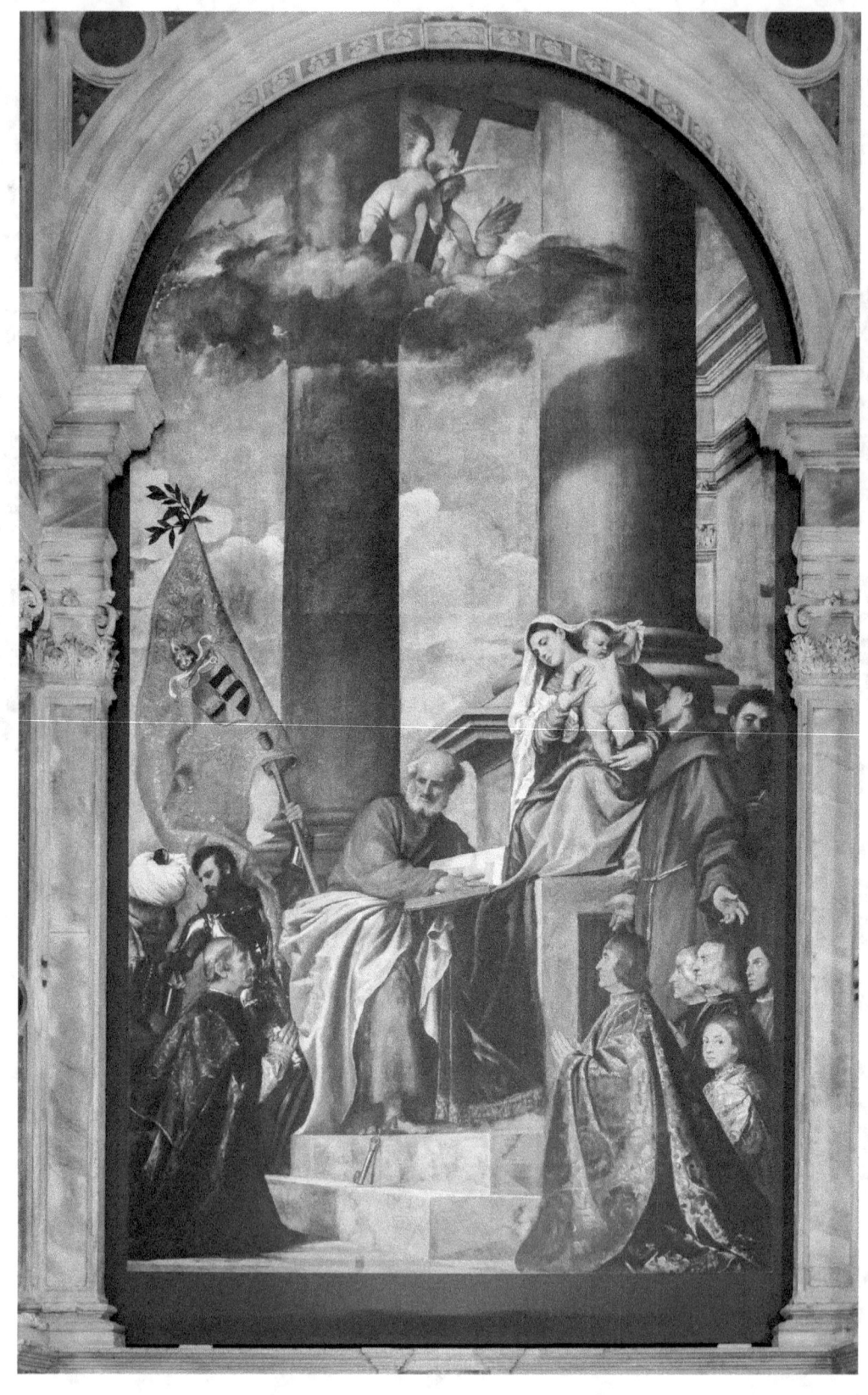

Titian, Pesaro Altarpiece, 1519-26, Friari , Venice

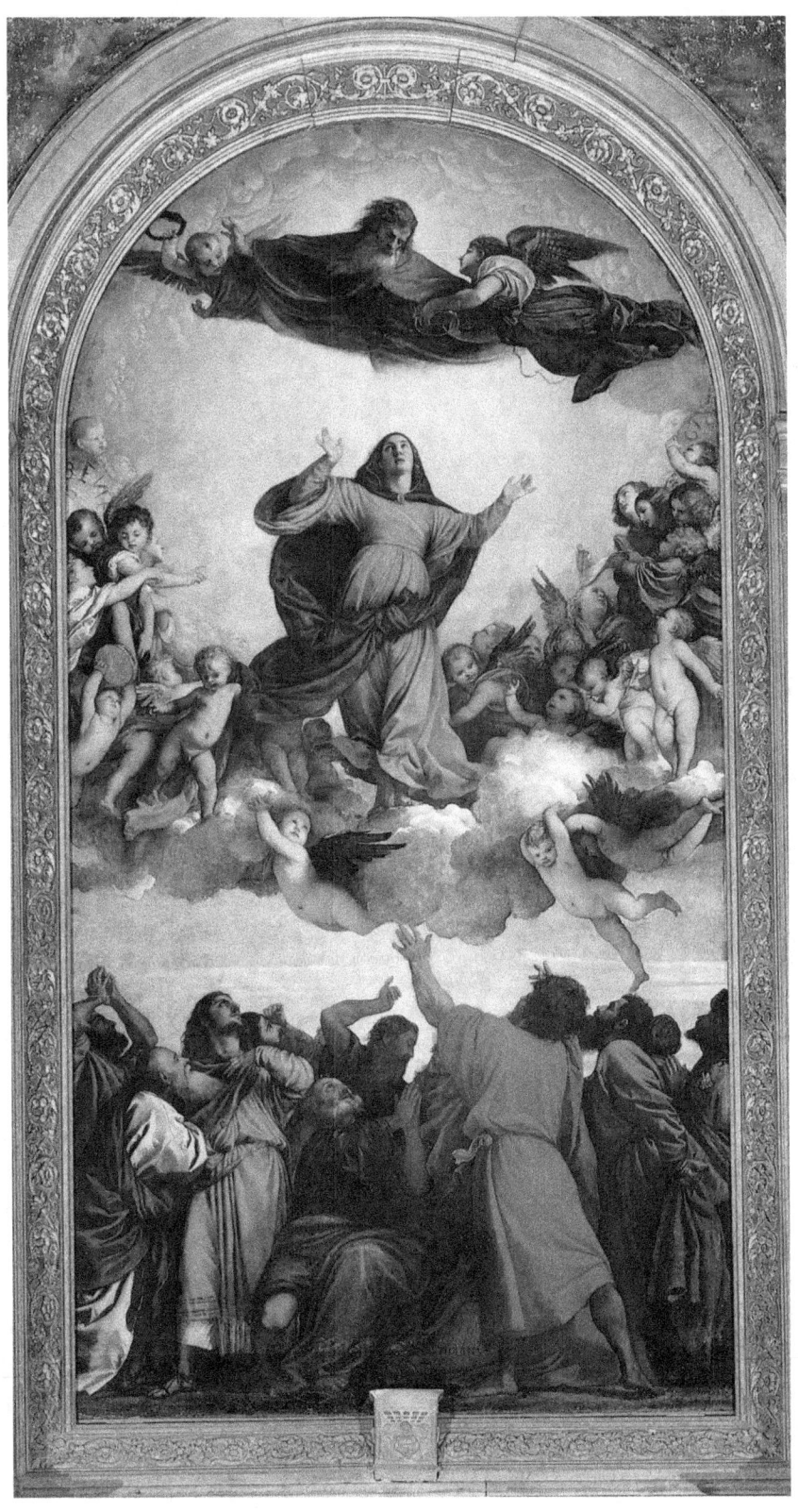

Titian, Assumption of the Virgin, 1517-18, Venice

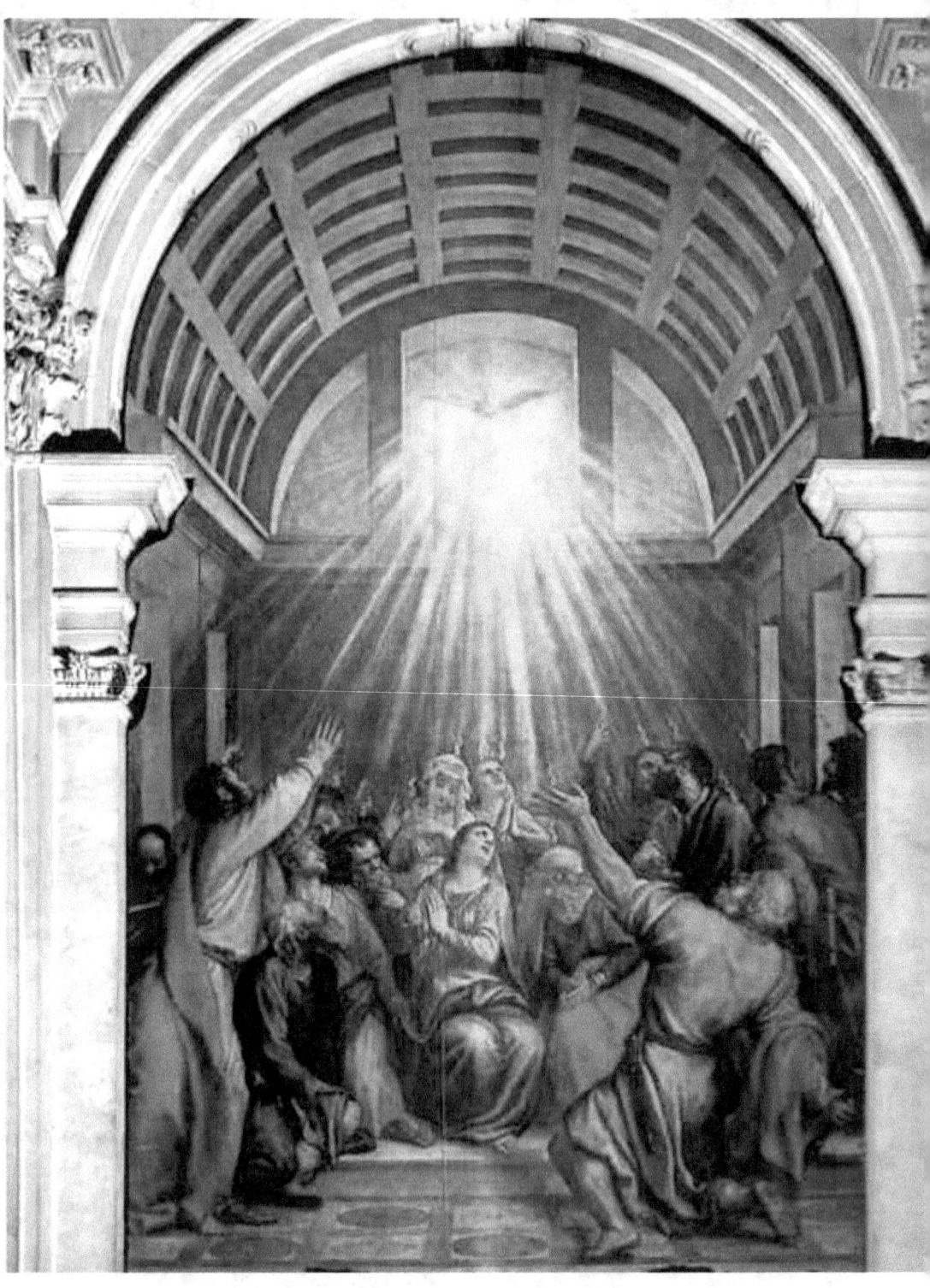

Titian, The Descent of the Holy Spirit, Venice

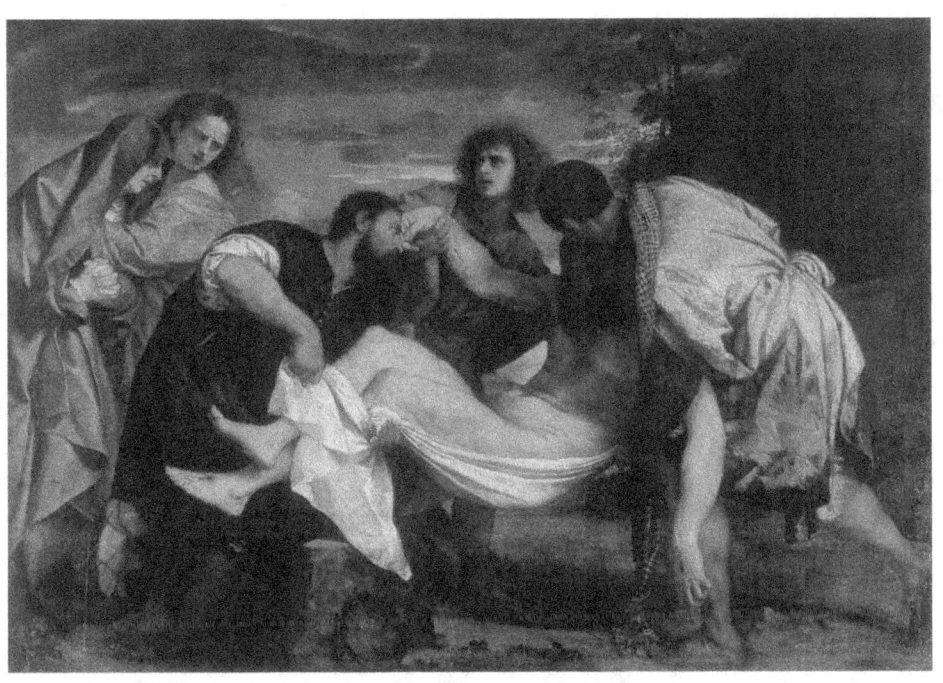

Titian, The Entombment, 1523-26, Louvre

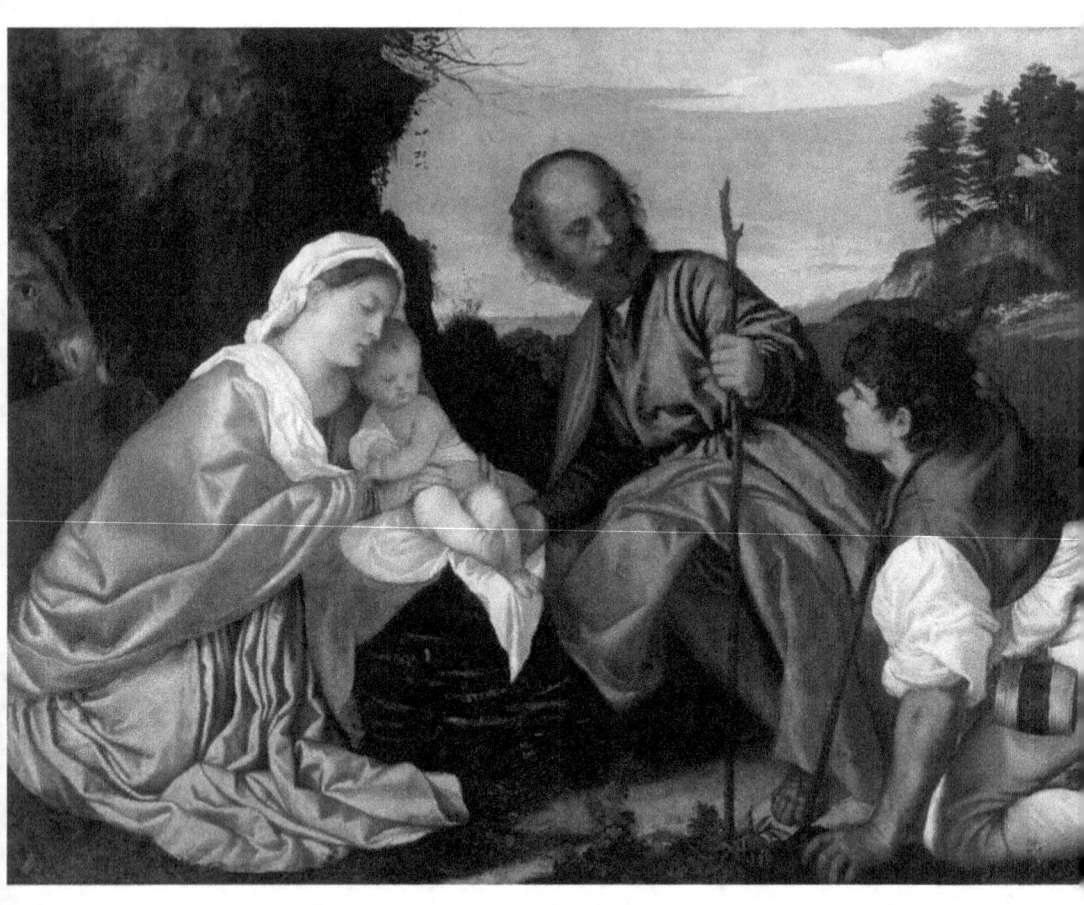

Titian, The Holy Family With a Shepherd, 1510,
National Gallery, Lndon

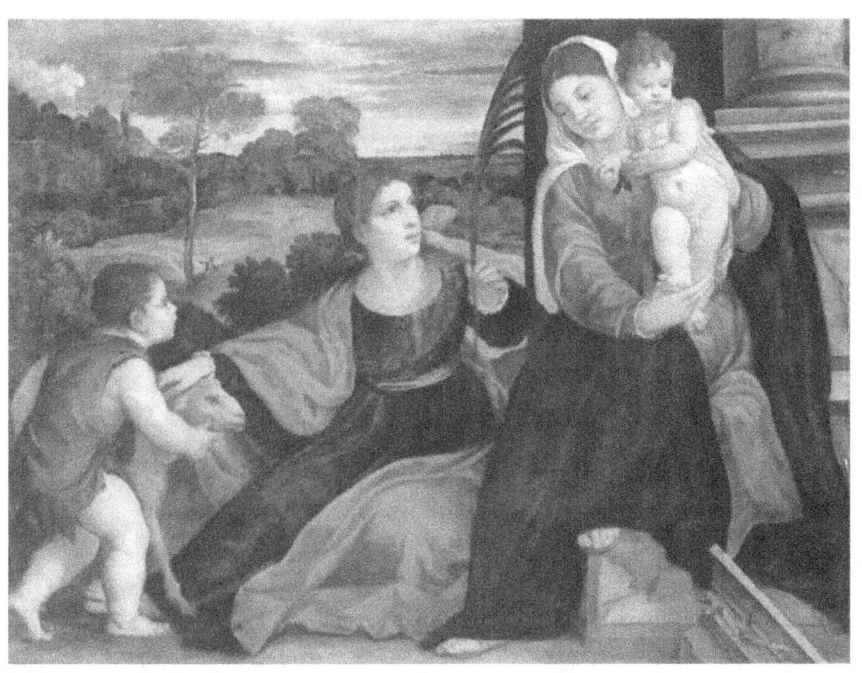

Titian, Madonna and Child With Saints Agnes and the Baptist, Dijon

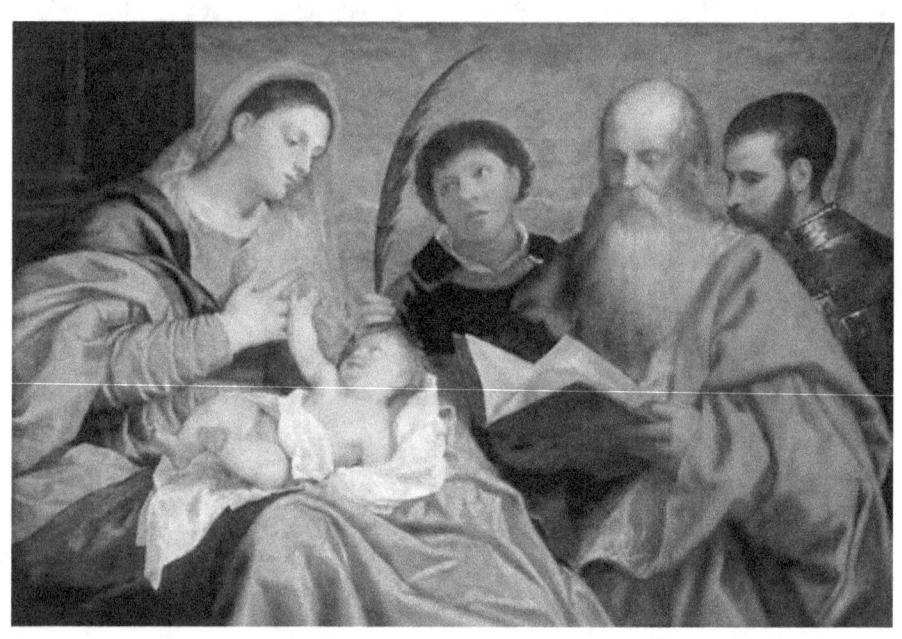

Titian, Madonna and Child With Saints, 1520, Vienna

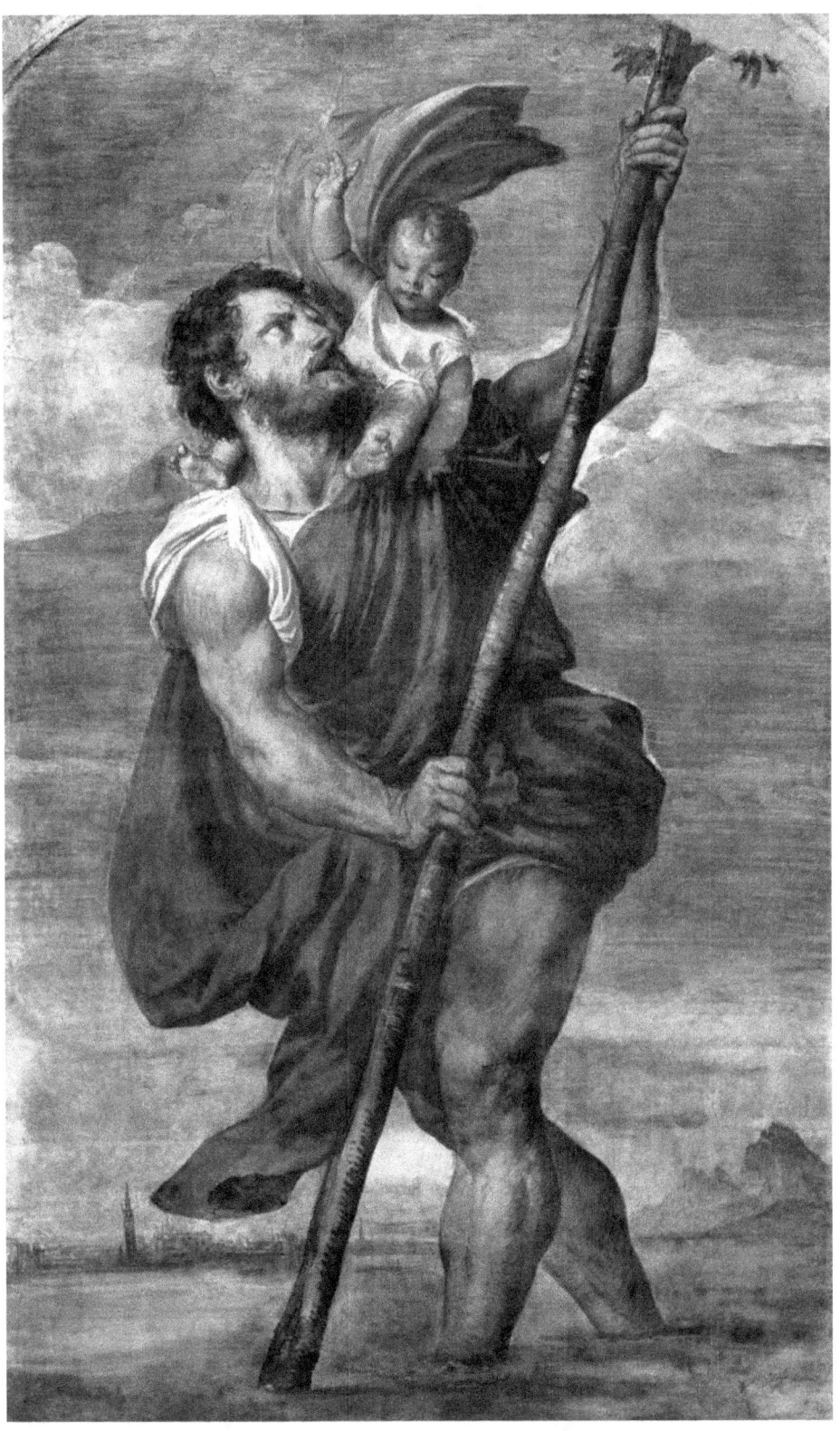

Titian, St Christopher, 1524, Venice

# CHAPTER II

*Frescoes of the Scuola del Santo – The "Herodias" type of picture – Holy Families and Sacred Conversations – Date of the "Cristo della Moneta" Is the "Concert" of the Pitti by Titian? – The "Bacchanal" of Alnwick Castle.*

It has been pointed out by Titian's biographers that the wars which followed upon the League of Cambrai had the effect of dispersing all over North Italy the chief Venetian artists of the younger generation. It was not long after this – on the death of his master Giorgione – that Sebastiano Luciani migrated to Rome and, so far as he could, shook off his allegiance to the new Venetian art; it was then that Titian temporarily left the city of his adoption to do work in fresco at Padua and Vicenza. If the date 1508, given by Vasari for the great frieze-like wood-engraving, *The Triumph of Faith*, be accepted, it must be held that it was executed before the journey to Padua. Ridolfi[*23] cites painted compositions of the *Triumph* as either the originals or the repetitions of the wood-engravings, for which Titian himself drew the blocks. The frescoes themselves, if indeed Titian carried them out on the walls of his house at Padua, as has been suggested, have perished; but that they ever came into existence there would not appear to be any direct evidence. The types, though broadened and coarsened in the process of translation into wood-engraving, are not materially at variance with those in the frescoes of the Scuola del Santo. But the movement, the spirit of the whole is essentially different. This mighty, onward-sweeping procession, with Adam and Eve, the Patriarchs, the Prophets and Sibyls, the martyred Innocents, the great chariot with Christ enthroned, drawn by the four Doctors of the Church and impelled forward by the Emblems of the four Evangelists, with a great company of Apostles and Martyrs following, has all the vigour and elasticity, all the decorative amplitude that is wanting in the frescoes of the Santo. It is obvious that inspiration was derived from the *Triumphs* of Mantegna, then already so widely popularised by numerous engravings. Titian and those under whose inspiration he worked here obviously intended an antithesis to the great series of canvases presenting the apotheosis of Julius Caesar, which were then to be seen in the not far distant Mantua. Have we here another pictorial commentary, like the famous *Cristo detta Moneta,* with which we shall have to deal presently, on the "Quod est Caesaris Caesari, quod est Dei Deo," which was the favourite device of Alfonso of Ferrara and the legend round his gold coins? The whole question is interesting, and deserves more careful consideration than can be accorded to it on the present occasion. Hardly again, until he reached extreme old age, did such an impulse of sacred passion colour the art of the painter of Cadore as here. In the earlier section of his life-work the *Triumph of Faith* constitutes a striking exception.

Passing over, as relatively unimportant, Titian's share in the much-defaced fresco decorations of the Scuola del Carmine, we come now to those more celebrated ones in the Scuola del Santo. Out of the sixteen frescoes executed in 1510-11 by Titian, in concert with Domenico Campagnola and other assistants of less fame, the following three are from the brush of the master himself: – *St. Anthony causes a new-born Infant to speak, testifying to the innocence of its Mother; St. Anthony heals the leg of a Youth; A jealous Husband puts to death his Wife, whom the Saint afterwards* *restores to life*. Here the figures, the composition, the beautiful landscape backgrounds bear unmistakably the trace of Giorgione's influence. The composition has just the timidity, the lack of rhythm and variety, that to the last marks that of Barbarelli. The figures have his naïve truth, his warmth and splendour of life, but not his gilding touch of spirituality to lift the uninspiring subjects a little above the actual. The *Nobleman putting to death his Wife* is dramatic, almost terrible in its fierce, awkward realism, yet it does not rise much higher in interpretation than what our neighbours would to-day call the *drame passionel*. The interest is much the same that is aroused in a student of Elizabethan literature by that study of murder, *Arden of Feversham*, not that higher attraction that he feels – horrors notwithstanding – for *The Maid's Tragedy* of Beaumont and Fletcher, or *The Duchess of Malfi* of Webster.[*24]

A convenient date for the magnificent *St. Mark enthroned, with SS. Sebastian, Roch, Cosmas, and Damianus*, is 1512, when Titian, having completed his share of the work at the Scuola del Santo, returned to Venice. True, it is still thoroughly Giorgionesque, except in the truculent *St. Mark*; but, then, as essentially so were the frescoes just terminated. The noble altar-piece[25] symbolises, or rather commemorates, the steadfastness of the State face to face with the terrors of the League of Cambrai: – on the one side St. Sebastian, standing, perhaps, for martyrdom by superior force of arms, St. Roch for plague (the plague of Venice in 1510); on the other, SS. Cosmas and Damianus, suggesting the healing of these evils. The colour is Giorgionesque in that truer sense in which Barbarelli's own is so to be described. Especially does it show points of contact with that of the so-called *Three Philosophers*, which, on the authority of Marcantonio Michiel (the *Anonimo*), is rightly or wrongly held to be one of the last works of the Castelfranco master. That is to say, it is both sumptuous and boldly contrasted in the local hues, the sovereign unity of general tone not being attained by any sacrifice or attenuation, by any undue fusion of these, as in some of the second-rate

Giorgionesques. Common to both is the use of a brilliant scarlet, which Giorgione successfully employs in the robe of the Trojan Aeneas, and Titian on a more extensive scale in that of one of the healing saints. These last are among the most admirable portrait-figures in the life-work of Titian. In them a simplicity, a concentration akin to that of Giovanni Bellini and Bartolommeo Montagna is combined with the suavity and flexibility of Barbarelli. The St. Sebastian is the most beautiful among the youthful male figures, as the *Venus* of Giorgione and the Venus of the *Sacred and Profane Love* are the most beautiful among the female figures to be found in the Venetian art of a century in which such presentments of youth in its flower abounded. There is something androgynous, in the true sense of the word, in the union of the strength and pride of lusty youth with a grace which is almost feminine in its suavity, yet not offensively effeminate. It should be noted that a delight in portraying the fresh comeliness, the elastic beauty of form proper to the youth just passing into the man was common to many Venetian painters at this stage, and coloured their art as it had coloured the whole art of Greece.

Hereabouts the writer would like to place the singularly attractive, yet a little puzzling, *Madonna and Child with St. Joseph and a Shepherd*, which is No. 4 in the National Gallery. The type of the landscape is early, and even for that time the execution in this particular is, for Titian, curiously small and wanting in breadth. Especially the projecting rock, with its fringe of half-bare shrubs profiled against the sky, recalls the backgrounds of the Scuola del Santo frescoes. The noble type and the stilted attitude of the *St. Joseph* suggest the *St. Mark* of the Salute. The frank note of bright scarlet in the jacket of the thick-set young shepherd, who calls up rather the downrightness of Palma than the idyllic charm of Giorgione, is to be found again in the Salute picture. The unusually pensive Madonna reminds the spectator, by a certain fleshiness and matronly amplitude of proportion, though by no means in sentiment, of the sumptuous dames who look on so unconcernedly in the *St. Anthony causing a new-born Infant to speak*, of the Scuola. Her draperies show, too, the jagged breaks and close parallel folds of the early time before complete freedom of design was attained.

The splendidly beautiful *Herodias with the head of St. John the Baptist*, in the Doria Gallery, formerly attributed to Pordenone, but by Morelli definitively placed among the Giorgionesque works of Titian, belongs to about the same time as the *Sacred and Profane Love*, and would therefore come in rather before than after the sojourn at Padua and Vicenza. The intention has been not so much to emphasise the tragic character of the motive as to exhibit to the highest advantage the voluptuous charm, the languid indifference of a Venetian beauty posing for Herod's baleful consort. Repetitions of this *Herodias* exist in the Northbrook Collection and in that of Mr. R.H. Benson. The latter, which is presumably from the workshop of the master, and shows variations in one or two unimportant particulars from the Doria picture, is here, failing the original, reproduced with the kind permission of the owner. A conception traceable back to Giorgione would appear to underlie, not only this Doria picture, but that *Herodias* which at Dorchester House is, for not obvious reasons, attributed to Pordenone, and another similar one by Palma Vecchio, of which a late copy exists in the collection of the Earl of Chichester. Especially is this community of origin noticeable in the head of St. John on the charger, as it appears in each of these works. All of them again show a family resemblance in this particular respect to the interesting full-length *Judith* at the Hermitage, now ascribed to Giorgione, to the over-painted half-length *Judith* in the Querini-Stampalia Collection at Venice, and to Hollar's print after a picture supposed by the engraver to give the portrait of Giorgione himself in the character of David, the slayer of Goliath.[*26] The sumptuous but much-injured *Vanitas*, which is No. 1110 in the Alte Pinakothek of Munich – a beautiful woman of the same opulent type as the *Herodias*, holding a mirror which reflects jewels and other symbols of earthly vanity – may be classed with the last-named work. Again we owe it to Morelli[27] that this painting, ascribed by Crowe and Cavalcaselle – as the *Herodias* was ascribed – to Pordenone, has been with general acceptance classed among the early works of Titian. The popular *Flora* of the Uffizi, a beautiful thing still, though all the bloom of its beauty has been effaced, must be placed rather later in this section of Titian's life-work, displaying as it does a technique more facile and accomplished, and a conception of a somewhat higher individuality. The model is surely the same as that which has served for the Venus of the *Sacred and Profane Love*, though the picture comes some years after that piece. Later still comes the so-called *Alfonso d'Este and Laura Dianti*, as to which something will be said farther on. Another puzzle is provided by the beautiful *"Noli me tangere"* of the National Gallery, which must necessarily have its place somewhere here among the early works. Giorgionesque the picture still is, and most markedly so in the character of the beautiful landscape; yet the execution shows an altogether unusual freedom and mastery for that period. The *Magdalen* is, appropriately enough, of the same type as the exquisite, golden blond courtezans – or, if you will, models – who constantly appear and reappear in this period of Venetian art. Hardly anywhere has the painter exhibited a more wonderful freedom and subtlety of brush than in the figure of the Christ, in which glowing flesh is so finely set off by the white of fluttering, half-transparent draperies. The canvas has exquisite colour, almost without colours; the only local tint of any very defined character being the dark red of the Magdalen's robe. Yet a certain affectation, a certain exaggeration of fluttering movement and strained attitude repel the beholder a little at first, and neutralise for him the rare beauties of the canvas. It is as if a wave of some strange transient influence had passed over Titian at this moment, then again to be dissipated.

But to turn now once more to the series of our master's Holy Families and Sacred Conversations which began with *La Zingarella*, and was continued with the *Virgin and Child with SS. Ulfo and Brigida* of Madrid. The most popular of all those belonging to this still early time is the *Virgin with the Cherries* in the Vienna Gallery. Here the painter is already completely himself. He will go much farther in breadth if not in polish, in transparency, in forcefulness, if not in attractiveness of colour; but he is now, in sacred art at any rate, practically free from outside influences. For the pensive girl-Madonna of Giorgione we now have the radiant young matron of Titian, joyous yet calm in her play with the infant Christ, while the Madonna of his master and friend was unrestful and full of tender foreboding even in seeming repose. Pretty close on this must have followed the *Madonna and Child with St. Stephen, St. Ambrose and St. Maurice*, No 439 in the Louvre, in which the rich colour-harmonies strike a somewhat deeper note. An atelier repetition of this fine original is No. 166 in the Vienna Gallery; the only material variation traceable in this last-named example being that in lieu of St. Ambrose, wearing a kind of biretta, we have St. Jerome bare-headed.

Very near in time and style to this particular series, with which it may safely be grouped, is the beautiful and finely preserved *Holy Family* in the Bridgewater Gallery, where it is still erroneously attributed to Palma Vecchio. It is to be found in the same private apartment on the groundfloor of Bridgewater House, that contains the *Three Ages*. Deep glowing richness of colour and smooth perfection without smallness of finish make this picture remarkable, notwithstanding its lack of any deeper significance. Nor must there be forgotten in an enumeration of the early Holy Families, one of the loveliest of all, the *Madonna and Child with the infant St. John and St. Anthony Abbot*, which adorns the Venetian section of the Uffizi Gallery. Here the relationship to Giorgione is more clearly shown than in any of these Holy Families of the first period, and in so far the painting, which cannot be placed very early among them, constitutes a partial exception in the series. The Virgin is of a more refined and pensive type than in the *Madonna with the Cherries* of Vienna, or the *Madonna with Saints*, No. 439 in the Louvre, and the divine Bambino less robust in build and aspect. The magnificent St. Anthony is quite Giorgion-esque in the serenity tinged with sadness of his contemplative mood.

Last of all in this particular group – another work in respect of which Morelli has played the rescuer – is the *Madonna and Child with Four Saints*, No. 168 in the Dresden Gallery, a much-injured but eminently Titianesque work, which may be said to bring this particular series to within a couple of years or so of the *Assunta* – that great landmark of the first period of maturity. The type of the Madonna here is still very similar to that in the *Madonna with the Cherries*.

Apart from all these sacred works, and in every respect an exceptional production, is the world-famous *Cristo della Moneta* of the Dresden Gallery. As to the exact date to be assigned to this panel among the early works of Titian considerable difficulty exists. For once agreeing with Crowe and Cavalcaselle, Morelli is inclined to disregard the testimony of Vasari, from whose text it would result that it was painted in or after the year 1514, and to place it as far back as 1508. Notwithstanding this weight of authority the writer is strongly inclined, following Vasari in this instance, and trusting to certain indications furnished by the picture itself, to return to the date 1514 or thereabouts. There is no valid reason to doubt that the *Christ of the Tribute-Money* was painted for Alfonso I. of Ferrara, and the less so, seeing that it so aptly illustrates the already quoted legend on his coins: "Quod est Caesaris Caesari, quod est Dei Deo." According to Vasari, it was painted *nella porta d'un armario* – that is to say, in the door of a press or wardrobe. But this statement need not be taken in its most literal sense. If it were to be assumed from this passage that the picture was painted on the spot, its date must be advanced to 1516, since Titian did not pay his first visit to Ferrara before that year. There is no sufficient ground, however, for assuming that he did not execute his wonderful panel in the usual fashion – that is to say, at home in Venice. The last finishing touches might, perhaps, have been given to it *in situ*, as they were to Bellini's

*Bacchanal,* done also for the Duke of Ferrara. The extraordinary finish of the painting, which is hardly to be paralleled in this respect in the life-work of the artist, may have been due to his desire to "show his hand" to his new patron in a subject which touched him so nearly. And then the finish is not of the Quattrocento type, not such as we find, for instance, in the *Leonardo Loredano* of Giovanni Bellini, the finest panels of Cima, or the early *Christ bearing the Cross* of Giorgione. In it exquisite polish of surface and consummate rendering of detail are combined with the utmost breadth and majesty of composition, with a now perfect freedom in the casting of the draperies. It is difficult, indeed, to imagine that this masterpiece – so eminently a work of the Cinquecento, and one, too, in which the master of Cadore rose superior to all influences, even to that of Giorgione – could have been painted in 1508, that is some two years before Bellini's *Baptism of Christ* in S. Corona, and in all probability before the *Three Philosophers* of Giorgione himself. The one of Titian's own early pictures with which it appears to the writer to have most in common – not so much in technique, indeed, as in general style – is the *St. Mark* of the Salute, and than this it is very much less Giorgionesque. To praise the *Cristo della Moneta* anew after it has been so incomparably well praised seems almost an impertinence. The soft radiance of the colour so well matches the tempered majesty, the infinite mansuetude of the conception; the spirituality, which is of the essence of the august subject, is so happily expressed, without any sensible diminution of the splendour of Renaissance art approaching its highest. And yet nothing could well be simpler than the scheme of colour as compared with the complex harmonies which Venetian art in a somewhat later phase affected. Frank contrasts are established between the tender, glowing flesh of the Christ, seen in all the glory of achieved manhood, and the coarse, brown skin of the son of the people who appears as the Pharisee; between the bright yet tempered red of His robe and the deep blue of His mantle. But the golden glow, which is Titian's own, envelops the contrasting figures and the contrasting hues in its harmonising atmosphere, and gives unity to the whole.[*28]

A small group of early portraits – all of them somewhat difficult to place – call for attention before we proceed. Probably the earliest portrait among those as yet recognised as from the hand of our painter – leaving out of the question the *Baffo* and the portrait-figures in the great *St. Mark* of the Salute – is the magnificent *Ariosto* in the Earl of Darnley's Collection at Cobham Hall.[*29] There is very considerable doubt, to say the least, as to whether this half-length really represents the court poet of Ferrara, but the point requires more elaborate discussion than can be here conceded to it. Thoroughly Giorgionesque is the soberly tinted yet sumptuous picture in its general arrangement, as in its general tone, and in this respect it is the fitting companion and the descendant of Giorgione's *Antonio Broccardo* at Buda-Pesth, of his *Knight of Malta* at the Uffizi. Its resemblance, moreover, is, as regards the general lines of the composition, a very striking one to the celebrated Sciarra *Violin-Player* by Sebastiano del Piombo, now in the gallery of Baron Alphonse Rothschild at Paris, where it is as heretofore given to Raphael.[*30] The handsome, manly head has lost both subtlety and character through some too severe process of cleaning, but Venetian art has hardly anything more magnificent to show than the costume, with the quilted sleeve of steely, blue-grey satin which occupies so prominent a place in the picture.

The so-called *Concert* of the Pitti Palace, which depicts a young Augustinian monk as he plays on a keyed instrument, having on one side of him a youthful cavalier in a plumed hat, on the other a bareheaded clerk holding a bass-viol, was, until Morelli arose, almost universally looked upon as one of the most typical Giorgiones.[*31] The most gifted of the purely aesthetic critics who have approached the Italian Renaissance, Walter Pater, actually built round this *Concert* his exquisite study on the School of Giorgione. There can be little doubt, notwithstanding, that Morelli was right in denying the authorship of Barbarelli, and tentatively, for he does no more, assigning the so subtly attractive and pathetic *Concert* to the early time of Titian. To express a definitive opinion on the latter point in the present state of the picture would be somewhat hazardous. The portrait of the modish young cavalier and that of the staid elderly clerk, whose baldness renders tonsure impossible – that is just those portions of the canvas which are least well preserved – are also those that least conclusively suggest our master. The passion-worn, ultra-sensitive physiognomy of the young Augustinian is, undoubtedly, in its very essence a Giorgionesque creation, for the fellows of which we must turn to the Castelfranco master's just now cited *Antonio Broccardo*, to his male portraits in Berlin and at the Uffizi, to his figure of the youthful Pallas, son of Evander, in the *Three Philosophers*. Closer to it, all the same, are the *Raffo* and the two portraits in the *St. Mark* of the Salute, and closer still is the supremely fine *Jeune Homme au Gant* of the Salon Carré, that later production of Vecelli's early time. The *Concert* of the Pitti, so far as it can be judged through the retouches that cover it, displays an art certainly not finer or more delicate, but yet in its technical processes broader, swifter, and more synthetic than anything that we can with certainty point to in the life-work of Barbarelli. The large but handsome and flexible hands of the player are much nearer in type and treatment to Titian than they are to his master. The beautiful motive – music for one happy moment uniting by invisible bonds of sympathy three human beings – is akin to that in the *Three Ages*, though there love steps in as the beautifier of rustic harmony. It is to be found also in Giorgione's *Concert Champêtre*, in the Louvre, in which the thrumming of the lute is, however, one among many delights appealing to the senses. This smouldering heat, this tragic passion in which youth revels, looking back already with discontent, yet forward also with unquenchable yearning, is the keynote of the Giorgionesque and the early Titianesque male portraiture. It is summed up by the *Antonio Broccardo* of the first, by the *Jeune Homme au Gant* of the second. Altogether other, and less due to a reaction from physical ardour, is the exquisite sensitiveness of Lorenzo Lotto, who sees most willingly in his sitters those qualities that are in the closest sympathy with his own highly-strung nature, and loves to present them as some secret, indefinable woe tears at their heart-strings. A strong element of the Giorgionesque pathos informs still and gives charm to the Sciarra *Violin-Player* of Sebastiano del Piombo; only that there it is already tempered by the haughty self-restraint more proper to Florentine and Roman portraiture. There is little or nothing to add after this as to the *Jeune Homme au Gant*, except that as a representation of aristocratic youth it has hardly a parallel among the master's works except, perhaps, a later and equally admirable, though less distinguished, portrait in the Pitti.

Not until Van Dyck, refining upon Rubens under the example of the Venetians, painted in the *pensieroso* mood his portraits of high-bred English cavaliers in all the pride of adolescence or earliest manhood, was this particular aspect of youth in its flower again depicted with the same felicity.[*32]

To Crowe and Cavalcaselle's pages the reader must be referred for a detailed and interesting account of Titian's intrigues against the venerable Giovanni Bellini in connection with the Senseria, or office of broker, to the merchants of the Fondaco de' Tedeschi. We see there how, on the death of the martial pontiff, Julius the Second, Pietro Bembo proposed to Titian to take service with the new Medici Pope, Leo the Tenth (Giovanni de' Medici), and how Navagero dissuaded him from such a step. Titian, making the most of his own magnanimity, proceeds to petition the Doge and Signori for the first vacant broker's patent for life, on the same conditions and with the same charges and exemptions as are conceded to Giovanni Bellini. The petition is presented on the 31st of May 1513, and the Council of Ten on that day moves and carries a resolution accepting Titian's offer with all the conditions attached. Though he has arrived at the extreme limit of his splendid career, old Gian Bellino, who has just given new proof of his still transcendent power in the great altar-piece of

S. Giovanni Crisostomo (1513), which is in some respects the finest of all his works, declines to sit still under the encroachments of his dangerous competitor, younger than himself by half a century. On the 24th of March 1514 the Council of Ten revokes its decree of the previous May, and formally declares that Titian is not to receive his broker's patent on the first vacancy, but must wait his turn. Seemingly nothing daunted, Titian petitions again, asking for the reversion of the particular broker's patent which will become vacant on the death of Giovanni Bellini; and this new offer, which stipulates for certain special payments and provisions, is accepted by the Council. Titian, like most other holders of the much-coveted office, shows himself subsequently much more eager to receive its not inconsiderable emoluments than to finish the pictures, the painting of which is the one essential duty attached to the office. Some further bargaining takes place with the Council on the 18th of January 1516, but, a few days after the death of Giovanni Bellini at the end of November in the same year, fresh resolutions are passed postponing the grant to Titian of Bellini's patent; notwithstanding which, there is conclusive evidence of a later date to show that he is allowed the full enjoyment of his "Senseria in Fontego di Tedeschi" (sic), with all its privileges and immunities, before the close of this same year, 1516.

It is in this year that Titian paid his first visit to Ferrara, and entered into relations with Alfonso I., which were to become more intimate as the position of the master became greater and more universally recognised in Italy. It was here, as we may safely assume, that he completed, or, it may be, repaired, Giovanni Bellini's last picture, the great *Bacchanal* or *Feast of the Gods on Earth*, now at Alnwick Castle. It is there that he obtained the commission for two famous works, the *Worship of Venus* and the *Bacchanal*, designed, in continuation of the series commenced with Bellini's *Feast of the Gods*, to adorn a favourite apartment in Alfonso's castle of Ferrara; the series being completed a little later on by that crown and climax of the whole set, the *Bacchus and*

*Ariadne* of the National Gallery.

Bellini appears in an unfamiliar phase in this final production of his magnificent old age, on which the signature, together with the date, 1514, so carefully noted by Vasari, is still most distinctly to be read. Much less Giorgionesque – if the term be in this case permissible – and more Quattrocentist in style than in the immediately preceding altar-piece of S. Giovanni Crisostomo, he is here hardly less interesting. All admirers of his art are familiar with the four beautiful *Allegories* of the Accademia delle Belle Arti at Venice, which constitute, besides the present picture, almost his sole excursion into the regions of pagan mythology and symbolism. These belong, however, to a considerably earlier period of his maturity, and show a fire which in the *Bacchanal* has died out.[*33] Vasari describes this *Bacchanal* as "one of the most beautiful works ever executed by Gian Bellino," and goes on to remark that it has in the draperies "a certain angular (or cutting) quality in accordance with the German style." He strangely attributes this to an imitation of Dürer's *Rosenkranzfest*, painted some eight years previously for the Church of San Bartolommeo, adjacent to the Fondaco de' Tedeschi. This particularity, noted by the author of the *Vite*, and, in some passages, a certain hardness and opacity of colour, give rise to the surmise that, even in the parts of the picture which belong to Bellini, the co-operation of Basaiti may be traced. It was he who most probably painted the background and the figure of St. Jerome in the master's altar-piece finished in the preceding year for S. Giovanni Crisostomo; it was he, too, who to a great extent executed, though he cannot have wholly devised, the Bellinesque *Madonna in Glory with Eight Saints* in the Church of San Pietro Martire at Murano, which belongs to this exact period. Even in the *Madonna* of the Brera Gallery (1510), which shows Gian Bellino's finest landscape of the late time, certain hardnesses of colour in the main group suggest the possibility of a minor co-operation by Basaiti. Some passages of the *Bacchanal*, however – especially the figures of the two blond, fair-breasted goddesses or nymphs who, in a break in the trees, stand relieved against the yellow bands of a sunset sky – are as beautiful as anything that Venetian art in its Bellinesque phase has produced up to the date of the picture's appearance. Very suggestive of Bellini is the way in which the hair of some of the personages is dressed in heavy formal locks, such as can only be produced by artificial means. These are to be found, no doubt, chiefly in his earliest or Paduan period, when they are much more defined and rigid. Still this coiffure – for as such it must be designated – is to be found more or less throughout the master's career. It is very noticeable in the *Allegories* just mentioned.

Infinitely pathetic is the old master's vain attempt to infuse into the chosen subject the measure of Dionysiac vehemence that it requires. An atmosphere of unruffled peace, a grand serenity, unconsciously betraying life-weariness, replaces the amorous unrest that courses like fire through the veins of his artistic offspring, Giorgione and Titian. The audacious gestures and movements naturally belonging to this rustic festival, in which the gods unbend and, after the homelier fashion of mortals, rejoice, are indicated; but they are here gone through, it would seem, only *pour la forme*. A careful examination of the picture substantially confirms Vasari's story that the *Feast of the Gods* was painted upon by Titian, or to put it otherwise, suggests in many passages a Titianesque hand. It may well be, at the same time, that Crowe and Cavalcaselle are right in their conjecture that what the younger master did was rather to repair injury to the last work of the elder and supplement it by his own than to complete a picture left unfinished by him. The whole conception, the *charpente*, the contours of even the landscape are attributable to Bellini. His are the carefully-defined, naked tree-trunks to the right, with above in the branches a pheasant, and on a twig, in the immediate foreground of the picture, a woodpecker; his is the rocky formation of the foreground with its small pebbles.[*34] Even the tall, beetling crag, crowned with a castle sunset-lit – so confidently identified with the rock of Cadore and its castle – is Bellinesque in conception, though not in execution. By Titian, and brushed in with a loose breadth that might be taken to betray a certain impatience and lack of interest, are the rocks, the cloud-flecked blue sky, the uplands and forest-growth to the left, the upper part of the foliage that caps the hard, round tree-trunks to the right. If it is Titian that we have here, as certainly appears most probable, he cannot be deemed to have exerted his full powers in completing or developing the Bellinesque landscape. The task may well, indeed, have presented itself to him as an uninviting one. There is nothing to remind the beholder, in conception or execution, of the exquisite Giorgionesque landscapes in the *Three Ages* and the *Sacred and Profane Love*, while the broader handling suggests rather the technical style, but in no way the beauty of the sublime prospect which opens out in the *Bacchus and Ariadne*.

# CHAPTER III

*The "Worship of Venus" and "Bacchanal" Place in Art of the "Assunta" – The "Bacchus and Ariadne" – So-called Portraits of Alfonso of Ferrara and Laura Dianti – The "St. Sebastian" of Brescia – Altar-pieces at Ancona and in the Vatican – The "Entombment" of the Louvre – The "Madonna di Casa Pesaro" – Place among Titian's works of "St. Peter Martyr."*

In the year in which Titian paid his first visit to Ferrara, Ariosto brought out there his first edition of the *Orlando Farioso*.[*35] A greater degree of intimacy between poet and painter has in some quarters been presupposed than probably existed at this stage of Titian's career, when his relation to Alfonso and the Ferrarese Court was far from being as close as it afterwards became. It has accordingly been surmised that in the *Worship of Venus* and the *Bacchanal*, painted for Alfonso, we have proof that he yielded to the influence of the romantic poet who infused new life-blood into the imaginative literature of the Italian Renaissance. In their frank sensuousness, in their fulness of life, in their unforced marriage of humanity to its environment, these very pictures are, however, essentially Pagan and Greek, not by any process of cold and deliberate imitation, but by a similar natural growth from a broad groundwork provided by Nature herself. It was the passionate and unbridled Dosso Dossi who among painters stood in the closest relation to Ariosto, both in his true vein of romanticism and his humorous eccentricity.

In the *Worship of Venus* and the *Bacchanal* we have left behind already the fresh morning of Titian's genius, represented by the Giorgionesque works already enumerated, and are rapidly approaching its bright noon. Another forward step has been taken, but not without some evaporation of the subtle Giorgionesque perfume exhaled by the more delicate flowers of genius of the first period. The *Worship of Venus* might be more appropriately named *Games of the Loves in Honour of Venus*. The subject is taken from the *Imagines*[*36] *of Philostratus,* a renowned Greek sophist, who, belonging to a late period of the Roman Empire, yet preserved intact the self-conscious grace and charm of the Hellenistic mode of conception. The theme is supplied by a series of paintings, supposed to have been seen by him in a villa near Naples, but by one important group of modern scholars held to be creations of the author's fertile brain. Before a statue of Venus more or less of the Praxitelean type – a more earthly sister of those which have been named the "Townley Venus" and the "Vénus d'Arles" – myriads of Loves sport, kissing, fondling, leaping, flying, playing rhythmic games, some of them shooting arrows at the opposing faction, to which challenge merry answer is made with the flinging of apples. Incomparable is the vigour, the life, the joyousness of the whole, and incomparable must have been the splendour of the colour before the outrages of time (and the cleaner) dimmed it. These delicious pagan *amorini* are the successors of the angelic *putti* of an earlier time, whom the Tuscan sculptors of the Quattrocento had already converted into more joyous and more earthly beings than their predecessors had imagined. Such painters of the North, in touch with the South, as Albrecht Dürer, Mabuse, and Jacob Cornelissen van Oostsanen, delighted in scattering through their sacred works these lusty, thick-limbed little urchins, and made them merrier and more mischievous still, with their quaint Northern physiognomy. To say nothing on this occasion of Albani, Poussin, and the Flemish sculptors of the seventeenth century, with Du Quesnoy and Van Opstal at their head, Rubens and Van Dyck derived their chief inspiration in similar subjects from these Loves of Titian.[*37]

The sumptuous *Bacchanal*, for which, we are told, Alfonso gave the commission and supplied the subject in 1518, is a performance of a less delicate charm but a more realistic vigour than its companion. From certain points of analogy with an *Ariadne* described by Philostratus, it has been very generally assumed that we have here a representation of the daughter of Minos consoled already for the departure of Theseus, whose sail gleams white on the blue sea in the distance. No Dionysus is, however, seen here among the revellers, who, in their orgies, do honour to the god, Ariadne's new lover. The revel in a certain audacious abandon denotes rather the festival from which the protagonists have retired, leaving the scene to the meaner performers. Even a certain agreement in pose between the realistic but lovely figure of the Bacchante, overcome with the fumes of wine, and the late classic statues then, and until lately, entitled *The Sleeping Ariadne*, does not lead the writer to believe that we have here the new spouse of Dionysus so lately won back from despair. The undraped figure,[*38] both in its attitude and its position in the picture, recalls the half-draped Bacchante, or goddess, in Bellini's *Bacchanal* at Alnwick. Titian's lovely mortal here may rank as a piece of flesh with Correggio's dazzling *Antiope* in the Louvre, but not with Giorgione's *Venus* or Titian's own *Antiope*, in which a certain feminine dignity spiritualises and shields from scorn beauty unveiled and otherwise defenceless. The climax of the splendid and distinctively Titianesque colour-harmony is the agitated crimson garment of the brown-limbed dancer who, facing his white-robed partner, turns his back to the spectator. This has the strongly marked yellowish lights that we find again in the streaming robe of Bacchus in the National Gallery picture, and yet again in the garment of Nicodemus in the *Entombment*.

The charming little *Tambourine Player*, which is No. 181 in the

Vienna Gallery, may be placed somewhere near the time of the great works just now described, but rather before than after them.

What that is new remains to be said about the *Assunta*, or *Assumption of the Virgin*, which was ordered of Titian as early as 1516, but not shown to the public on the high altar of Santa Maria de' Frari until the 20th of March 1518? To appreciate the greatest of extant Venetian altar-pieces at its true worth it is necessary to recall what had and what had not appeared at the time when it shone undimmed upon the world. Thus Raphael had produced the *Stanze*, the *Cartoons*, the *Madonnas of Foligno* and *San Sisto*, but not yet the *Transfiguration;* Michelangelo had six years before uncovered his *magnum opus*, the Ceiling of the Sixtine Chapel; Andrea del Sarto had some four years earlier completed his beautiful series of frescoes at the Annunziata in Florence. Among painters whom, origin notwithstanding, we must group as Venetians, Palma had in 1515 painted for the altar of the Bombardieri at S. Maria Formosa his famous *Santa Barbara;* Lorenzo Lotto in the following year had produced his characteristic and, in its charm of fluttering movement, strangely unconventional altar-piece for S. Bartolommeo at Bergamo, the *Madonna with Ten Saints*. In none of these masterpieces of the full Renaissance, even if they had all been seen by Titian, which was far from being the case, was there any help to be derived in the elaboration of a work which cannot be said to have had any precursor in the art of Venice. There was in existence one altar-piece dealing with the same subject from which Titian might possibly have obtained a hint. This was the *Assumption of the Virgin* painted by Dürer in 1509 for Jacob Heller, and now only known by Paul Juvenel's copy in the Municipal Gallery at Frankfort. The group of the Apostles gazing up at the Virgin, as she is crowned by the Father and the Son, was at the time of its appearance, in its variety as in its fine balance of line, a magnificent novelty in art. Without exercising a too fanciful ingenuity, it would be possible to find points of contact between this group and the corresponding one in the *Assunta*. But Titian could not at that time have seen the original of the Heller altar-piece, which was in the Dominican Church at Frankfort, where it remained for a century.[*39] He no doubt did see the *Assumption* in the *Marienleben* completed in 1510; but then this, though it stands in a definite relation to the Heller altar-piece, is much stiffer and more formal – much less likely to have inspired the master of Cadore. The *Assunta* was already in Vasari's time much dimmed, and thus difficult to see in its position on the high altar. Joshua Reynolds, when he visited the Frari in 1752, says that "he saw it near; it was most terribly dark but nobly painted." Now, in the Accademia delle Belle Arti, it shines forth again, not indeed uninjured, but sufficiently restored to its pristine beauty to vindicate its place as one of the greatest productions of Italian art at its highest. The sombre, passionate splendours of the colouring in the lower half, so well adapted to express the supreme agitation of the moment, so grandly contrast with the golden glory of the skies through which the Virgin is triumphantly borne, surrounded by myriads of angels and cherubim, and awaited by the Eternal. This last is a figure the divine serenity of which is the strongest contrast to those terrible representations of the Deity, so relentless in their superhuman majesty, which, in the ceiling of the Sixtine, move through the Infinite and fill the beholder with awe. The over-substantial, the merely mortal figure of the Virgin, in her voluminous red and blue draperies, has often been criticised, and not without some reason. Yet how in this tremendous ensemble, of which her form is, in the more exact sense, the centre of attraction and the climax, to substitute for Titian's conception anything more diaphanous, more ethereal? It is only when we strive to replace the colossal figure in the mind's eye, by a design of another and a more spiritual character, that the difficulty in all its extent is realised.

Placed as the *Assunta* now is in the immediate neighbourhood of one of Tintoretto's best-preserved masterpieces, the *Miracolo del Schiavo*, it undergoes an ordeal from which, in the opinion of many a modern connoisseur and lover of Venetian art, it does not issue absolutely triumphant. Titian's turbulent rival is more dazzling, more unusual, more overpowering in the lurid splendour of his colour; and he has that unique power of bringing the spectator to a state of mind, akin in its agitation to his own, in which he gladly renounces his power and right to exercise a sane judgment. When he is thoroughly penetrated with his subject, Tintoretto soars perhaps on a stronger pinion and higher above the earth than the elder master. Yet in fulness and variety of life, in unexaggerated dignity, in coherence, in richness and beauty, if not in poetic significance of colour, in grasp of humanity and nature, Titian stands infinitely above his younger competitor. If, unhappily, it were necessary to make a choice between the life-work of the one and the life-work of the other – making the world the poorer by the loss of Titian or Tintoretto – can it be doubted for a moment what the choice would be, even of those who abdicate when they are brought face to face with the mighty genius of the latter?

But to return for a moment to the *Assunta*. The enlargement of dimensions, the excessive vehemence of movement in the magnificent group of the Apostles is an exaggeration, not a perversion, of truth. It carries the subject into the domain of the heroic, the immeasurable, without depriving it of the great pulsation of life. If in sublime beauty and intellectuality the figures, taken one by one, cannot rank with the finest of those in Raphael's *Cartoons*, yet they preserve in a higher degree, with dramatic unity and truth, this precious quality of vitality. The expressiveness, the interpretative force of the gesture is the first thought, its rhythmic beauty only the second. This is not always the case with the *Cartoons*, and the reverse process, everywhere adhered to in the *Transfiguration*, is what gives to that overrated last work of Sanzio its painfully artificial character. Titian himself in the *St. Sebastian* of Brescia, and above all in the much-vaunted masterpiece, *The Martyrdom of St. Peter the Dominican*, sins in the same direction, but exceptionally only, and, as it were, against his better self.

Little wonder that the Franciscan Fathers were at first uncertain, and only half inclined to be enthusiastic, when they entered into possession of a work hitherto without parallel in Italian or any other art.[*40] What is great, and at the same time new, must inevitably suffer opposition at the outset. In this case the public, admitted on the high festival of St. Bernardino's Day in the year 1518 to see the vast panel, showed themselves less timorous, more enthusiastically favourable than the friars had been. Fra Germano, the guardian of Santa Maria de' Frari, and the chief mover in the matter, appears to have offered an apology to the ruffled painter, and the Fathers retained the treasure as against the Imperial Envoy, Adorno, who had seen and admired Titian's wonderful achievement on the day of its ceremonial introduction to the Venetians.

To the year 1519 belongs the *Annunciation* in the Cathedral of Treviso, the merit of which, in the opinion of the writer, has been greatly overstated. True, the Virgin, kneeling in the foreground as she awaits the divine message, is of unsurpassable suavity and beauty; but the foolish little archangel tumbling into the picture and the grotesquely ill-placed donor go far to mar it. Putting aside for the moment the beautiful and profoundly moving representations of the subject due to the Florentines and the Sienese – both sculptors and painters – south of the Alps, and to the Netherlanders north of them, during the whole of the fifteenth century, the essential triviality of the conception in the Treviso picture makes such a work as Lorenzo Lotto's pathetic *Annunciation* at Recanati, for all its excess of agitation, appear dignified by comparison. Titian's own *Annunciation*, bequeathed to the Scuola di S. Rocco by Amelio Cortona, and still to be seen hung high up on the staircase there, has a design of far greater gravity and appropriateness, and is in many respects the superior of the better known picture.

Now again, a few months after the death of Alfonso's Duchess, – the passive, and in later life estimable Lucrezia Borgia, whose character has been wilfully misconceived by the later historians and poets, – our master proceeds by the route of the Po to Ferrara, taking with him, we are told, the finished *Bacchanal*, already described above. He appears to have again visited the Court in 1520, and yet again in the early part of 1523. On which of these visits he took with him and completed at Ferrara (?) the last of the Bacchanalian series, our *Bacchus and Ariadne*, is not quite clear. It will not be safe to put the picture too late in the earlier section of Vecelli's work, though, with all its freshness of inspiration and still youthful passion, it shows a further advance on the *Worship of Venus* and the *Bacchanal*, and must be deemed to close the great series inaugurated by the *Feast of the Gods* of Gian Bellino. To the two superb fantasies of Titian already described our National Gallery picture is infinitely superior, and though time has not spared it, any more than it has other great Venetian pictures of the golden time, it is in far better condition than they are. In the *Worship of Venus* and the *Bacchanal* the allegiance to Giorgiono has been partly, if not wholly, shaken off; the naïveté remains, but not the infinite charm of the earlier Giorgionesque pieces. In the *Bacchus and Ariadne* Titian's genius flames up with an intensity of passion such as will hardly again be seen to illuminate it in an imaginative subject of this class. Certainly, with all the beauties of the *Venuses*, of the *Diana and Actaeon*, the *Diana and Calisto*, the *Rape of Europa*, we descend lower and lower in the quality of the conception as we advance, though the brush more and more reveals its supreme accomplishment, its power to summarise and subordinate. Only in those later pieces, the *Venere del Pardo* of the Louvre and the *Nymph and Shepherd* of Vienna, is there a moment of pause, a return to the painted poem of the earlier times, with its exquisite naïveté and mitigated sensuousness.

The *Bacchus and Ariadne* is a Titian which even the Louvre, the Museum of the Prado, and the Vienna Gallery, rich as they are in our master's works, may envy us. The picture is, as it were, under the eye of most readers, and in some shape or form is familiar to all who are interested in Italian art. This time Titian had no second-rate Valerius Flaccus or subtilising Philostratus to guide him, but Catullus himself, whose *Epithalamium Pelei et Thetidos* he followed with a closeness which did not prevent the pictorial interpretation from being a new creation of the subject, thrilling through with the same noble frenzy that had animated the original. How is it possible to better express the *At parte ex aliâ florens volitabat Iacchus.... Te quaerens, Ariadna, tuoque incensus amore* of the Veronese poet than by the youthful, eager movement of the all-conquering god in the canvas of the Venetian? Or to paraphrase with a more penetrating truth those other lines: *Horum pars tecta quatiebant cuspide thyrsos; Pars e divolso iactabant membra iuvenco; Pars sese tortis serpentibus incingebant?* Ariadne's crown of stars – the *Ex Ariadneis aurea temporibus Fixa corona* of the poem – shines in Titian's sky with a sublime radiance which corresponds perfectly to the description, so august in its very conciseness, of Catullus. The splendour of the colour in this piece – hardly equalled in its happy audacity, save by the *Madonna del Coniglio* or *Vierge au Lapin* of the Louvre,[*41] would be a theme delightful to dwell upon, did the prescribed limits of space admit of such an indulgence. Even here, however, where in sympathy with his subject, all aglow with the delights of sense, he has allowed no conventional limitation to restrain his imagination from expressing itself in appropriately daring chromatic harmonies, he cannot be said to have evoked difficulties merely for the sake of conquering them. This is not the sparkling brilliancy of those Veronese transformed into Venetians – Bonifazio Primo and Paolo Caliari; or the gay, stimulating colour-harmony of the Brescian Romanino; or the more violent and self-assertive splendour of Gaudenzio Ferrari; or the mysterious glamour of the poet-painter Dosso Dossi. With Titian the highest degree of poetic fancy, the highest technical accomplishment, are not allowed to obscure the true Venetian dignity and moderation in the use of colour, of which our master may in the full Renaissance be considered the supreme exponent.

The ever-popular picture in the Salon Carré of the Louvre

now known as *Alfonso I. of Ferrara and Laura Dianti,* but in the collection of Charles I. called, with no nearer approach to the truth, *Titian's Mistress after the Life,* comes in very well at this stage. The exuberant beauty, with the skin of dazzling fairness and the unbound hair of rippling gold, is the last in order of the earthly divinities inspired by Giorgione – the loveliest of all in some respects, the most consummately rendered, but the least significant, the one nearest still to the realities of life. The chief harmony is here one of dark blue, myrtle green, and white, setting off flesh delicately rosy, the whole enframed in the luminous half-gloom of a background shot through here and there with gleams of light. Vasari described how Titian painted, *ottimamente con un braccio sopra un gran pezzo d' artiglieria,* the Duke Alfonso, and how he portrayed, too, the Signora Laura, who afterwards became the wife of the duke, *che è opera stupenda.* It is upon this foundation, and a certain real or fancied resemblance between the cavalier who in the background holds the mirror to his splendid *donna* and the *Alfonso of Ferrara* of the Museo del Prado, that the popular designation of this lovely picture is founded, which probably, like so many of its class, represents a fair Venetian courtesan with a lover proud of her fresh, yet full-blown beauty. Now, however, the accomplished biographer of Velazquez, Herr Carl Justi,[*42] comes forward with convincing arguments to show that the handsome *insouciant* personage, with the crisply curling dark hair and beard, in Titian's picture at Madrid cannot possibly be, as has hitherto been almost universally assumed, Alfonso I. of Ferrara, but may very probably be his son, Ercole II. This alone invalidates the favourite designation of the Louvre picture, and renders it highly unlikely that we have here the "stupendous" portrait of the Signora Laura mentioned by Vasari. A comparison of the Madrid portrait with the so-called *Giorgio Cornaro* of Castle Howard – a famous portrait by Titian of a gentleman holding a hawk, and having a sporting dog as his companion, which was seen at the recent Venetian exhibition of the New Gallery – results in something like certainty that in both is the same personage portrayed. It is not only that the quality and cast of the close curling hair and beard are the same in both portraits, and that the handsome features agree exceedingly well; the sympathetic personage gives in either case the same impression of splendid manhood fully and worthily enjoyed, yet not abused. This means that if the Madrid portrait be taken to present the gracious Ercole II. of Ferrara, then must it be held that also in the Castle Howard picture is Alfonso's son and successor portrayed. In the latter canvas, which bears, according to Crowe and Cavalcaselle, the later signature "Titianus F.," the personage is, it may be, a year or two older. Let it be borne in mind that only on the *back* of the canvas is, or rather was, to be found the inscription: "Georgius Cornelius, frater Catterinae Cipri et Hierusalem Reginae (*sic*)," upon the authority of which it bears its present designation.

The altar-piece, *The Virgin and Child with Angels, adored by St. Francis, St. Blaise, and a Donor,* now in San Domenico, but formerly in San Francesco at Ancona, bears the date 1520 and the signature "Titianus Cadorinus pinsit," this being about the first instance in which the later spelling "Titianus" appears. If as a pictorial achievement it cannot rank with the San Niccolò and the Pesaro altar-pieces, it presents some special points of interest which make it easily distinguishable from these. The conception is marked by a peculiar intensity but rarely to be met with in our master at this stage, and hardly in any other altar-piece of this particular type. It reveals a passionate unrest, an element of the uncurbed, the excessive, which one expects to find rather in Lorenzo Lotto than in Titian, whose dramatic force is generally, even in its most vigorous manifestations, well under control. The design suggests that in some shape or other the painter was acquainted with Raphael's *Madonna di Foligno*; but it is dramatic and real where the Urbinate's masterpiece was lofty and symbolical. Still Titian's St. Francis, rapt in contemplation, is sublime in steadfastness and intensity of faith; the kneeling donor is as pathetic in the humility of his adoration as any similar figure in a Quattrocento altar-piece, yet his expressive head is touched with the hand of a master of the full Renaissance. An improved version of the upper portion of the Ancona picture, showing the Madonna and Child with angels in the clouds, appears a little later on in the S. Niccolò altar-piece.

Coming to the important altar-piece completed in 1522 for the Papal Legate, Averoldo, and originally placed on the high altar in the Church of SS. Nazzaro e Celso at Brescia, we find a marked change of style and sentiment. The *St. Sebastian* presently to be referred to, constituting the right wing of the altar-piece, was completed before the rest,[*43] and excited so great an interest in Venice that Tebaldi, the agent of Duke Alfonso, made an attempt to defeat the Legate and secure the much-talked-of piece for his master. Titian succumbed to an offer of sixty ducats in ready money, thus revealing neither for the first nor the last time the least attractive yet not the least significant side of his character. But at the last moment Alfonso, fearing to make an enemy of the Legate, drew back and left to Titian the discredit without the profit of the transaction. The central compartment of the Brescia altar-piece presents *The Resurrection*, the upper panels on the left and right show together the *Annunciation*, the lower left panel depicts the patron saints, Nazarus and Celsus, with the kneeling donor, Averoldo; the lower right panel has the famous *St. Sebastian*[*44] in the foreground, and in the landscape the Angel ministering to St. Roch. The *St. Sebastian* is neither more nor less than the magnificent academic study of a nude athlete bound to a tree in such fashion as to bring into violent play at one and the same moment every muscle in his splendidly developed body. There is neither in the figure nor in the beautiful face framed in long falling hair any pretence at suggesting the agony or the ecstasy of martyrdom. A wide gulf indeed separates the mood and the method of this superb bravura piece from the reposeful charm of the Giorgionesque saint in the *St. Mark* of the Salute, or the healthy realism of the unconcerned *St. Sebastian* in the S. Niccolò altar-piece. Here, as later on with the *St. Peter Martyr*, those who admire in Venetian art in general, and in that of Titian in particular, its freedom from mere rhetoric and the deep root that it has in Nature, must protest that in this case moderation and truth are offended by a conception in its very essence artificial. Yet, brought face to face with the work itself, they will put aside the role of critic, and against their better judgment pay homage unreservedly to depth and richness of colour, to irresistible beauty of modelling and painting.[*45] Analogies have been drawn between the *Medicean Faun* and the *St. Sebastian*, chiefly on account of the strained position of the arms, and the peculiar one of the right leg, both in the statue and the painting; but surely the most obvious and natural resemblance, notwithstanding certain marked variations, is to the figure of Laocoon in the world-famous group of the Vatican. Of this a model had been made by Sansovino for Cardinal Domenico Grimani, and of that model a cast was kept in Titian's workshop, from which he is said to have studied.

In the *Madonna di S. Niccolò*, which was painted or rather finished in the succeeding year, 1523, for the little Church of S. Niccolò de' Frari, and is now in the Pinacoteca of the Vatican, the keynote is suavity, unbroken richness and harmony, virtuosity, but not extravagance of technique. The composition must have had much greater unity before the barbarous shaving off, when the picture went to Rome, of the circular top which it had in common with the *Assunta*, the Ancona, and the Pesaro altar-pieces. Technically superior to the second of these great works, it is marked by no such unity of dramatic action and sentiment, by no such passionate identification of the artist with his subject. It is only in passing from one of its beauties to another that its artistic worth can be fully appreciated. Then we admire the rapt expression, not less than the wonderfully painted vestments of the *St. Nicholas*,[*46] the mansuetude of the *St. Francis*, the Venetian loveliness of the *St. Catherine*, the palpitating life of the *St. Sebastian*. The latter is not much more than a handsome, over-plump young gondolier stripped and painted as he was –

contemplating, if anything, himself. The figure is just as Vasari describes it, *ritratto dal' vivo e senza artificio niuno.* The royal saint of Alexandria is a sister in refined elegance of beauty and costume, as in cunning elaboration of coiffure, to the *St. Catherine* of the *Madonna del Coniglio,* and the not dissimilar figure in our own *Holy Family with St. Catherine* at the National Gallery.

The fresco showing St. Christopher wading through the Lagunes with the infant Christ on his shoulder, painted at the foot of a staircase in the Palazzo Ducale leading from the Doge's private apartments to the Senate Hall, belongs either to this year, 1523, or to 1524. It is, so far as we know, Titian's first performance as a *frescante* since the completion, twelve years previously, of the series at the Scuola del Santo of Padua. As it at present appears, it is broad and solid in execution, rich and brilliant in colour for a fresco, very fairly preserved – deserving, in fact, of a much better reputation as regards technique than Crowe and Cavalcaselle have made for it. The movement is broad and true, the rugged realism of the conception not without its pathos; yet the subject is not lifted high above the commonplace by that penetrating spirit of personal interpretation which can transfigure truth without unduly transforming it. In grandeur of design and decorative character, it is greatly exceeded by the magnificent drawing in black chalk, heightened with white, of the same subject, by Pordenone, in the British Museum. Even the colossal, half-effaced *St. Christopher with the Infant Christ,* painted by the same master on the wall of a house near the Town Hall at Udine, has a finer swing, a more resistless energy.

Where exactly in the life-work of Titian are we to place the *Entombment* of the Louvre, to which among his sacred works, other than altar-pieces of vast dimensions, the same supreme rank may be accorded which belongs to the *Bacchus and Ariadne* among purely secular subjects? It was in 1523 that Titian acquired a new and illustrious patron in the person of Federigo Gonzaga II., Marquess of Mantua, son of that most indefatigable of collectors, the Marchioness Isabella d'Este Gonzaga, and nephew of Alfonso of Ferrara. The *Entombment* being a "Mantua piece," [*47] Crowe and Cavalcaselle have not unnaturally assumed that it was done expressly for the Mantuan ruler, in which case, as some correspondence published by them goes to show, it must have been painted at, or subsequently to, the latter end of 1523. Judging entirely by the style and technical execution of the canvas itself, the writer feels strongly inclined to place it earlier by some two years or thereabouts – that is to say, to put it back to a period pretty closely following upon that in which the *Worship of Venus* and the *Bacchanal* were painted. Mature as Titian's art here is, it reveals, not for the last time, the influence of Giorgione with which its beginnings were saturated. The beautiful head of St. John shows the Giorgionesque type and the Giorgionesque feeling at its highest. The Joseph of Arimathea has the robustness and the passion of the Apostles in the *Assunta*, the crimson coat of Nicodemus, with its high yellowish lights, is such as we meet with in the *Bacchanal.* The Magdalen, with her features distorted by grief, resembles – allowing for the necessary differences imposed by the situation – the women making offering to the love-goddess in the *Worship of Venus*. The figure of the Virgin, on the other hand, enveloped from head to foot in her mantle of cold blue, creates a type which would appear to have much influenced Paolo Veronese and his school. To define the beauty, the supreme concentration of the *Entombment*, without by dissection killing it, is a task of difficulty. What gives to it that singular power of enchanting the eye and enthralling the spirit, the one in perfect agreement with the other, is perhaps above all its unity, not only of design, but of tone, of informing sentiment. Perfectly satisfying balance and interconnection of the two main groups just stops short of too obvious academic grace – the well-ordered movement, the sweeping rhythm so well serving to accentuate the mournful harmony which envelops the sacred personages, bound together by the bond of the same great sorrow, and from them communicates itself, as it were, to the beholder. In the colouring, while nothing jars or impairs the concert of the tints taken as a whole, each one stands out, affirming, but not noisily asserting, its own splendour and its own special significance. And yet the yellow of the Magdalen's dress, the deep green of the coat making ruddier the embrowned flesh of sturdy Joseph of Arimathea, the rich shot crimson of Nicodemus's garment, relieved with green and brown, the chilling white of the cloth which supports the wan limbs of Christ, the blue of the Virgin's robe, combine less to produce the impression of great pictorial magnificence than to heighten that of solemn pathos, of portentous tragedy.

Of the frescoes executed by Titian for Doge Andrea Gritti in the Doge's chapel in 1524 no trace now remains. They consisted of a lunette about the altar,[*48] with the Virgin and Child between St. Nicholas and the kneeling Doge, figures of the four Evangelists on either side of the altar, and in the lunette above the entrance St. Mark seated on a lion.

The *Madonna di Casa Pesaro*, which Titian finished in 1526, after having worked upon it for no less than seven years, is perhaps the masterpiece of the painter of Cadore among the extant altar-pieces of exceptional dimensions, if there be excepted its former companion at the Frari, the *Assunta*. For ceremonial dignity, for well-ordered pomp and splendour, for the dexterous combination, in a composition of quite sufficient *vraisemblance*, of divine and sacred with real personages, it has hardly a rival among the extant pictures of its class. And yet, apart from amazement at the pictorial skill shown, at the difficulties overcome, at the magnificence tempered by due solemnity of the whole, many of us are more languidly interested by this famous canvas than we should care to confess. It would hardly be possible to achieve a more splendid success with the prescribed subject and the material at hand. It is the subject itself that must be deemed to be of the lower and less interesting order. It necessitates the pompous exhibition of the Virgin and Child, of St. Peter and other attendant saints, united by an invisible bond of sympathy and protection, not to a perpetually renewed crowd of unseen worshippers outside the picture, as in Giorgione's *Castelfranco Madonna*, but merely to the Pesaro family, so proud in their humility as they kneel in adoration, with Jacopo Pesaro, Bishop of Paphos (Baffo), at their head. The natural tie that should unite the sacred personages to the whole outer world, and with it their power to impress, is thus greatly diminished, and we are dangerously near to a condition in which they become merely grand conventional figures in a decorative ensemble of the higher order. To analyse the general scheme or the details of the glorious colour-harmony, which has survived so many drastic renovations and cleanings, is not possible on this occasion, or indeed necessary. The magic of bold and subtle chiaroscuro is obtained by the cloud gently descending along the two gigantic pillars which fill all the upper part of the arched canvas, dark in the main, but illuminated above and below by the light emanating from the divine putti; the boldest feature in the scheme is the striking cinnamon-yellow mantle of St. Peter, worn over a deep blue tunic, the two boldly contrasting with the magnificent dark-red and gold banner of the Borgias crowned with the olive branch Peace.[*49] This is an unexpected note of the most stimulating effect, which braces the spectator and saves him from a surfeit of richness. Thus, too, Titian went to work in the *Bacchus and Ariadne* – giving forth a single clarion note in the scarlet scarf of the fugitive daughter of Minos. The writer is unable to accept as from the master's own hand the unfinished *Virgin and Child* which, at the Uffizi, generally passes for the preliminary sketch of the central group in the Pesaro altar-piece. The original sketch in red chalk for the greater part of the composition is in the Albertina at Vienna. The collection of drawings in the Uffizi holds a like original study for the kneeling Baffo.

By common consent through the centuries which have succeeded the placing of Titian's world-renowned *Martyrdom of St. Peter the Dominican* on the altar of the Brotherhood of St. Peter Martyr, in the vast Church of SS. Giovanni e Paolo, it has been put down as his masterpiece, and as one of the most triumphant achievements of the Renaissance at its maturity. On the 16th of August 1867 – one of the blackest of days in the calendar for the lover of Venetian art – the *St. Peter Martyr* was burnt in the Cappella del Rosario of SS. Giovanni e Paolo, together with one of Giovanni Bellini's finest altar-pieces, the *Virgin and Child with Saints and Angels,* painted in 1472. Some malign influence had caused the temporary removal to the chapel of these two priceless works during the repair of the first and second altars to the right of the nave. Now the many who never knew the original are compelled to form their estimate of the *St. Peter Martyr* from the numerous existing copies and prints of all kinds that remain to give some sort of hint of what the picture was. Any appreciation of the work based on a personal impression may, under the circumstances, appear over-bold. Nothing could well be more hazardous, indeed, than to judge the world's greatest colourist by a translation into black-and-white, or blackened paint, of what he has conceived in the myriad hues of nature. The writer, not having had the good fortune to see the original, has not fallen under the spell of the marvellously suggestive colour-scheme. This Crowe and Cavalcaselle minutely describe, with its prevailing blacks and whites furnished by the robes of the Dominicans, with its sombre, awe-inspiring landscape, in which lurid storm-light is held in check by the divine radiance falling almost perpendicularly from the angels above – with its single startling note of red in the hose of the executioner. It is, therefore, with a certain amount of reluctance that he ventures to own that the composition, notwithstanding its largeness and its tremendous swing, notwithstanding the singular felicity with which it is framed in the overpoweringly grand landscape, has always seemed to him strained and unnatural in its most essential elements. What has been called its Michelangelism has very ingeniously been attributed to the passing influence of Buonarroti, who, fleeing from Florence, passed some months at Venice in 1829, and to that of his adherent Sebastiano Luciani, who, returning to his native city some time after the sack of Rome, had remained there until March in the same year. All the same, is not the exaggeration in the direction of academic loftiness and the rhetoric of passion based rather on the Raphaelism of the later time as it culminated in the *Transfiguration*? All through the wonderful career of the Urbinate, beginning with the Borghese *Entombment*, and going on through the *Spasimo di Sicilia* to the end, there is this tendency to consider the nobility, the academic perfection of a group, a figure, a pose, a gesture in priority to its natural dramatic significance. Much less evident is this tendency in Raphael's greatest works, the *Stanze* and the *Cartoons*, in which true dramatic significance and the sovereign beauties of exalted style generally go hand in hand. The *Transfiguration* itself is, however, the most crying example of the reversal of the natural order in the inception of a great work. In it are many sublime beauties, many figures of unsurpassable majesty if we take them separately. Yet the whole is a failure, or rather two failures, since there are two pictures instead of one in the same frame. Nature, instead of being broadened and developed by art, is here stifled. In the *St. Peter Martyr* the tremendous figure of the attendant friar fleeing in frenzied terror, with vast draperies all fluttering in the storm-wind, is in attitude and gesture based on nothing in nature. It is a stage-dramatic effect, a carefully studied attitude that we have here, though of the most imposing kind. In the same way the relation of the executioner to the martyred saint, who in the moment of supreme agony appeals to Heaven, is an academic and conventional rather than a true one based on natural truth. Allowing for the point of view exceptionally adopted here by Titian, there is, all the same, extraordinary intensity of a kind in the *dramatis personae* of the gruesome scene – extraordinary facial expressiveness. An immense effect is undoubtedly made, but not one of the highest sublimity that can come only from truth, which, raising its crest to the heavens, must ever have its feet firmly planted on earth. Still, could one come face to face with this academic marvel as one can still with the *St. Sebastian* of Brescia, criticism would no doubt be silent, and the magic of the painter *par excellence* would assert itself. Very curiously it is not any more less contemporary copy – least of all that by Ludovico Cardi da Cigoli now, as a miserable substitute for the original, at SS. Giovanni e Paolo – that gives this impression that Titian in the original would have prevailed over the recalcitrant critic of his great work. The best notion of the *St. Peter Martyr* is, so far as the writer is aware, to be derived from an apparently faithful modern copy by Appert, which hangs in the great hall of the École des Beaux-Arts in Paris. Even through this recent repetition the beholder divines beauties, especially in the landscape, which bring him to silence, and lead him, without further carping, to accept Titian as he is. A little more and, criticism notwithstanding, one would find oneself agreeing with Vasari, who, perceiving in the great work a more strict adherence to those narrower rules of art which he had learnt to reverence, than can, as a rule, be discovered in Venetian painting, described it as *la più compiuta, la più celebrata, e la maggiore e meglio intesa e condotta che altra, la quale in tutta la sua vita Tiziano abbia fatto* (sic) *ancor mai.*

It was after a public competition between Titian, Palma, and Pordenone, instituted by the Brotherhood of St. Peter Martyr, that the great commission was given to the first-named master. Palma had arrived at the end of his too short career, since he died in this same year, 1828. Of Pordenone's design we get a very good notion from the highly-finished drawing of the *Martyrdom of St. Peter* in the Uffizi, which is either by or, as the writer believes, after the Friulan painter, but is at any rate in conception wholly his. Awkward and abrupt as this may seem in some respects, as compared with Titian's astonishing performance, it represents the subject with a truer, a more tragic pathos. Sublime in its gravity is the group of pitying angels aloft, and infinitely touching the Dominican saint who, in the moment of violent death, still asserts his faith. Among the drawings which have been deemed to be preliminary sketches for the *St. Peter Martyr* are: a pen-and-ink sketch in the Louvre showing the assassin chasing the companion of the victim; another, also in the Louvre, in which the murderer gazes at the saint lying dead; yet another at Lille, containing on one sheet thumb-nail sketches of (or from) the attendant friar, the actual massacre, and the angels in mid-air. At the British Museum is the drawing of a soldier attacking the prostrate Dominican, which gives the impression of being an adaptation or variation of that drawing by Titian for the fresco of the Scuola del Santo, *A Nobleman murdering his Wife*, which is now, as has been pointed out above, at the École des Beaux-Arts of Paris. As to none of the above-mentioned drawings does the writer feel any confidence that they can be ascribed to the hand of Titian himself.[*50]

# NOTES

1. Herr Franz Wickhoff in his now famous article "Giorgione's Bilder zu Römischen Heldengedichten" (*Jahrbuch der Königlich Preussischen Kunstsammlungen*: Sechzehnter Band, I. Heft) has most ingeniously, and upon what may be deemed solid grounds, renamed this most Giorgionesque of all Giorgiones after an incident in the *Thebaid* of Statius, *Adrastus and Hypsipyle*. He gives reasons which may be accepted as convincing for entitling the *Three Philosophers*, after a familiar incident in Book viii. of the *Aeneid*, "Aeneas, Evander, and Pallas contemplating the Rock of the Capitol." His not less ingenious explanation of Titian's *Sacred and Profane Love* will be dealt with a little later on. These identifications are all-important, not only in connection with the works themselves thus renamed, and for the first time satisfactorily explained, but as compelling the students of Giorgione partly to reconsider their view of his art, and, indeed, of the Venetian idyll generally.

2. For many highly ingenious interpretations of Lotto's portraits and a sustained analysis of his art generally, Mr. Bernard Berenson's *Lorenzo Lotto* should be consulted. See also M. Emile Michel's article, "Les Portraits de Lorenzo Lotto," in the *Gazette des Beaux Arts*, 1896, vol. i.

3. For these and other particulars of the childhood of Titian, see Crowe and Cavalcaselle's elaborate *Life and Times of Titian* (second edition, 1881), in which are carefully summarised all the general and local authorities on the subject.

4. *Life and Times of Titian*, vol. i. p. 29.

5. *Die Galerien zu München und Dresden*, p. 75.

6. Carlo Ridolfi (better known as a historian of the Venetian school of art than as a Venetian painter of the late time) expressly states that Palma came young to Venice and learnt much from Titan: "*C' egli apprese certa*

*dolcezza di colorire che si avvicina alle opere prime dello stesso Tiziano"* (Lermolieff: *Die Galerien zu München und Dresden*).

7. Vasari, *Le Vite: Giorgione da Castelfranco.*

8. One of these is a description of wedding festivities presided over by the Queen at Asolo, to which came, among many other guests from the capital by the Lagunes, three Venetian gentlemen and three ladies. This gentle company, in a series of conversations, dwell upon, and embroider in many variations, that inexhaustible theme, the love of man for woman. A subject this which, transposed into an atmosphere at once more frankly sensuous and of a higher spirituality, might well have served as the basis for such a picture as Giorgione's *Fête Champêtre* in the Salon Carré of the Louvre!

9. *Magazine of Art*, July 1895.

10. *Life and Times of Titian*, vol. i. p. 111.

11. Mentioned in one of the inventories of the king's effects, taken after his execution, as *Pope Alexander and Seignior Burgeo (Borgia) his son.*

12. *La Vie et l'Oeuvre du Titien*, 1887.

13. The inscription on a cartellino at the base of the picture, "Ritratto di uno di Casa Pesaro in Venetia che fu fatto generale di Sta chiesa. Titiano fecit," is unquestionably of much later date than the work itself. The cartellino is entirely out of perspective with the marble floor to which it is supposed to adhere. The part of the background showing the galleys of Pesaro's fleet is so coarsely repainted that the original touch cannot be distinguished. The form "Titiano" is not to be found in any authentic picture by Vecelli. "Ticianus," and much more rarely "Tician," are the forms for the earlier time; "Titianus" is, as a rule, that of the later time. The two forms overlap in certain instances to be presently mentioned.

14. Kugler's *Italian Schools of Painting*, re-edited by Sir Henry Layard.

15. Marcantonio Michiel, who saw this *Baptism* in the year 1531 in the house of M. Zuanne Ram at S. Stefano in Venice, thus describes it: "La tavola del S. Zuane che battezza Cristo nel Giordano, che è nel fiume insino alle ginocchia, con el bel paese, ed esso M. Zuanne Ram ritratto sino al cinto, e con la schena contro li spettatori, fu de man de Tiziano" (*Notizia d' Opere di Disegno*, pubblicata da J. Jacopo Morelli, Ed. Frizzoni, 1884).

16. This picture having been brought to completion in 1510, and Cima's great altar-piece with the same subject, behind the high-altar in the Church of S. Giovanni in Bragora at Venice, being dated 1494, the inference is irresistible that in this case the head of the school borrowed much and without disguise from the painter who has always been looked upon as one of his close followers. In size, in distribution, in the

arrangement and characterisation of the chief groups, the two altar-pieces are so nearly related that the idea of a merely accidental and family resemblance must be dismissed. This type of Christ, then, of a perfect, manly beauty, of a divine meekness tempering majesty, dates back, not to Gian Bellino, but to Cima. The preferred type of the elder master is more passionate, more human. Our own *Incredulity of St. Thomas*, by Cima, in the National Gallery, shows, in a much more perfunctory fashion, a Christ similarly conceived; and the beautiful *Man of Sorrows* in the same collection, still nominally ascribed to Giovanni Bellini, if not from Cima's own hand, is at any rate from that of an artist dominated by his influence. When the life-work of the Conegliano master has been more closely studied in connection with that of his contemporaries, it will probably appear that he owes very much less to Bellini than it has been the fashion to assume. The idea of an actual subordinate co-operation with the *caposcuola*, like that of Bissolo, Rondinelli, Basaiti, and so many others, must be excluded. The earlier and more masculine work of Cima bears a definite relation to that of Bartolommeo Montagna.

17. The *Tobias and the Angel* shows some curious points of contact with the large *Madonna and Child with St. Agnes and St. John* by Titian, in the Louvre – a work which is far from equalling the S. Marciliano picture throughout in quality. The beautiful head of the St. Agnes is but that of the majestic archangel in reverse; the St. John, though much younger than the Tobias, has very much the same type and movement of the head. There is in the Church of S. Caterina at Venice a kind of paraphrase with many variations of the S. Marciliano Titian, assigned by Ridolfi to the great master himself, but by Boschini to Santo Zago (Crowe and Cavalcaselle, vol. ii. p. 432). Here the adapter has ruined Titian's great conception by substituting his own trivial archangel for the superb figure of the original (see also a modern copy of this last piece in the Schack Gallery at Munich). A reproduction of the Titian has for purposes of comparison been placed at the end of the present monograph (p. 99).

18. Vasari places the *Three Ages* after the first visit to Ferrara, that is almost as much too late as he places the *Tobias* of S. Marciliano too early. He describes its subject as "un pastore ignudo ed una forese chi li porge certi flauti per che suoni."

19. From an often-cited passage in the *Anonimo*, describing Giorgione's great *Venus* now in the Dresden Gallery, in the year 1525, when it was in the house of Jeronimo Marcello at Venice, we learn that it was finished by Titian. The text says: "La tela della Venere nuda, che dorme ni uno paese con Cupidine, fu de mano de Zorzo da Castelfranco; ma lo paese e Cupidine furono finiti da Tiziano." The Cupid, irretrievably

damaged, has been altogether removed, but the landscape remains, and it certainly shows a strong family resemblance to those which enframe the figures in the *Three Ages, Sacred and Profane Love,* and the *"Noli me tangere"* of the National Gallery. The same *Anonimo* in 1530 saw in the house of Gabriel Vendramin at Venice a *Dead Christ supported by an Angel,* from the hand of Giorgone, which, according to him, had been retouched by Titian. It need hardly be pointed out, at this stage, that the work thus indicated has nothing in common with the coarse and thoroughly second-rate *Dead Christ supported by Child-Angels,* still to be seen at the Monte di Pietà of Treviso. The engraving of a *Dead Christ supported by an Angel,* reproduced in M. Lafenestre's *Vie et Oeuvre du Titien* as having possibly been derived from Giorgione's original, is about as unlike his work or that of Titian as anything in sixteenth-century Italian art could possibly be. In the extravagance of its mannerism it comes much nearer to the late style of Pordenone or to that of his imitators.

20. *Jahrbuch der Preussischen Kunstsammlungen,* Heft I. 1895.

21. See also as to these paintings by Giorgione, the *Notizia d' Opere di Disegno,* pubblicata da D. Jacopo Morelli, Edizione Frizzoni, 1884.

22. M. Thausing, *Wiener Kunstbriefe,* 1884.

23. *Le Meraviglie dell' Arte.*

24. The original drawing by Titian for the subject of this fresco is to be found among those publicly exhibited at the École des Beaux Arts of Paris. It is in error given by Morelli as in the Malcolm Collection, and curiously enough M. Georges Lafenestre repeats this error in his *Vie et Oeuvre du Titien.* The drawing differs so essentially from the fresco that it can only be considered as a discarded design for it. It is in the style which Domenico Campagnola, in his Giorgionesque-Titianesque phase, so assiduously imitates.

25. One of the many inaccuracies of Vasari in his biography of Titian is to speak of the *St. Mark* as "una piccola tavoletta, un S. Marco a sedere in mezzo a certi santi."

26. In connection with this group of works, all of them belonging to the quite early years of the sixteenth century, there should also be mentioned an extraordinarily interesting and as yet little known *Herodias with the head of St. John the Baptist* by Sebastiano Luciani, bearing the date 1510. This has recently passed into the rich collection of Mr. George Salting. It shows the painter admirably in his purely Giorgionesque phase, the authentic date bearing witness that it was painted during the lifetime of the Castelfranco master. It groups therefore with the great altar-piece by Sebastiano at S. Giovanni Crisostomo in Venice, with Sir Francis Cook's

injured but still lovely *Venetian Lady as the Magdalen* (the same ruddy blond model), and with the four Giorgionesque *Saints* in the Church of S. Bartolommeo al Rialto.

27. *Die Galerien zu München und Dresden*, p. 74.

28. The *Christ* of the Pitti Gallery – a bust-figure of the Saviour, relieved against a level far-stretching landscape of the most solemn beauty – must date a good many years after the *Cristo della Moneta*. In both works the beauty of the hand is especially remarkable. The head of the Pitti *Christ* in its present state might not conclusively proclaim its origin; but the pathetic and intensely significant landscape is one of Titian's loveliest.

29. Last seen in public at the Old Masters' Exhibition of the Royal Academy in 1895.

30. An ingenious suggestion was made, when the *Ariosto* was last publicly exhibited, that it might be that *Portrait of a Gentleman of the House of Barbarigo* which, according to Vasari, Titian painted with wonderful skill at the age of eighteen. The broad, masterly technique of the Cobham Hall picture in no way accords, however, with Vasari's description, and marks a degree of accomplishment such as no boy of eighteen, not even Titian, could have attained. And then Vasari's "giubbone di raso inargentato" is not the superbly luminous steel-grey sleeve of this *Ariosto*, but surely a vest of satin embroidered with silver. The late form of signature, "Titianus F.," on the stone balustrade, which is one of the most Giorgionesque elements of the portrait, is disquieting, and most probably a later addition. It seems likely that the balustrade bore originally only the "V" repeated, which curiously enough occurs also on the similar balustrade of the beautiful *Portrait of a young Venetian*, by Giorgione, first cited as such by Morelli, and now in the Berlin Gallery, into which it passed from the collection of its discoverer, Dr. J.P. Richter. The signature "Ticianus" occurs, as a rule, on pictures belonging to the latter half of the first period. The works in the earlier half of this first period do not appear to have been signed, the "Titiano F." of the *Baffo* inscription being admittedly of later date. Thus that the *Cristo della Moneta* bears the "Ticianus F." on the collar of the Pharisee's shirt is an additional argument in favour of maintaining its date as originally given by Vasari (1514), instead of putting it back to 1508 or thereabouts. Among a good many other paintings with this last signature may be mentioned the *Jeune Homme au Gant* and *Vierge au Lapin* of the Louvre; the *Madonna with St. Anthony Abbot* of the Uffizi; the *Bacchus and Ariadne*, the *Assunta*, the *St. Sebastian* of Brescia (dated 1522). The *Virgin and Child with St. Catherine* of the National Gallery, and the *Christ with the Pilgrims at Emmaus* of the

Louvre – neither of them early works – are signed "Tician." The usual signature of the later time is "Titianus F.," among the first works to show it being the Ancona altar-piece and the great *Madonna di San Niccolò* now in the Pinacoteca of the Vatican. It has been incorrectly stated that the late *St. Jerome* of the Brera bears the earlier signature, "Ticianus F." This is not the case. The signature is most distinctly "Titianus," though in a somewhat unusual character.

31. Crowe and Cavalcaselle describe it as a "picture which has not its equal in any period of Giorgione's practice" (*History of Painting in North Italy*, vol. ii.).

32. Among other notable portraits belonging to this early period, but to which within it the writer hesitates to assign an exact place, are the so-called *Titian's Physician Parma*, No. 167 in the Vienna Gallery; the first-rate *Portrait of a Young Man* (once falsely named *Pietro Aretino*), No. 1111 in the Alte Pinakothek of Munich; the so-called *Alessandro de' Medici* in the Hampton Court Gallery. The last-named portrait is a work injured, no doubt, but of extraordinary force and conciseness in the painting, and of no less singular power in the characterisation of a sinister personage whose true name has not yet been discovered.

33. The fifth *Allegory*, representing a sphinx or chimaera – now framed with the rest as the centre of an ensemble – is from another and far inferior hand, and, moreover, of different dimensions. The so-called *Venus* of the Imperial Gallery at Vienna is, notwithstanding the signature of Bellini and the date (MDXV.), by Bissolo.

34. In Bellini's share in the landscape there is not a little to remind the beholder of the *Death of St. Peter Martyr* to be found in the Venetian room of the National Gallery, where it is still assigned to the great master himself, though it is beyond reasonable doubt by one of his late pupils or followers.

35. The enlarged second edition, with the profile portrait of Ariosto by Titian, did not appear until 1532. Among the additions then made were the often-quoted lines in which the poet, enumerating the greatest painters of the time, couples Titian with Leonardo, Andrea Mantegna, Gian Bellino, the two Dossi, Michelangelo, Sebastiano, and Raffael (33rd canto, 2nd ed.).

36. Filostratou Eikonwn ErwteV

37. Let the reader, among other things of the kind, refer to Rubens's *Jardin à Amour*, made familiar by so many repetitions and reproductions, and to Van Dyck's *Madone aux Perdrix* at the Hermitage (see Portfolio: *The Collections of Charles I.*). Rubens copied, indeed, both the *Worship of Venus* and the *Bacchanal*, some time between 1601 and 1608, when the

pictures were at Rome. These copies are now in the Museum at Stockholm. The realistic vigour of the *Bacchanal* proved particularly attractive to the Antwerp master, and he in more than one instance derived inspiration from it. The ultra-realistic *Bacchus seated on a Barrel*, in the Gallery of the Hermitage at St. Petersburg, contains in the chief figure a pronounced reminiscence of Titian's picture; while the unconventional attitude of the amorino, or Bacchic figure, in attendance on the god, is imitated without alteration from that of the little toper whose action Vasari so explicitly describes.

38. Vasari's simple description is best: "Una donna nuda che dorme, tanto bella che pare viva, insieme con altre figure."

39. Moritz Thausing's *Albrecht Dürer*, Zweiter Band, p. 14.

40. Crowe and Cavalcaselle, *Life and Times of Titian*, vol. i. p. 212.

41. It appears to the writer that this masterpiece of colour and reposeful charm, with its wonderful gleams of orange, pale turquoise, red, blue, and golden white, with its early signature, "Ticianus F.," should be placed not later than this period. Crowe and Cavalcaselle assign it to the year 1530, and hold it to be the *Madonna with St. Catherine*, mentioned in a letter of that year written by Giacomo Malatesta to Federigo Gonzaga at Mantua. Should not this last picture be more properly identified with our own superb *Madonna and Child with St. John and St. Catherine*, No. 635 in the National Gallery, the style of which, notwithstanding the rather Giorgionesque type of the girlish Virgin, shows further advance in a more sweeping breadth and a larger generalisation? The latter, as has already been noted, is signed "Tician."

42. "Tizian und Alfons von Este," *Jahrbuch der Königlich Preussischen Kunstsammlungen*, Fünfzehnter Band, II. Heft, 1894.

43. Crowe and Cavalcaselle, *Life and Times of Titian*, vol. i. pp. 237-240.

44. On the circular base of the column upon which the warrior-saint rests his foot is the signature "Ticianus faciebat MDXXII." This, taken in conjunction with the signature "Titianus" on the Ancona altar-piece painted in 1520, tends to show that the line of demarcation between the two signatures cannot be absolutely fixed.

45. Lord Wemyss possesses a repetition, probably from Titian's workshop, of the *St. Sebastian*, slightly smaller than the Brescia original. This cannot have been the picture catalogued by Vanderdoort as among Charles I.'s treasures, since the latter, like the earliest version of the *St. Sebastian*, preceding the definitive work, showed the saint tied not to a tree, but to a column, and in it the group of St. Roch and the Angel was replaced by the figures of two archers shooting.

46. Ridolfi, followed in this particular by Crowe and Cavalcaselle, sees in the upturned face of the *St. Nicholas* a reflection of that of Laocoon in the Vatican group.

47. It passed with the rest of the Mantua pictures into the collection of Charles I., and was after his execution sold by the Commonwealth to the banker and dealer Jabach for £120. By the latter it was made over to Louis XIV., together with many other masterpieces acquired in the same way.

48. Crowe and Cavalcaselle, *Life and Times of Titian*, vol. i. pp. 298, 299.

49. The victory over the Turks here commemorated was won by Baffo in the service of the Borgia Pope, Alexander VI., some twenty-three years before. This gives a special significance to the position in the picture of St. Peter, who, with the keys at his feet, stands midway between the Bishop and the Virgin. We have seen Baffo in one of Titian's earliest works (*circa* 1503) recommended to St. Peter by Alexander VI. just before his departure for this same expedition.

50. It has been impossible in the first section of these remarks upon the work of the master of Cadore to go into the very important question of the drawings rightly and wrongly ascribed to him. Some attempt will be made in the second section, to be entitled *The Later Work of Titian*, to deal summarily with this branch of the subject, which has been placed on a more solid basis since Giovanni Morelli disentangled the genuine landscape drawings of the master from those of Domenico Campagnola, and furnished a firm basis for further study.

# THE LATER WORK OF TITIAN

# THE LATER WORK OF TITIAN

## CLAUDE PHILLIPS

*Keeper of the Wallace Collection*

CRESCENT MOON

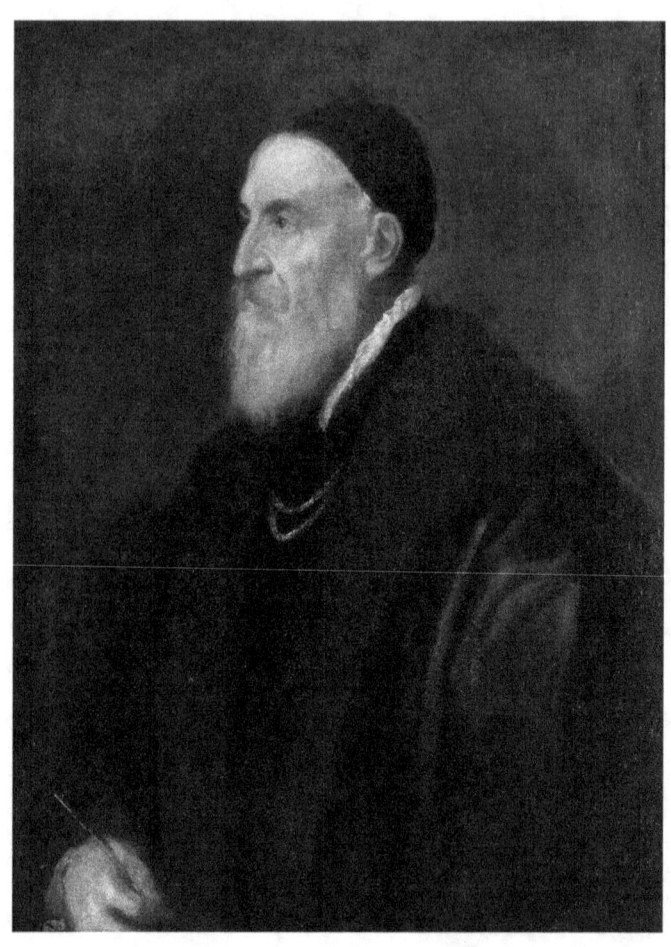

Titian, Self-Portrait, 1565, Prado, Madrid

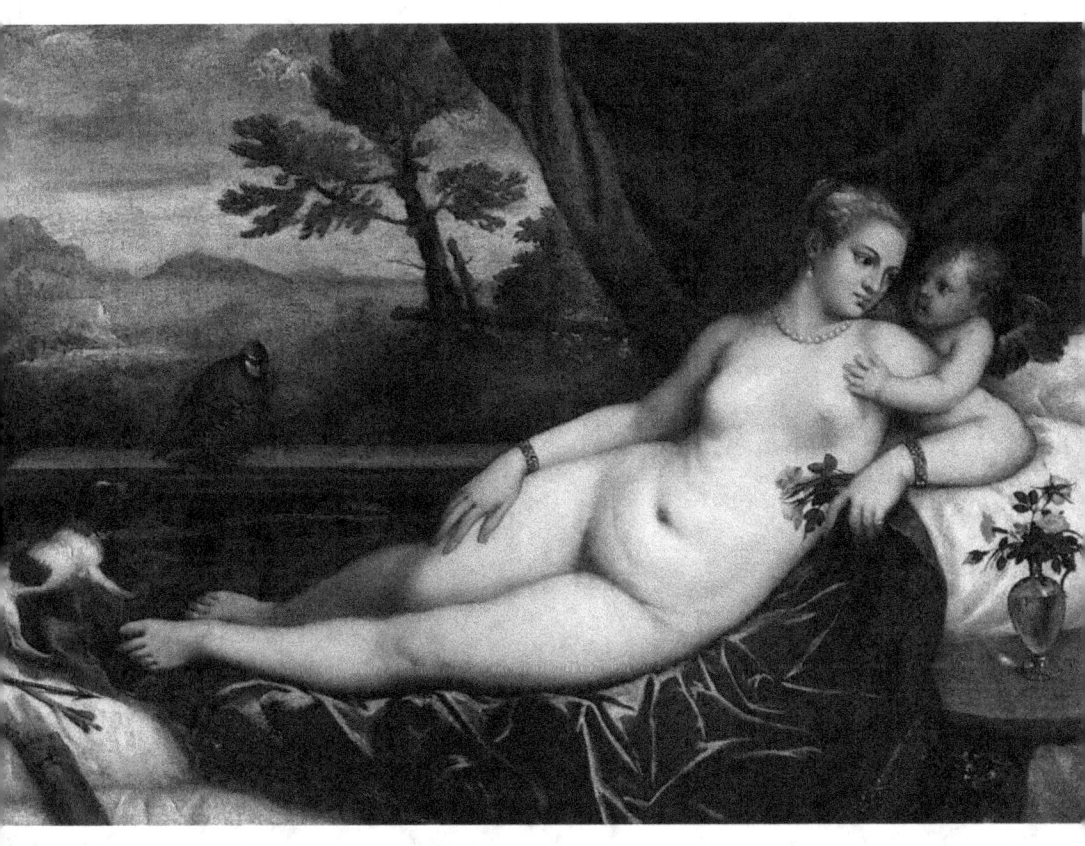

Titian, Venus and Cupid, 1550, Uffizi

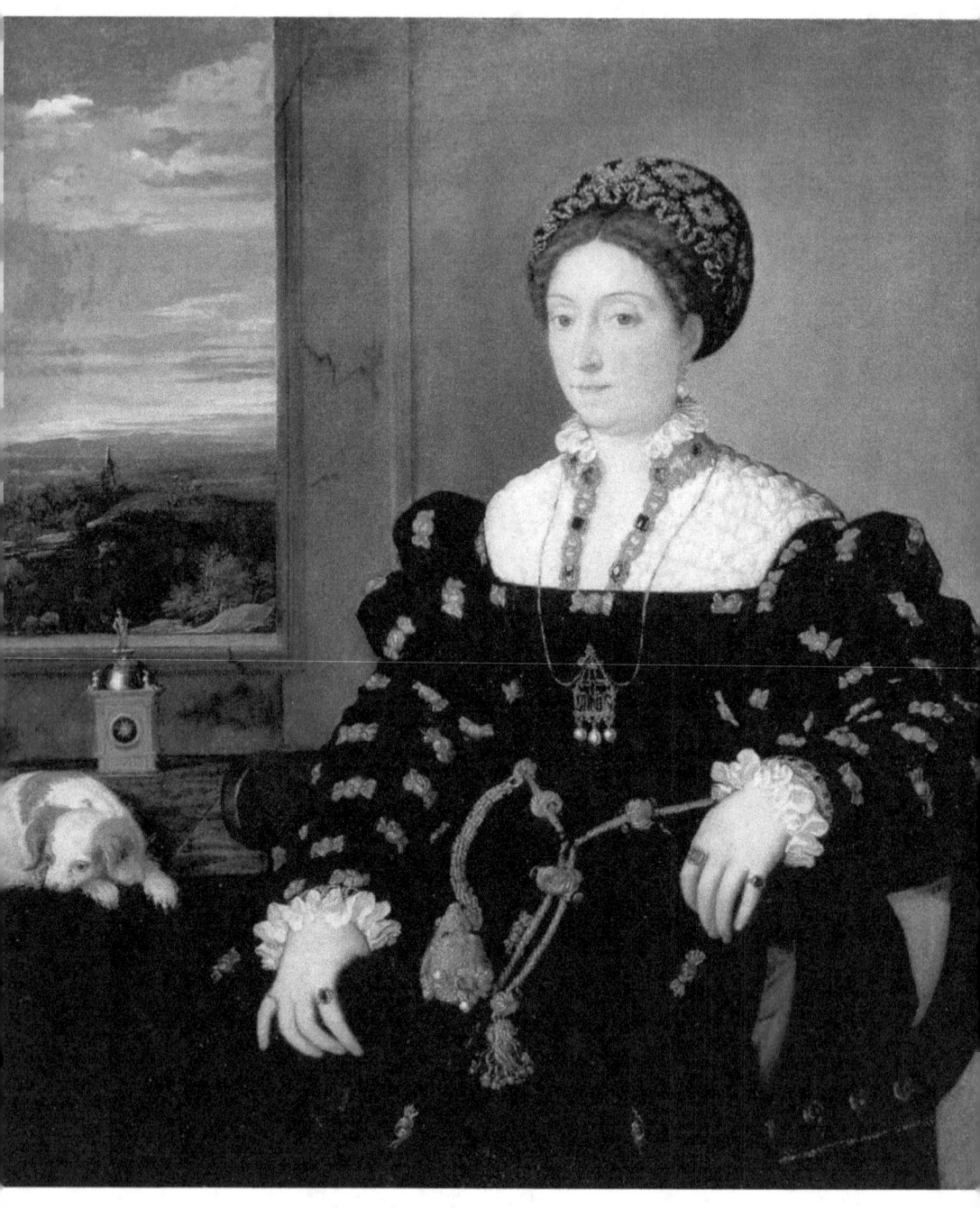

Titian, Portrait of Eleonora Gonzaga, 1538, Uffizi

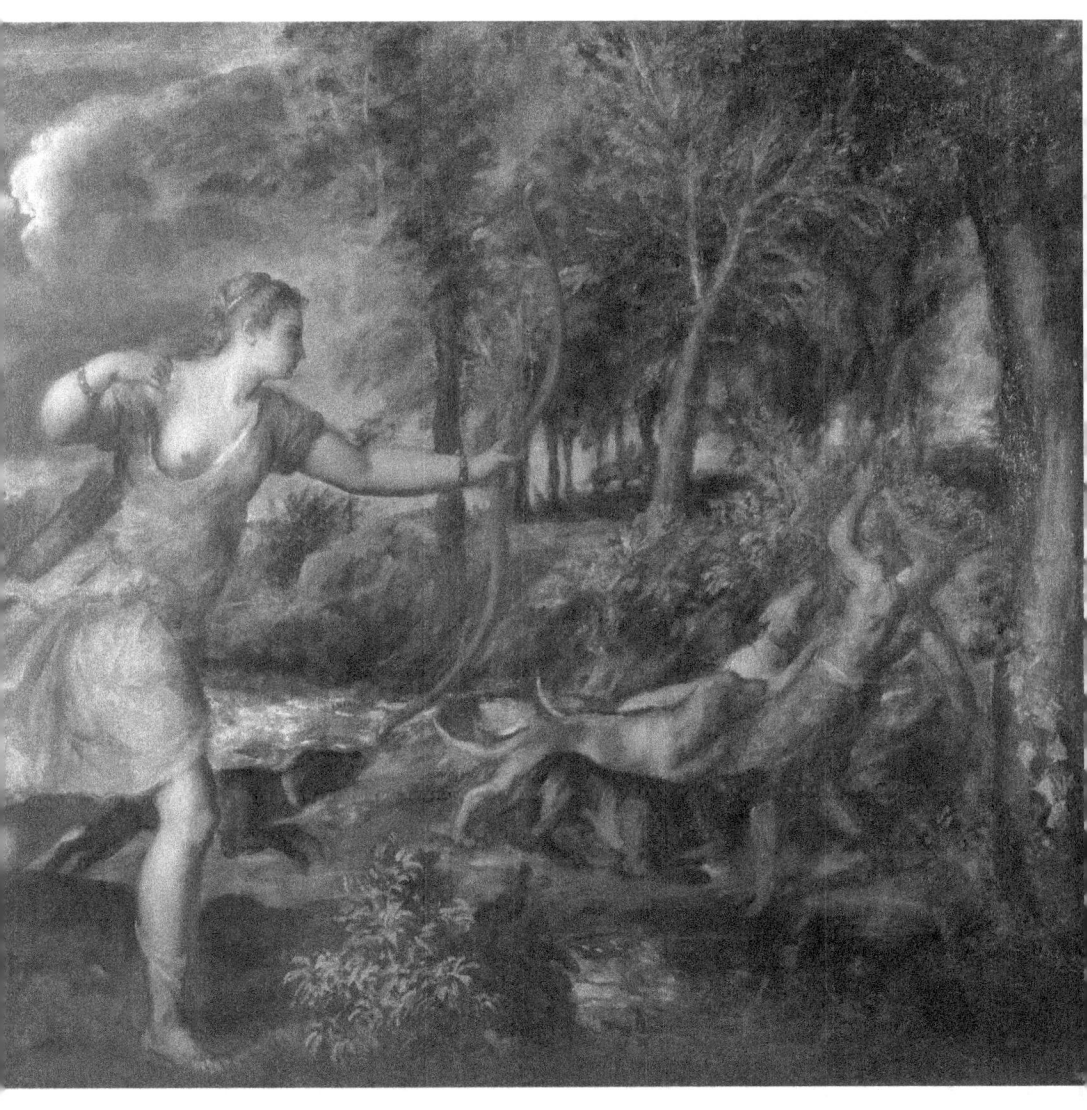

Titian, The Death of Actaeon 1559-75
National Gallery, London

# CHAPTER I

*Friendship with Aretino – Its effect on Titian's art – Characteristics of the middle period – "Madonna with St. Catherine" of National Gallery – Portraits not painted from life – "Magdalen" of the Pitti – First Portrait of Charles V. – Titian the painter, par excellence, of aristocratic traits – The "d'Avalos Allegory" – Portrait of Cardinal Ippolito de' Medici – S. Giovanni Elemosinario altar-piece.*

Having followed Titian as far as the year 1530, rendered memorable by that sensational, and, of its kind, triumphant achievement, *The Martyrdom of St. Peter the Dominican*, we must retrace our steps some three years in order to dwell a little upon an incident which must appear of vital importance to those who seek to understand Titian's life, and, above all, to follow the development of his art during the middle period of splendid maturity reaching to the confines of old age. This incident is the meeting with Pietro Aretino at Venice in 1527, and the gradual strengthening by mutual service and mutual inclination of the bonds of a friendship which is to endure without break until the life of the Aretine comes, many years later, to a sudden and violent end. Titian was at that time fifty years of age, and he might thus be deemed to have over-passed the age of sensuous delights. Yet it must be remembered that he was in the fullest vigour of manhood, and had only then arrived at the middle point of a career which, in its untroubled serenity, was to endure for a full half-century more, less a single year. Three years later on, that is to say in the middle of August 1530, the death of his wife Cecilia, who had borne to him Pomponio, Orazio, and Lavinia, left him all disconsolate, and so embarrassed with the cares of his young family that he was compelled to appeal to his sister Orsa, who thereupon came from Cadore to preside over his household. The highest point of celebrity, of favour with princes and magnates, having been attained, and a certain royalty in Venetian art being already conceded to him, there was no longer any obstacle to the organising of a life in which all the refinements of culture and all the delights of sense were to form the most agreeable relief to days of continuous and magnificently fruitful labour. It is just because Titian's art of this great period of some twenty years so entirely accords with what we know, and may legitimately infer, to have been his life at this time, that it becomes important to consider the friendship with Aretino and the rise of the so-called Triumvirate, which was a kind of Council of Three, having as its *raison d'être* the mutual furtherance of material interests, and the pursuit of art, love, and pleasure. The third member of the Triumvirate was Jacopo Tatti or del Sansovino, the Florentine sculptor, whose fame and fortune were so far above his deserts as an artist. Coming to Venice after the sack of Rome, which so entirely for the moment disorganised art and artists in the pontifical city, he elected to remain there notwithstanding the pressing invitations sent to him by Francis the First to take service with him. In 1529 he was appointed architect of San Marco, and he then by his adhesion completed the Triumvirate which was to endure for more than a quarter of a century.

It has always excited a certain sense of distrust in Titian, and caused the world to form a lower estimate of his character than it would otherwise have done, that he should have been capable of thus living in the closest and most fraternal intimacy with a man so spotted and in many ways so infamous as Aretino. Without precisely calling Titian to account in set terms, his biographers Crowe and Cavalcaselle, and above all M. Georges Lafenestre in *La Vie et L'Oeuvre du Titien*, have relentlessly raked up Aretino's past before he came together with the Cadorine, and as pitilessly laid bare that organised system of professional sycophancy, adulation, scurrilous libel, and blackmail, which was the foundation and the backbone of his life of outward pomp and luxurious ease at Venice. By them, as by his other biographers, he has been judged, not indeed unjustly, yet perhaps too much from the standard of our own time, too little from that of his own. With all his infamies, Aretino was a man whom sovereigns and princes, nay even pontiffs, delighted to honour, or rather to distinguish by honours. The Marquess Federigo Gonzaga of Mantua, the Duke Guidobaldo II. of Urbino, among many others, showed themselves ready to propitiate him; and such a man as Titian the worldly-wise, the lover of splendid living to whom ample means and the fruitful favour of the great were a necessity; who was grasping yet not avaricious, who loved wealth chiefly because it secured material consideration and a life of serene enjoyment; such a man could not be expected to rise superior to the temptations presented by a friendship with Aretino, or to despise the immense advantages which it included. As he is revealed by his biographers, and above all by himself, Aretino was essentially "good company." He could pass off his most flagrant misdeeds, his worst sallies, with a certain large and Rabelaisian gaiety; if he made money his chief god, it was to spend it in magnificent clothes and high living, but also at times with an intelligent and even a beneficent liberality. He was a fine though not an unerring connoisseur of art, he had a passionate love of music, and an unusually exquisite perception of the beauties of Nature.

To hint that the lower nature of the man corrupted that of Titian, and exercised a disintegrating influence over his art, would be to go far beyond the requirements of the case. The great

Venetian, though he might at this stage be much nearer to earth than in those early days when he was enveloped in the golden glow of Giorgione's overmastering influence, could never have lowered himself to the level of those too famous *Sonetti Lussuriosi* which brought down the vengeance of even a Medici Pope (Clement VII.) upon Aretino the writer, Giulio Romano the illustrator, and Marcantonio Raimondi the engraver. Gracious and dignified in sensuousness he always remained even when, as at this middle stage of his career, the vivifying shafts of poetry no longer pierced through, and transmuted with their vibration of true passion, the fair realities of life. He could never have been guilty of the frigid and calculated indecency of a Giulio Romano; he could not have cast aside all conventional restraints, of taste as well as of propriety, as Rubens and even Rembrandt did on occasion; but as Van Dyck, the child of Titian almost as much as he was the child of Rubens, ever shrank from doing. Still the ease and splendour of the life at Biri Grande – that pleasant abode with its fair gardens overlooking Murano, the Lagoons, and the Friulan Alps, to which Titian migrated in 1531 – the Epicureanism which saturated the atmosphere, the necessity for keeping constantly in view the material side of life, all these things operated to colour the creations which mark this period of Titian's practice, at which he has reached the apex of pictorial achievement, but shows himself too serene in sensuousness, too unruffled in the masterly practice of his profession to give to the heart the absolute satisfaction that he affords to the eyes. This is the greatest test of genius of the first order – to preserve undimmed in mature manhood and old age the gift of imaginative interpretation which youth and love give, or lend, to so many who, buoyed up by momentary inspiration, are yet not to remain permanently in the first rank. With Titian at this time supreme ability is not invariably illumined from within by the lamp of genius; the light flashes forth nevertheless, now and again, and most often in those portraits of men of which the sublime *Charles V. at Mühlberg* is the greatest. Towards the end the flame will rise once more and steadily burn, with something on occasion of the old heat, but with a hue paler and more mysterious, such as may naturally be the outward symbol of genius on the confines of eternity.

The second period, following upon the completion of the *St. Peter Martyr*, is one less of great altar-pieces and *poesie* such as the miscalled *Sacred and Profane Love* (*Medea and Venus*), the *Bacchanals*, and the *Bacchus and Ariadne*, than it is of splendid nudities and great portraits. In the former, however mythological be the subject, it is generally chosen but to afford a decent pretext for the generous display of beauty unveiled. The portraits are at this stage less often intimate and soul-searching in their summing up of a human personality than they are official presentments of great personages and noble dames; showing them, no doubt, without false adulation or cheap idealisation, yet much as they desire to appear to their allies, their friends, and their subjects, sovereign in natural dignity and aristocratic grace, yet essentially in a moment of representation. Farther on the great altar-pieces reappear more sombre, more agitated in passion, as befits the period of the sixteenth century in which Titian's latest years are passed, and the patrons for whom he paints. Of the *poesie* there is then a new upspringing, a new efflorescence, and we get by the side of the *Venus and Adonis*, the *Diana and Actæon*, the *Diana and Calisto*, the *Rape of Europa*, such pieces of a more exquisite and penetrating poetry as the *Venere del Pardo* of Paris, and the *Nymph and Shepherd* of Vienna.

This appears to be the right place to say a word about the magnificent engraving by Van Dalen of a portrait, no longer known to exist, but which has, upon the evidence apparently of the print, been put down as that of Titian by himself. It represents a bearded man of some thirty-five years, dressed in a rich but sombre habit, and holding a book. The portrait is evidently not that of a painter by himself, nor does it represent Titian at any age; but it finely suggests, even in black and white, a noble original by the master. Now, a comparison with the best authenticated portrait of Aretino, the superb three-quarter length painted in 1545, and actually at the Pitti Palace, reveals certain marked similarities of feature and type, notwithstanding the very considerable difference of age between the personages represented. Very striking is the agreement of eye and nose in either case, while in the younger as in the older man we note an idiosyncrasy in which vigorous intellect as well as strong sensuality has full play. Van Dalen's engraving very probably reproduces one of the lost portraits of Aretino by Titian. In Crowe and Cavalcaselle's *Biography* (vol. i. pp. 317-319) we learn from correspondence interchanged in the summer of 1527 between Federigo Gonzaga, Titian, and Aretino, that the painter, in order to propitiate the Mantuan ruler, sent to him with a letter, the exaggerated flattery of which savours of Aretino's precept and example, portraits of the latter and of Signor Hieronimo Adorno, another "faithful servant" of the Marquess. Now Aretino was born in 1492, so that in 1527 he would be thirty-five, which appears to be just about the age of the vigorous and splendid personage in Van Dalen's print.

Some reasons were given in the former section of this mono-graph[*1] for the assertion that the *Madonna with St. Catherine*, mentioned in a letter from Giacomo Malatesta to the Marchese Federigo Gonzaga, dated February 1530, was not, as is assumed by Crowe and Cavalcaselle, the *Madonna del Coniglio* of the Louvre, but the *Madonna and Child with St. John the Baptist and St. Catherine*, which is No. 635 at the National Gallery.[*2] Few pictures of the master have been more frequently copied and adapted than this radiantly beautiful piece, in which the dominant chord of the scheme of colour is composed by the cerulean blues of the heavens and the Virgin's entire dress, the deep luscious greens of the landscape, and the peculiar, pale, citron hue, relieved with a crimson girdle, of the robe worn by the St. Catherine, a splendid Venetian beauty of no very refined type or emotional intensity. Perfect repose and serenity are the keynote of the conception, which in its luxuriant beauty has little of the power to touch that must be conceded to the more naïve and equally splendid *Madonna del Coniglio*.[*3] It is above all in the wonderful Venetian landscape – a mountain-bordered vale, along which flocks and herds are being driven, under a sky of the most intense blue – that the master shows himself supreme. Nature is therein not so much detailed as synthesised with a sweeping breadth which makes of the scene not the reflection of one beautiful spot in the Venetian territory, but without loss of essential truth or character a very type of Venetian landscape of the sixteenth century. These herdsmen and their flocks, and also the note of warning in the sky of supernatural splendour, recall the beautiful Venetian storm-landscape in the royal collection at Buckingham Palace. This has been very generally attributed to Titian himself,[*4] and described as the only canvas still extant in which he has made landscape his one and only theme. It has, indeed, a rare and mysterious power to move, a true poetry of interpretation. A fleeting moment, full of portent as well as of beauty, has been seized; the smile traversed by a frown of the stormy sky, half overshadowing half revealing the wooded slopes, the rich plain, and the distant mountains, is rendered with a rare felicity. The beauty is, all the same, in the conception and in the thing actually seen – much less in the actual painting. It is hardly possible to convince oneself, comparing the work with such landscape backgrounds as those in this picture at the National Gallery in the somewhat earlier *Madonna del Coniglio,* and the gigantic *St. Peter Martyr,* or, indeed, in a score of other genuine productions, that the depth, the vigour, the authority of Titian himself are here to be recognised. The weak treatment of the great Titianesque tree in the foreground, with its too summarily indicated foliage – to select only one detail that comes naturally to hand – would in itself suffice to bring such an attribution into question.

Vasari states, speaking confessedly from hearsay, that in 1530, the Emperor Charles V. being at Bologna, Titian was summoned thither by Cardinal Ippolito de' Medici, using Aretino as an intermediary, and that he on that occasion executed a most admirable portrait of His Majesty, all in arms, which had so much success that the artist received as a present a thousand scudi. Crowe and Cavalcaselle, however, adduce strong evidence to prove that Titian was busy in Venice for Federigo Gonzaga at the time of the Emperor's first visit, and that he only proceeded to Bologna in July to paint for the Marquess of Mantua the portrait of a Bolognese beauty, *La Cornelia*, the lady-in-waiting of the Countess Pepoli, whom Covas, the all-powerful political secretary of Charles the Fifth, had seen and admired at the splendid entertainments given by the Pepoli to the Emperor. Vasari has in all probability confounded this journey of Charles in 1530 with that subsequent one undertaken in 1532 when Titian not only portrayed the Emperor, but also painted an admirable likeness of Ippolito de' Medici presently to be described. He had the bad luck on this occasion to miss the lady Cornelia, who had retired to Nuvolara, indisposed and not in good face. The letter written by our painter to the Marquess in connection with this incident[*5] is chiefly remarkable as affording evidence of his too great anxiety to portray the lady without approaching her, relying merely on the portrait, "che fece quel altro pittore della detta Cornelia"; of his unwillingness to proceed to Nuvolara, unless the picture thus done at second hand should require alteration. In truth we have lighted here upon one of Titian's most besetting sins, this willingness, this eagerness, when occasion offers, to paint portraits without direct reference to the model. In this connection we are reminded that he never saw Francis the First, whose likeness he notwithstanding painted with so showy and superficial a magnificence as to make up to the casual observer for the absence of true vitality;[*6] that the Empress Isabella, Charles V.'s consort, when at the behest of the monarch he produced her sumptuous but lifeless and empty portrait, now in the great gallery of the Prado, was long since dead. He consented, basing his picture upon a likeness of much earlier date, to paint Isabella d'Este Gonzaga as a young woman when she was already an old one, thereby flattering an amiable and natural weakness in this great princess and unrivalled dilettante, but impairing his own position as an artist of supreme rank.[*7] It is not necessary to include in this category the popular *Caterina Cornaro* of the Uffizi, since it is confessedly nothing but a fancy portrait, making no reference to the true aspect at any period of the long-since deceased queen of Cyprus, and, what is more, no original Titian, but at the utmost an atelier piece from his *entourage*. Take, however, as an instance the *Francis the First*, which was painted some few years later than the time at which we have now arrived, and at about the same period as the *Isabella d'Este*. Though as a *portrait d'apparat* it makes its effect, and reveals the sovereign accomplishment of the master, does it not shrink into the merest insignificance when compared with such renderings from life as the successive portraits of *Charles the Fifth*, the *Ippolito de' Medici*, the *Francesco Maria della Rovere*? This is as it must and should be, and Titian is not the less great, but the greater, because he cannot convincingly evolve at second hand the true human individuality, physical and mental, of man or woman.

It was in the earlier part of 1531 that Titian painted for Federigo Gonzaga a *St. Jerome* and a *St. Mary Magdalene*, destined for the famous Vittoria Colonna, Marchioness of Pescara, who had expressed to the ruler of Mantua the desire to possess such a picture. Gonzaga writes to the Marchioness on March 11, 1831[*8]: – "Ho subito mandate a Venezia e scritto a Titiano, quale è forse il piu eccellente in quell' arte che a nostri tempi si ritrovi, ed è tutto mio, ricercandolo con grande instantia a volerne fare una bella lagrimosa piu che si so puo, e farmela haver presto." The passage is worth quoting as showing the estimation in which Titian was held at a court which had known and still knew the greatest Italian masters of the art.

It is not possible at present to identify with any extant painting the *St. Jerome*, of which we know that it hung in the private apartments of the Marchioness Isabella at Mantua. The writer is unable to accept Crowe and Cavalcaselle's suggestion that it may be the fine moonlight landscape with St. Jerome in prayer which is now in the Long Gallery of the Louvre. This piece, if indeed it be by Titian, which is by no means certain, must belong to his late time. The landscape, which is marked by a beautiful and wholly unconventional treatment of moonlight, for which it would not be easy to find a parallel in the painting of the time, is worthy of the Cadorine, and agrees well, especially in the broad treatment of foliage, with, for instance, the background in the late *Venus and Cupid* of the Tribuna.[*9] The figure of St. Jerome, on the other hand, does not in the peculiar tightness of the modelling, or in the flesh-tints, recall Titian's masterly synthetic way of going to work in works of this late period. The noble *St. Jerome* of the Brera, which indubitably belongs to a well-advanced stage in the late time, will be dealt with in its right place. Though it does not appear probable that we have, in the much-admired *Magdalen* of the Pitti, the picture here referred to – this last having belonged to Francesco Maria della Rovere, Duke of Urbino, and representing, to judge by style, a somewhat more advanced period in the painter's career – it may be convenient to mention it here. As an example of accomplished brush-work, of handling careful and yet splendid in breadth, it is indeed worthy of all admiration. The colours of the fair human body, the marvellous wealth of golden blond hair, the youthful flesh glowing semi-transparent, and suggesting the rush of the blood beneath; these are also the colours of the picture, aided only by the indefinite landscape and the deep blue sky of the background. If this were to be accepted as the *Magdalen* painted for Federigo Gonzaga, we must hold, nevertheless, that Titian with his masterpiece of painting only half satisfied the requirements of his patron. *Bellissima* this Magdalen undoubtedly is, but hardly *lagrimosa pin che si puo*. She is a *belle pécheresse* whose repentance sits all too lightly upon her, whose consciousness of a physical charm not easily to be withstood is hardly disguised. Somehow, although the picture in no way oversteps the bounds of decency, and cannot be objected to even by the most over-scrupulous, there is latent in it a jarring note of unrefinement in the presentment of exuberant youth and beauty which we do not find in the more avowedly sensuous *Venus of the Tribuna*. This last is an avowed act of worship by the artist of the naked human body, and as such, in its noble frankness, free from all offence, except to those whose scruples in matters of art we are not here called upon to consider. From this *Magdalen* to that much later one of the Hermitage, which will be described farther on, is a great step upwards, and it is a step which, in passing from the middle to the last period, we shall more than once find ourselves taking.

It is impossible to give even in outline here an account of Titian's correspondence and business relations with his noble and royal patrons, instructive as it is to follow these out, and to see how, under the influence of Aretino, his natural eagerness to grasp in every direction at material advantages is sharpened; how he becomes at once more humble and more pressing, covering with the manner and the tone appropriate to courts the reiterated demands of the keen and indefatigable man of business. It is the less necessary to attempt any such account in these pages – dealing as we are chiefly with the work and not primarily with the life of Titian – seeing that in Crowe and Cavalcaselle's admirable biography this side of the subject, among many others, is most patiently and exhaustively dealt with.

In 1531 we read of a *Boy Baptist* by Titian sent by Aretino to Maximian Stampa, an imperialist partisan in command of the castle of Milan. The donor particularly dwells upon "the beautiful curl of the Baptist's hair, the fairness of his skin, etc.," a description which recalls to us, in striking fashion, the little St. John in the *Virgin and Child with St. Catherine* of the National Gallery, which belongs, as has been shown, to the same time.

It was on the occasion of the second visit of the Emperor and his court to Bologna at the close of 1532 that Titian first came in personal contact with Charles V., and obtained from that monarch his first sitting. In the course of an inspection, with Federigo Gonzaga himself as cicerone, of the art treasures preserved in the palace at Mantua, the Emperor saw the portrait by Titian of

Federigo, and was so much struck with it, so intent upon obtaining a portrait of himself from the same brush, that the Marquess wrote off at once pressing our master to join him without delay in his capital. Titian preferred, however, to go direct to Bologna in the train of his earlier patron Alfonso d'Este. It was on this occasion that Charles's all-powerful secretary, the greedy, overbearing Covos, exacted as a gift from the agents of the Duke of Ferrara, among other things, a portrait of Alfonso himself by Titian; and in all probability obtained also a portrait from the same hand of Ercole d'Este, the heir-apparent. There is evidence to show that the portrait of Alfonso was at once handed over to, or appropriated by, the Emperor.

Whether this was the picture described by Vasari as representing the prince with his arm resting on a great piece of artillery, does not appear. Of this last a copy exists in the Pitti Gallery which Crowe and Cavalcaselle have ascribed to Dosso Dossi, but the original is nowhere to be traced. The Ferrarese ruler is, in this last canvas, depicted as a man of forty or upwards, of resolute and somewhat careworn aspect. It has already been demonstrated, on evidence furnished by Herr Carl Justi, that the supposed portrait of Alfonso, in the gallery of the Prado at Madrid, cannot possibly represent Titian's patron at any stage of his career, but in all probability, like the so-called *Giorgio Cornaro* of Castle Howard, is a likeness of his son and successor, Ercole II.

Titian's first portrait of the Emperor, a full-length in which he appeared in armour with a generalissimo's baton of command, was taken in 1556 from Brussels to Madrid, after the formal ceremony of abdication, and perished, it would appear, in one of the too numerous fires which have devastated from time to time the royal palaces of the Spanish capital and its neighbourhood. To the same period belongs, no doubt, the noble full-length of Charles in gala court costume which now hangs in the *Sala de la Reina Isabel* in the Prado Gallery, as a pendant to Titian's portrait of Philip II. in youth. Crowe and Cavalcaselle assume that not this picture, but a replica, was the one which found its way into

Charles I.'s collection, and was there catalogued by Van der Doort as "the Emperor Charles the Fifth, brought by the king from Spain, being done at length with a big white Irish dog" – going afterwards, at the dispersal of the king's effects, to Sir Balthasar Gerbier for £150. There is, however, no valid reason for doubting that this is the very picture owned for a time by Charles I., and which busy intriguing Gerbier afterwards bought, only to part with it to Cardenas the Spanish ambassador.[*10] Other famous originals by Titian were among the choicest gifts made by Philip IV. to Prince Charles at the time of his runaway expedition to Madrid with the Duke of Buckingham, and this was no doubt among them. Confirmation is supplied by the fact that the references to the existence of this picture in the royal palaces of Madrid are for the reigns of Philip II., Charles II., and Charles III., thus leaving a large gap unaccounted for. Dimmed as the great portrait is, robbed of its glow and its chastened splendour in a variety of ways, it is still a rare example of the master's unequalled power in rendering race, the unaffected consciousness of exalted rank, natural as distinguished from assumed dignity. There is here no demonstrative assertion of *grandeza*, no menacing display of truculent authority, but an absolutely serene and simple attitude such as can only be the outcome of a consciousness of supreme rank and responsibility which it can never have occurred to any one to call into question. To see and perpetuate these subtle qualities, which go so far to redeem the physical drawbacks of the House of Hapsburg, the painter must have had a peculiar instinct for what is aristocratic in the higher sense of the word – that is, both outwardly and inwardly distinguished. This was indeed one of the leading characteristics of Titian's great art, more especially in portraiture. Giorgione went deeper, knowing the secret of the soul's refinement, the aristocracy of poetry and passion; Lotto sympathetically laid bare the heart's secrets and showed the pathetic helplessness of humanity. Tintoretto communicated his own savage grandeur, his own unrest, to those whom he depicted; Paolo Veronese charmed without *arrière-pensée* by the intensity of vitality which with perfect simplicity he preserved in his sitters. Yet to Titian must be conceded absolute supremacy in the rendering not only of the outward but of the essential dignity, the refinement of type and bearing, which without doubt come unconsciously to those who can boast a noble and illustrious ancestry.

Again the writer hesitates to agree with Crowe and Cavalcaselle when they place at this period, that is to say about 1533, the superb *Allegory* of the Louvre (No. 1589), which is very generally believed to represent the famous commander Alfonso d'Avalos, Marqués del Vasto, with his family. The eminent biographers of Titian connect the picture with the return of d'Avalos from the campaign against the Turks, undertaken by him in the autumn of 1532, under the leadership of Croy, at the behest of his imperial master. They hazard the surmise that the picture, though painted after Alfonso's return, symbolises his departure for the wars, "consoled by Victory, Love, and Hymen." A more natural conclusion would surely be that what Titian has sought to suggest is the return of the commander to enjoy the hard-earned fruits of victory.

The Italo-Spanish grandee was born at Naples in 1502, so that at this date he would have been but thirty-one years of age, whereas the mailed warrior of the *Allegory* is at least forty, perhaps older. Moreover, and this is the essential point, the technical qualities of the picture, the wonderful easy mastery of the handling, the peculiarities of the colouring and the general tone, surely point to a rather later date, to a period, indeed, some ten years ahead of the time at which we have arrived. If we are to accept the tradition that this Allegory, or quasi-allegorical portrait-piece, giving a fanciful embodiment to the pleasures of martial domination, of conjugal love, of well-earned peace and plenty, represents d'Avalos, his consort Mary of Arragon, and their family – and a comparison with the well-authenticated portrait of Del Vasto in the *Allocution* of Madrid does not carry with it entire conviction – we must perforce place the Louvre picture some ten years later than do Crowe and Cavalcaselle. Apart from the question of identification, it appears to the writer that the technical execution of the piece would lead to a similar conclusion.[*11]

To this year, 1533, belongs one of the masterpieces in portraiture of our painter, the wonderful *Cardinal Ippolito de' Medici in a Hungarian habit* of the Pitti. This youthful Prince of the Church, the natural son of Giuliano de' Medici, Duke of Nemours, was born in 1511, so that when Titian so incomparably portrayed him, he was, for all the perfect maturity of his virile beauty, for all the perfect self-possession of his aspect, but twenty-two years of age. He was the passionate worshipper of the divine Giulia Gonzaga, whose portrait he caused to be painted by Sebastiano del Piombo. His part in the war undertaken by Charles V. in 1532, against the Turks, had been a strange one. Clement VII., his relative, had appointed him Legate and sent him to Vienna at the head of three hundred musketeers. But when Charles withdrew from the army to return to Italy, the Italian contingent, instead of going in pursuit of the Sultan into Hungary, opportunely mutinied, thus affording to their pleasure-loving leader the desired pretext for riding back with them through the Austrian provinces, with eyes wilfully closed the while to their acts of depredation. It was in the rich and fantastic habit of a Hungarian captain that the handsome young Medici was now painted by Titian at Bologna, the result being a portrait unique of its kind even in his life-work. The sombre glow of the supple, youthful flesh, the red-brown of the rich velvet habit which defines the perfect shape of Ippolito, the red of the fantastic plumed head-dress worn by him with such sovereign ease, make up a deep harmony, warm, yet not in the technical sense hot, and of indescribable effect. And this effect is centralised in the uncanny glance, the mysterious aspect of the man whom, as we see him here, a woman might love for his beauty, but a man would do well to distrust. The smaller portrait painted by Titian about the same time of the young Cardinal fully armed – the one which, with the Pitti picture, Vasari saw in the closet (*guardaroba*) of

Cosimo, Duke of Tuscany – is not now known to exist.[*12]

It may be convenient to mention here one of the most magnificent among the male portraits of Titian, the *Young Nobleman* in the Sala di Marte of the Pitti Gallery, although its exact place in the middle time of the artist it is, failing all data on the point, not easy to determine. At Florence there has somehow been attached to it the curious name *Howard duca di Norfolk*,[*13] but upon what grounds, if any, the writer is unable to state. The master of Cadore never painted a head more finely or with a more exquisite finesse, never more happily characterised a face, than that of this resolute, self-contained young patrician with the curly chestnut hair and the short, fine beard and moustache – a personage high of rank, doubtless, notwithstanding the studied simplicity of his dress. Because we know nothing of the sitter, and there is in his pose and general aspect nothing sensational, this masterpiece is, if not precisely not less celebrated among connoisseurs, at any rate less popular with the larger public, than it deserves to be.[*14]

The noble altar-piece in the church of S. Giovanni Elemosinario at Venice showing the saint of that name enthroned, and giving alms to a beggar, belongs to the close of 1533 or thereabouts, since the high-altar was finished in the month of October of that year. According to Vasari, it must be regarded as having served above all to assert once for all the supremacy of Titian over Pordenone, whose friends had obtained for him the commission to paint in competition with the Cadorine an altar-piece for one of the apsidal chapels of the church, where, indeed, his work is still to be seen.[*15] Titian's canvas, like most of the great altar-pieces of the middle time, was originally arched at the top; but the vandalism of a subsequent epoch has, as in the case of the *Madonna di S. Niccola*, now in the Vatican, made of this arch a square, thereby greatly impairing the majesty of the general effect. Titian here solves the problem of combining the strong and simple decorative aspect demanded by the position of the work as the central feature of a small church, with the utmost pathos and dignity, thus doing incomparably in his own way – the way of the colourist and the warm, the essentially human realist – what Michelangelo had, soaring high above earth, accomplished with unapproachable sublimity in the *Prophets* and *Sibyls* of the Sixtine Chapel.

The colour is appropriately sober, yet a general tone is produced of great strength and astonishing effectiveness. The illumination is that of the open air, tempered and modified by an overhanging canopy of green; the great effect is obtained by the brilliant grayish white of the saint's alb, dominating and keeping in due balance the red of the rochet and the under-robes, the cloud-veiled sky, the marble throne or podium, the dark green hanging. This picture must have had in the years to follow a strong and lasting influence on Paolo Veronese, the keynote to whose audaciously brilliant yet never over-dazzling colour is this use of white and gray in large dominating masses. The noble figure of S. Giovanni gave him a prototype for many of his imposing figures of bearded old men. There is a strong reminiscence, too, of the saint's attitude in one of the most wonderful of extant Veroneses – that sumptuous altar-piece *SS. Anthony, Cornelius, and Cyprian with a Page*, in the Brera, for which he invented a harmony as delicious as it is daring, composed wholly of violet-purple, green, and gold.

# CHAPTER II

*Francesco Maria della Rovere – Titian and Eleonora Gonzaga – The "Venus with the Shell" – Titian's later ideals – The "Venus of Urbino" – The "Bella di Tiziano" – The "Twelve Cæsars" – Titian and Pordenone – The "Battle of Cadore" – Portraits of the Master by himself – The "Presentation in the Temple" – The "Allocation" of Madrid – The Ceiling Pictures of Santo Spirito – First Meeting with Pope Paul III. – The "Ecce Homo" of Vienna – "Christ with the Pilgrims at Emmaus."*

Within the years 1532 and 1538, or thereabouts, would appear to fall Titian's relations with another princely patron, Francesco Maria della Rovere, Duke of Urbino, the nephew of the redoubtable Pope Julius II., whose qualities of martial ardour and unbridled passion he reproduced in an exaggerated form. By his mother, Giovanna da Montefeltro, he descended also from the rightful dynasty of Urbino, to which he succeeded in virtue of adoption. His life of perpetual strife, of warfare in defence of his more than once lost and reconquered duchy, and as the captain first of the army of the Church, afterwards of the Venetian forces, came to an abrupt end in 1538. With his own hand he had, in the ardent days of his youth, slain in the open streets of Ravenna the handsome, sinister Cardinal Alidosi, thereby bringing down upon himself the anathemas of his uncle, Julius II., and furnishing to his successor, the Medici pope Leo X., the best possible excuse for the sequestration of the duchy of Urbino in favour of his own house. He himself died by poison, suspicion resting upon the infamous Pier Luigi Farnese, the son of Paul III.

Francesco Maria had espoused Eleonora Gonzaga, the sister of Titian's protector, Federigo, and it is probably through the latter that the relations with our master sprang up to which we owe a small group of his very finest works, including the so-called *Venus of Urbino* of the Tribuna, the *Girl in a Fur Cloak* of the Vienna Gallery, and the companion portraits of Francesco Maria and Eleonora which are now in the Venetian Gallery at the Uffizi. The fiery leader of armies had, it should be remembered, been brought up by Guidobaldo of Montefeltro, one of the most amiable and enlightened princes of his time, and, moreover, his consort Eleonora was the daughter of Isabella d'Este Gonzaga, than whom the Renaissance knew no more enthusiastic or more discriminating patron of art.

A curious problem meets us at the outset. We may assume with some degree of certainty that the portraits of the duke and duchess belong to the year 1537. Stylistic characteristics point to the conclusion that the great *Venus* of the Tribuna, the so-called *Bella di Tiziano*, and the *Girl in the Fur Cloak* – to take only undoubted originals – belong to much the same stage of Titian's practice as the companion portraits at the Uffizi. Eleonora Gonzaga, a princess of the highest culture, the daughter of an admirable mother, the friend of Pietro Bembo, Sadolet, and Baldassarre Castiglione, was at this time a matron of some twenty years' standing; at the date when her avowed portrait was painted she must have been at the very least forty. By what magic did Titian manage to suggest her type and physiognomy in the famous pictures just now mentioned, and yet to plunge the duchess into a kind of *Fontaine de Jouvence*, realising in the divine freshness of youth and beauty beings who nevertheless appear to have with her some kind of mystic and unsolved connection? If this was what he really intended – and the results attained may lead us without temerity to assume as much – no subtler or more exquisite form of flattery could be conceived. It is curious to note that at the same time he signally failed with the portrait of her mother, Isabella d'Este, painted in 1534, but showing the Marchioness of Mantua as a young woman of some twenty-five years, though she was then sixty. Here youth and a semblance of beauty are called up by the magic of the artist, but the personality, both physical and mental, is lost in the effort. But then in this last case Titian was working from an early portrait, and without the living original to refer to.

But, before approaching the discussion of the *Venus of Urbino*, it is necessary to say a word about another *Venus* which must have been painted some years before this time, revealing, as it does, a completely different and, it must be owned, a higher ideal. This is the terribly ruined, yet still beautiful, *Venus Anadyomene*, or *Venus of the Shell*, of the Bridgewater Gallery, painted perhaps at the instigation of some humanist, to realise a description of the world-famous painting of Apelles. It is not at present possible to place this picture with anything approaching to chronological exactitude. It must have been painted some years after the *Bacchus and Ariadne* of the National Gallery, some years before the *Venus* of the Tribuna, and that is about as near as surmise can get. The type of the goddess in the Ellesmere picture recalls somewhat the *Ariadne* in our masterpiece at the National Gallery, but also, albeit in a less material form, the *Magdalens* of a later time. Titian's conception of perfect womanhood is here midway between his earlier Giorgionesque ideal and the frankly sensuous yet grand luxuriance of his maturity and old age. He never, even in the days of youth and Giorgionesque enchantment, penetrated so far below the surface as did his master and friend Barbarelli. He could not equal him in giving, with the undisguised physical allurement which belongs to the true woman, as distinguished from the ideal conception compounded of womanhood's finest attributes, that sovereignty of amorous yet of spiritual charm which is its complement and its corrective.[*16]

Still with Titian, too, in the earlier years, woman, as presented in the perfection of mature youth, had, accompanying and elevating her bodily loveliness, a measure of that higher and nobler feminine attractiveness which would enable her to meet man on equal terms, nay, actively to exercise a dominating influence of fascination. In illustration of this assertion it is only necessary to refer to the draped and the undraped figure in the *Medea and Venus (Sacred and Profane Love)* of the Borghese Gallery, to the *Herodias* of the Doria Gallery, to the *Flora* of the Uffizi. Here, even when the beautiful Venetian courtesan is represented or suggested, what the master gives is less the mere votary than the priestess of love. Of this power of domination, this feminine royalty, the *Venus Anadyomene* still retains a measure, but the *Venus of Urbino* and the splendid succession of Venuses and Danaës, goddesses, nymphs, and heroines belonging to the period of the fullest maturity, show woman in the phase in which, renouncing her power to enslave, she is herself reduced to slavery.

These glowing presentments of physical attractiveness embody a lower ideal – that of woman as the plaything of man, his precious possession, his delight in the lower sense. And yet Titian expresses this by no means exalted conception with a grand candour, an absence of *arrière-pensée* such as almost purges it of offence. It is Giovanni Morelli who, in tracing the gradual descent from his recovered treasure, the *Venus* of Giorgione in the Dresden Gallery,[*17] through the various Venuses of Titian down to those of the latest manner, so finely expresses the essential difference between Giorgione's divinity and her sister in the Tribuna. The former sleeping, and protected only by her sovereign loveliness, is safer from offence than the waking goddess – or shall we not rather say woman? – who in Titian's canvas passively waits in her rich Venetian bower, tended by her handmaidens. It is again Morelli[*18] who points out that, as compared with Correggio, even Giorgione – to say nothing of Titian – is when he renders the beauty of woman or goddess a realist. And this is true in a sense, yet not altogether. Correggio's *Danaë*, his *Io*, his *Leda*, his *Venus*, are in their exquisite grace of form and movement farther removed from the mere fleshly beauty of the undraped model than are the goddesses and women of Giorgione. The passion and throb of humanity are replaced by a subtler and less easily explicable charm; beauty becomes a perfectly balanced and finely modulated harmony. Still the allurement is there, and it is more consciously and more provocatively exercised than with Giorgione, though the fascination of Correggio's divinities asserts itself less directly, less candidly. Showing through the frankly human loveliness of Giorgione's women there is after all a higher spirituality, a deeper intimation of that true, that clear-burning passion, enveloping body and soul, which transcends all exterior grace and harmony, however exquisite it may be in refinement of voluptuousness.[*19]

It is not, indeed, by any means certain that we are justified in seriously criticising as a *Venus* the great picture of the Tribuna. Titian himself has given no indication that the beautiful Venetian woman who lies undraped after the bath, while in a sumptuous chamber, furnished according to the mode of the time, her handmaidens are seeking for the robes with which she will adorn herself, is intended to present the love-goddess, or even a beauty masquerading with her attributes. Vasari, who saw it in the picture-closet of the Duke of Urbino, describes it, no doubt, as "une Venere giovanetta a giacere, con fieri e certi panni sottili attorno." It is manifestly borrowed, too – as is now universally acknowledged – from Giorgione's *Venus* in the Dresden Gallery, with the significant alteration, however, that Titian's fair one voluptuously dreams awake, while Giorgione's goddess more divinely reposes, and sleeping dreams loftier dreams. The motive is in the borrowing robbed of much of its dignity and beauty, and individualised in a fashion which, were any other master than Titian in question, would have brought it to the verge of triviality. Still as an example of his unrivalled mastery in rendering the glow and semi-transparency of flesh, enhanced by the contrast with white linen – itself slightly golden in tinge; in suggesting the appropriate atmospheric environment; in giving the full splendour of Venetian colour, duly subordinated nevertheless to the main motive, which is the glorification of a beautiful human body as it is; in all these respects the picture is of superlative excellence, a representative example of the master and of Venetian art, a piece which it would not be easy to match even among his own works.

More and more, as the supreme artist matures, do we find him disdaining the showier and more evident forms of virtuosity. His colour is more and more marked in its luminous beauty by reticence and concentration, by the search after such a main colour-chord as shall not only be beautiful and satisfying in itself, but expressive of the motive which is at the root of the picture. Play of light over the surfaces and round the contours of the human form; the breaking-up and modulation of masses of colour by that play of light; strength, and beauty of general tone – these are now Titian's main preoccupations. To this point his perfected technical art has legitimately developed itself from the Giorgionesque ideal of colour and tone-harmony, which was essentially the same in principle, though necessarily in a less advanced stage, and more diversified by exceptions. Our master became, as time went on, less and less interested in the mere dexterous juxtaposition of brilliantly harmonising and brilliantly contrasting tints, in piquancy, gaiety, and sparkle of colour, to be achieved for its own sake. Indeed this phase of Venetian sixteenth-century colour belongs rather to those artists who issued from Verona – to the Bonifazi, and to Paolo Veronese – who in this respect, as generally in artistic temperament, proved themselves the natural successors of Domenico and Francesco Morone, of Girolamo dai Libri, of Cavazzola.

Yet when Titian takes colour itself as his chief motive, he can vie with the most sumptuous of them in splendour, and eclipse them all by the sureness of his taste. A good example of this is the celebrated *Bella di Tiziano* of the Pitti Gallery, another work which, like the *Venus of Urbino*, recalls the features without giving the precise personality of Eleonora Gonzaga. The beautiful but somewhat expressionless head with its crowning glory of bright hair, a waving mass of Venetian gold, has been so much injured by rubbing down and restoration that we regret what has been lost even more than we enjoy what is left. But the surfaces of the fair and exquisitely modelled neck and bosom have been less cruelly treated; the superb costume retains much of its pristine splendour. With its combination of brownish-purple velvet, peacock-blue brocade, and white lawn, its delicate trimmings of gold, and its further adornment with small knots, having in them, now at any rate, but an effaced note of red, the gown of *La Bella* has remained the type of what is most beautiful in Venetian costume as it was in the earlier half of the sixteenth century. In richness and ingenious elaboration, chastened by taste, it far transcends the over-splendid and ponderous dresses in which later on the patrician dames portrayed by Veronese and his school loved to array themselves. A bright note of red in the upper jewel of one earring, now, no doubt, cruder than was originally intended, gives a fillip to the whole, after a fashion peculiar to Titian.

The *Girl in the Fur Cloak*, No 197 in the Imperial Gallery at Vienna, shows once more in a youthful and blooming woman the features of Eleonora. The model is nude under a mantle of black satin lined with fur, which leaves uncovered the right breast and both arms. The picture is undoubtedly Titian's own, and fine in quality, but it reveals less than his usual graciousness and charm. It is probably identical with the canvas described in the often-quoted catalogue of Charles I.'s pictures as "A naked woman putting on her smock, which the king changed with the Duchess of Buckingham for one of His Majesty's Mantua pieces." It may well have suggested to Rubens, who must have seen it among the King's possessions on the occasion of his visit to London, his superb, yet singularly unrefined, *Hélène Fourment in a Fur*

*Mantle*, now also in the Vienna Gallery.

The great portraits of the Duke and Duchess of Urbino in the Uffizi belong, as has already been noted, to 1537. Francesco Maria, here represented in the penultimate year of his stormy life, assumes deliberately the truculent warrior, and has beyond reasonable doubt made his own pose in a portrait destined to show the leader of armies, and not the amorous spouse or the patron of art and artists. Praise enthusiastic, but not excessive, has ever been and ever will be lavished on the breadth and splendid decision of the painting; on the magnificent rendering of the suit of plain but finely fashioned steel armour, with its wonderful reflections; on the energy of the virile countenance, and the appropriate concentration and simplicity of the whole. The superb head has, it must be confessed, more grandeur and energy than true individuality or life. The companion picture represents Eleonora Gonzaga seated near an open window, wearing a sombre but magnificent costume, and, completing it, one of those turbans with which the patrician ladies of North Italy, other than those of Venice, habitually crowned their locks. It has suffered in loss of freshness and touch more than its companion. Fine and accurate as the portrait is, much as it surpasses its pendant in subtle truth of characterisation, it has in the opinion of the writer been somewhat overpraised. For once, Titian approaches very nearly to the northern ideal in portraiture, underlining the truth with singular accuracy, yet with some sacrifice of graciousness and charm. The daughter of the learned and brilliant Isabella looks here as if, in the decline of her beauty, she had become something of a *précieuse* and a prude, though it would be imprudent to assert that she was either the one or the other. Perhaps the most attractive feature of the whole composition is the beautiful landscape so characteristically stretching away into the far blue distance, suggested rather than revealed through the open window. This is such a picture as might have inspired the Netherlander Antonio Moro, just because it is Italian art of the Cinquecento with a difference, that is, with a certain admixture of northern downrightness and literalness of statement.

About this same time Titian received from the brother of this princess, his patron and admirer Federigo Gonzaga, the commission for the famous series of the *Twelve Cæsars*, now only known to the world by stray copies here and there, and by the grotesquely exaggerated engravings of Ægidius Sadeler. Giulio Romano having in 1536[*20] completed the Sala di Troja in the Castello of Mantua, and made considerable progress with the apartments round about it, Federigo Gonzaga conceived the idea of devoting one whole room to the painted effigies of the *Twelve Cæsars* to be undertaken by Titian. The exact date when the *Cæsars* were delivered is not known, but it may legitimately be inferred that this was in the course of 1537 or the earlier half of 1538. Our master's pictures were, according to Vasari, placed in an *anticamera* of the Mantuan Palace, below them being hung twelve *storie a olio* – histories in oils – by Giulio Romano.[*21] The *Cæsars* were all half-lengths, eleven out of the twelve being done by the Venetian master and the twelfth by Giulio Romano himself.[*22] Brought to England with the rest of the Mantua pieces purchased by Daniel Nys for Charles I., they suffered injury, and Van Dyck is said to have repainted the *Vitellius*, which was one of several canvases irretrievably ruined by the quicksilver of the frames during the transit from Italy.[*23] On the disposal of the royal collection after Charles Stuart's execution the *Twelve Cæsars* were sold by the State – not presented, as is usually asserted – to the Spanish Ambassador Cardenas, who gave £1200 for them. On their arrival in Spain with the other treasures secured on behalf of Philip IV., they were placed in the Alcazar of Madrid, where in one of the numerous fires which successively devastated the royal palace they must have perished, since no trace of them is to be found after the end of the seventeenth century. The popularity of Titian's decorative canvases is proved by the fact that Bernardino Campi of Cremona made five successive sets of copies from them – for Charles V., d'Avalos, the Duke of Alva, Rangone, and another Spanish grandee. Agostino

Caracci subsequently copied them for the palace of Parma, and traces of yet other copies exist. Numerous versions are shown in private collections, both in England and abroad, purporting to be from the hand of Titian, but of these none – at any rate none of those seen by the writer – are originals or even Venetian copies. Among the best are the examples in the collection of Earl Brownlow and at the royal palace of Munich respectively, and these may possibly be from the hand of Campi. Although we are expressly told in Dolce's *Dialogo* that Titian "painted the *Twelve Cæsars*, taking them in part from medals, in part from antique marbles," it is perfectly clear that of the exact copying of antiques – such as is to be noted, for instance, in those marble medallions by Donatello which adorn the courtyard of the Medici Palace at Florence – there can have been no question. The attitudes of the *Cæsars*, as shown in the engravings and the extant copies, exclude any such supposition. Those who have judged them from those copies and the hideous grotesques of Sadeler have wondered at the popularity of the originals, somewhat hastily deeming Titian to have been here inferior to himself. Strange to say, a better idea of what he intended, and what he may have realised in the originals, is to be obtained from a series of small copies now in the Provincial Museum of Hanover, than from anything else that has survived.[*24] The little pictures in question, being on copper, cannot well be anterior to the first part of the seventeenth century, and they are not in themselves wonders. All the same they have a unique interest as proving that, while adopting the pompous attitudes and the purely decorative standpoint which the position of the pictures in the Castello may have rendered obligatory, Titian managed to make of his Emperors creatures of flesh and blood; the splendid Venetian warrior and patrician appearing in all the glory of manhood behind the conventional dignity, the self-consciousness of the Roman type and attitude.

These last years had been to Titian as fruitful in material gain as in honour. He had, as has been seen, established permanent and intimate relations not only with the art-loving rulers of the

North Italian principalities, but now with Charles V. himself, mightiest of European sovereigns, and, as a natural consequence, with the all-powerful captains and grandees of the Hispano-Austrian court. Meanwhile a serious danger to his supremacy had arisen. At home in Venice his unique position was threatened by Pordenone, that masterly and wonderfully facile *frescante* and painter of monumental decorations, who had on more than one occasion in the past been found in competition with him.

The Friulan, after many wanderings and much labour in North Italy, had settled in Venice in 1535, and there acquired an immense reputation by the grandeur and consummate ease with which he had carried out great mural decorations, such as the façade of Martin d'Anna's house on the Grand Canal, comprising in its scheme of decoration a Curtius on horse-back and a flying Mercury which according to Vasari became the talk of the town.[*25] Here, at any rate, was a field in which even Titian himself, seeing that he had only at long intervals practised in fresco painting, could not hope to rival Pordenone. The Friulan, indeed, in this his special branch, stood entirely alone among the painters of North Italy.

The Council of Ten in June 1537 issued a decree recording that Titian had since 1516 been in possession of his *senseria*, or broker's patent, and its accompanying salary, on condition that he should paint "the canvas of the land fight on the side of the Hall of the Great Council looking out on the Grand Canal," but that he had drawn his salary without performing his promise. He was therefore called upon to refund all that he had received for the time during which he had done no work. This sharp reminder operated as it was intended to do. We see from Aretino's correspondence that in November 1537 Titian was busily engaged on the great canvas for the Doges' Palace. This tardy recognition of an old obligation did not prevent the Council from issuing an order in November 1538 directing Pordenone to paint a picture for the Sala del Gran Consiglio, to occupy the space next to that reserved for Titian's long-delayed battle-piece.

That this can never have been executed is clear, since Pordenone, on receipt of an urgent summons from Ercole II., Duke of Ferrara, departed from Venice in the month of December of the same year, and falling sick at Ferrara, died so suddenly as to give rise to the suspicion of foul play, which too easily sprang up in those days when ambition or private vengeance found ready to hand weapons so many and so convenient. Crowe and Cavalcaselle give good grounds for the assumption that, in order to save appearances, Titian was supposed – replacing and covering the battle-piece which already existed in the Great Hall – to be presenting the Battle of Spoleto in Umbria, whereas it was clear to all Venetians, from the costumes, the banners, and the landscape, that he meant to depict the Battle of Cadore fought in 1508. The latter was a Venetian victory and an Imperial defeat, the former a Papal defeat and an Imperial victory. The all-devouring fire of 1577 annihilated the *Battle of Cadore* with too many other works of capital importance in the history both of the primitive and the mature Venetian schools. We have nothing now to show what it may have been, save the print of Fontana, and the oil painting in the Venetian Gallery of the Uffizi, reproducing on a reduced scale part only of the big canvas. This last is of Venetian origin, and more or less contemporary, but it need hardly be pointed out that it is a copy from, not a sketch for, the picture.

To us who know the vast battle-piece only in the feeble echo of the print and the picture just now mentioned, it is a little difficult to account for the enthusiasm that it excited, and the prominent place accorded to it among the most famous of the Cadorine's works. Though the whole has abundant movement and passion, and the *mise-en-scène* is undoubtedly imposing, the combat is not raised above reality into the region of the higher and more representative truth by any element of tragic vastness and significance. Even though the Imperialists are armed more or less in the antique Roman fashion, to distinguish them from the Venetians, who appear in the accoutrements of their own day, it is still that minor and local combat the *Battle of Cadore* that we have before us, and not, above and beyond this battle, War, as some masters of the century, gifted with a higher power of evocation, might have shown it. Even as the fragment of Leonardo da Vinci's *Battle of Anghiari* survives in the free translation of Rubens's well-known drawing in the Louvre, we see how he has made out of the unimportant cavalry combat, yet without conventionality or undue transposition, a representation unequalled in art of the frenzy generated in man and beast by the clash of arms and the scent of blood. And Rubens, too, how incomparably in the *Battle of the Amazons* of the Pinakothek at Munich, he evokes the terrors, not only of one mortal encounter, but of War – the hideous din, the horror of man let loose and become beast once more, the pitiless yell of the victors, the despairing cry of the vanquished, the irremediable overthrow! It would, however, be foolhardy in those who can only guess at what the picture may have been to arrogate to themselves the right of sitting in judgment on Vasari and those contemporaries who, actually seeing, enthusiastically admired it. What excited their delight must surely have been Titian's magic power of brush as displayed in individual figures and episodes, such as that famous one of the knight armed by his page in the immediate foreground.

Into this period of our master's career there fit very well the two portraits in which he appears, painted by himself, on the confines of old age, vigorous and ardent still, fully conscious, moreover, though without affectation, of pre-eminent genius and supreme artistic rank. The portraits referred to are those very similar ones, both of them undoubtedly originals, which are respectively in the Berlin Gallery and the Painters' Gallery of the Uffizi. It is strange that there should exist no certain likeness of the master of Cadore done in youth or earlier manhood, if there be excepted the injured and more than doubtful production in the Imperial Gallery of Vienna, which has pretty generally been supposed to be an original auto-portrait belonging to this period. In the Uffizi and Berlin pictures Titian looks about sixty years old, but may be a little more or a little less. The latter is a half-length, showing him seated and gazing obliquely out of the picture with a majestic air, but also with something of combativeness and disquietude, an element, this last, which is traceable even in some of the earlier portraits, but not in the mythological *poesie* or any sacred work. More and more as we advance through the final period of old age do we find this element of disquietude and misgiving asserting itself in male portraiture, as, for instance, in the *Maltese Knight* of the Prado, the *Dominican Monk* of the Borghese, the *Portrait of a Man with a Palm Branch* of the Dresden Gallery. The atmosphere of sadness and foreboding enveloping man is traceable back to Giorgione; but with him it comes from the plenitude of inner life, from the gaze turned inwards upon the mystery of the human individuality rather than outwards upon the inevitable tragedies of the exterior life common to all. This same atmosphere of passionate contemplativeness enwraps, indeed, all that Giorgione did, and is the cause that he sees the world and himself lyrically, not dramatically; the flame of aspiration burning steadily at the heart's core and leaving the surface not indeed unruffled, but outwardly calm in its glow. Titian's is the more dramatic temperament in outward things, but also the more superficial. It must be remembered, too, that arriving rapidly at the maturity of his art, and painting all through the period of the full Renaissance, he was able with far less hindrance from technical limitations to express his conceptions to the full. His portraiture, however, especially his male portraiture, was and remained in its essence a splendid and full-blown development of the Giorgionesque ideal. It was grander, more accomplished, and for obvious reasons more satisfying, yet far less penetrating, less expressive of the inner fibre, whether of the painter or of his subject.

But to return to the portrait of Berlin. It is in parts unfinished, and therefore the more interesting as revealing something of the methods employed by the master in this period of absolute mastery, when his palette was as sober in its strength as it was rich and harmonious; when, as ever, execution was a way to an end, and therefore not to be vain-gloriously displayed merely for its own sake. The picture came, with very many other masterpieces of the Italian and Netherlandish schools, from the Solly collection, which formed the nucleus of the Berlin Gallery. The Uffizi portrait emerges noble still, in its semi-ruined state, from a haze of restoration and injury, which has not succeeded in destroying the exceptional fineness and sensitiveness of the modelling. Although the pose and treatment of the head are practically identical with that in the Berlin picture, the conception seems a less dramatic one. It includes, unless the writer has misread it, an element of greater mansuetude and a less perturbed reflectiveness.

The double portrait in the collection of Her Majesty the Queen at Windsor Castle, styled *Titian and Franceschini*[*26] has no pretensions whatever to be even discussed as a Titian. The figure of the Venetian senator designated as Franceschini is the better performance of the two; the lifeless head of Titian, which looks very like an afterthought, has been copied, without reference to the relation of the two figures the one to the other, from the Uffizi picture, or some portrait identical with it in character. A far finer likeness of Titian than any of these is the much later one, now in the Prado Gallery; but this it will be best to deal with in its proper chronological order.

We come now to one of the most popular of all Titian's great canvases based on a sacred subject, the *Presentation in the Temple* in the Accademia delle Belle Arti at Venice. This, as Vasari expressly states, was painted for the Scuola di S. Maria della Carità, that is, for the confraternity which owned the very building where now the Accademia displays its treasures. It is the magnificent scenic rendering of a subject lending itself easily to exterior pomp and display, not so easily to a more mystic and less obvious mode of conception. At the root of Titian's design lies in all probability the very similar picture on a comparatively small scale by Cima da Conegliano, now No. 63 in the Dresden Gallery, and this last may well have been inspired by Carpaccio's *Presentation of the Virgin*, now in the Brera at Milan.[*27] The imposing canvases belonging to this particular period of Titian's activity, and this one in particular, with its splendid architectural framing, its wealth of life and movement, its richness and variety in type and costume, its fair prospect of Venetian landscape in the distance, must have largely contributed to form the transcendent decorative talent of Paolo Veronese. Only in the exquisitely fresh and beautiful figure of the childlike Virgin, who ascends the mighty flight of stone steps, clad all in shimmering blue, her head crowned with a halo of yellow light, does the artist prove that he has penetrated to the innermost significance of his subject. Here, at any rate, he touches the heart as well as feasts the eye. The thoughts of all who are familiar with Venetian art will involuntarily turn to Tintoretto's rendering of the same moving, yet in its symbolical character not naturally ultra-dramatic, scene. The younger master lends to it a significance so vast that he may be said to go as far beyond and above the requirements of the theme as Titian, with all his legitimate splendour and serene dignity, remains below it. With Tintoretto as interpreter we are made to see the beautiful episode as an event of the most tremendous import – one that must shake the earth to its centre. The reason of the onlooker may rebel against this portentous version, yet he is dominated all the same, is overwhelmed with something of the indefinable awe that has seized upon the bystanders who are witnesses of the scene.

But now to discuss a very curious point in connection with the actual state of Titian's important canvas. It has been very generally assumed – and Crowe and Cavalcaselle have set their seal on the assumption – that Titian painted his picture for a special place in the Albergo (now Accademia), and that this place is now architecturally as it was in Titian's time. Let them speak for themselves.

"In this room (in the Albergo), which is contiguous to the modern hall

in which Titian's *Assunta* is displayed, there were two doors for
which allowance was made in Titian's canvas; twenty-five feet – the
length of the wall – is now the length of the picture. When this vast
canvas was removed from its place, the gaps of the doors were filled
in with new linen, and painted up to the tone of the original...."

That the pieces of canvas to which reference is here made
were new, and not Titian's original work from the brush, was of
course well known to those who saw the work as it used to hang
in the Accademia. Crowe and Cavalcaselle give indeed the name
of a painter of this century who is responsible for them. Within
the last three years the new and enterprising director of the
Venice Academy, as part of a comprehensive scheme of
rearrangement of the whole collection, caused these pieces of new
canvas to be removed and then proceeded to replace the picture
in the room for which it is believed to have been executed, fitting
it into the space above the two doors just referred to. Many people
have declared themselves delighted with the alteration, looking
upon it as a tardy act of justice done to Titian, whose work, it is
assumed, is now again seen just as he designed it for the Albergo.
The writer must own that he has, from an examination of the
canvas where it is now placed, or replaced, derived an absolutely
contrary impression. First, is it conceivable that Titian in the
heyday of his glory should have been asked to paint such a
picture – not a mere mural decoration – for such a place? There is
no instance of anything of the kind having been done with the
canvases painted by Gentile Bellini, Carpaccio, Mansueti, and
others for the various *Scuole* of Venice. There is no instance of a
great decorative canvas by a sixteenth century master of the first
rank,[*28] other than a ceiling decoration, being degraded in the
first instance to such a use. And then Vasari, who saw the picture
in Venice, and correctly characterises it, would surely have
noticed such an extraordinary peculiarity as the abnormal shape
necessitated by the two doors. It is incredible that Titian, if so
unpalatable a task had indeed been originally imposed upon
him, should not have designed his canvas otherwise. The hole for

the right door coming in the midst of the monumental steps is just possible, though not very probable. Not so that for the left door, which, according to the present arrangement, cuts the very vitals out of one of the main groups in the foreground. Is it not to insult one of the greatest masters of all time thus to assume that he would have designed what we now see? It is much more likely that Titian executed his *Presentation* in the first place in the normal shape, and that vandals of a later time, deciding to pierce the room in the Scuola in which the picture is now once more placed with one, or probably two, additional doors, partially sacrificed it to the structural requirements of the moment. Monstrous as such barbarism may appear, we have already seen, and shall again see later on, that it was by no means uncommon in those great ages of painting, the sixteenth and seventeenth centuries.

When the untimely death of Pordenone, at the close of 1538, had extinguished the hopes of the Council that the grandiose facility of this master of monumental decoration might be made available for the purposes of the State, Titian having, as has been seen, made good his gravest default, was reinstated in his lucrative and by no means onerous office. He regained the *senseria* by decree of August 28, 1539. The potent d'Avalos, Marqués del Vasto, had in 1539 conferred upon Titian's eldest son Pomponio, the scapegrace and spendthrift that was to be, a canonry. Both to father and son the gift was in the future to be productive of more evil than good. At or about the same time he had commissioned of Titian a picture of himself haranguing his soldiers in the pompous Roman fashion; this was not, however, completed until 1541. Exhibited by d'Avalos to admiring crowds at Milan, it made a sensation for which there is absolutely nothing in the picture, as we now see it in the gallery of the Prado, to account; but then it would appear that it was irreparably injured in a fire which devastated the Alcazar of Madrid in 1621, and was afterwards extensively repainted. The Marquis and his son Francesco, both of them full-length figures, are placed on a low plinth, to the left, and from this point of vantage the Spanish leader addresses a company of foot-soldiers who with fine effect raise their halberds high into the air.[*29] Among these last tradition places a portrait of Aretino, which is not now to be recognised with any certainty. Were the pedigree of the canvas a less well-authenticated one, one might be tempted to deny Titian's authorship altogether, so extraordinary are, apart from other considerations, the disproportions in the figure of the youth Francesco. Restoration must in this instance have amounted to entire repainting. Del Vasto appears more robust, more martial, and slightly younger than the armed leader in the *Allegory* of the Louvre. If this last picture is to be accepted as a semi-idealised presentment of the Spanish captain, it must, as has already been pointed out, have been painted nearer to the time of his death, which took place in 1546. The often-cited biographers of our master are clearly in error in their conclusion that the painting described in the collection of Charles I. as "done by Titian, the picture of the Marquis Guasto, containing five half-figures so big as the life, which the king bought out of an Almonedo," is identical with the large sketch made by Titian as a preparation for the *Allocution* of Madrid. This description, on the contrary, applies perfectly to the *Allegory* of the Louvre, which was, as we know, included in the collection of Charles, and subsequently found its way into that of Louis Quatorze.

It was in 1542 that Vasari, summoned to Venice at the suggestion of Aretino, paid his first visit to the city of the Lagoons in order to paint the scenery and *apparato* in connection with a carnival performance, which included the representation of his fellow-townsman's *Talanta*.[*30] It was on this occasion, no doubt, that Sansovino, in agreement with Titian, obtained for the Florentine the commission to paint the ceilings of Santo Spirito in Isola – a commission which was afterwards, as a consequence of his departure, undertaken and performed by Titian himself, with whose grandiose canvases we shall have to deal a little later on. In weighing the value of Vasari's testimony with reference to the works of Vecellio and other Venetian painters more or less of his own time, it should be borne in mind that he paid two successive visits to Venice, enjoying there the company of the great painter and the most eminent artists of the day, and that on the occasion of Titian's memorable visit to Rome he was his close friend, cicerone, and companion. Allowing for the Aretine biographer's well-known inaccuracies in matters of detail and for his royal disregard of chronological order – faults for which it is manifestly absurd to blame him over-severely – it would be unwise lightly to disregard or overrule his testimony with regard to matters which he may have learned from the lips of Titian himself and his immediate entourage.

To the year 1542 belongs, as the authentic signature and date on the picture affirm, that celebrated portrait, *The Daughter of Roberto Strozzi*, once in the splendid palace of the family at Florence, but now, with some other priceless treasures having the same origin, in the Berlin Museum. Technically, the picture is one of the most brilliant, one of the most subtly exquisite, among the works of the great Cadorine's maturity. It well serves to show what Titian's ideal of colour was at this time. The canvas is all silvery gleam, all splendour and sober strength of colour – yet not of colours. These in all their plentitude and richness, as in the crimson drapery and the distant landscape, are duly subordinated to the main effect; they but set off discreetly the figure of the child, dressed all in white satin with hair of reddish gold, and contribute without fanfare to the fine and harmonious balance of the whole. Here, as elsewhere, more particularly in the work of Titian's maturity, one does not in the first place pause to pick out this or the other tint, this or the other combination of colours as particularly exquisite; and that is what one is so easily led to do in the contemplation of the Bonifazi and of Paolo Veronese.

As the portrait of a child, though in conception it reveals a marked progress towards the *intimité* of later times, the Berlin picture lacks something of charm and that quality which, for want of a better word, must be called loveableness. Or is it perhaps that the eighteenth and nineteenth centuries have spoilt us in this respect? For it is only in these latter days that to the child, in deliberate and avowed portraiture, is allowed that freakishness, that natural *espièglerie* and freedom from artificial control which has its climax in the unapproached portraits of Sir Joshua Reynolds. This is the more curious when it is remembered how tenderly, with what observant and sympathetic truth the relation of child to mother, of child to child, was noted in the innumerable "Madonnas" and "Holy Families" of the fifteenth and sixteenth centuries; how both the Italians, and following them the Netherlanders, relieved the severity of their sacred works by the delightful roguishness, the romping impudence of their little angels, their *putti*.

It has already been recorded that Titian, taking up the commission abandoned by Vasari, undertook a great scheme of pictorial decoration for the Brothers of Santo Spirito in Isola. All that he carried out for that church has now found its way into that of the Salute. The three ceiling pictures, *The Sacrifice of Isaac, Cain and Abel*, and *David victorious over Goliath*, are in the great sacristy of the church; the *Four Evangelists* and *Four Doctors* are in the ceiling of the choir behind the altar; the altar-piece, *The Descent of the Holy Spirit*, is in one of the chapels which completely girdle the circular church itself. The ceiling pictures, depicting three of the most dramatic moments in sacred history, have received the most enthusiastic praise from the master's successive biographers. They were indeed at the time of their inception a new thing in Venetian art. Nothing so daring as these foreshortenings, as these scenes of dramatic violence, of physical force triumphant, had been seen in Venice. The turbulent spirit was an exaggeration of that revealed by Titian in the *St. Peter Martyr*; the problem of the foreshortening for the purposes of ceiling decoration was superadded. It must be remembered, too, that even in Rome, the headquarters of the grand style, nothing precisely of the same kind could be said to exist. Raphael and his pupils either disdained, or it may be feared to approach, the problem. Neither in the ceiling decorations of the Farnesina nor in the Stanze is there any attempt on a large scale to *faire plafonner* the figures, that is, to paint them so that they might appear as they would actually be seen from below. Michelangelo himself, in the stupendous decoration of the ceiling to the Sixtine Chapel, had elected to treat the subjects of the flat surface which constitutes the centre and climax of the whole, as a series of pictures designed under ordinary conditions. It can hardly be doubted that Titian, in attempting these *tours de force*, though not necessarily or even probably in any other way, was inspired by Correggio. It would not be easy, indeed, to exaggerate the Venetian master's achievement from this point of view, even though in two at least of the groups – the *Cain and Abel* and the *David and Goliath* – the modern professor might be justified in criticising with considerable severity his draughtsmanship and many salient points in his design. The effect produced is tremendous of its kind. The power suggested is, however, brutal, unreasoning, not nobly dominating force; and this not alone in the *Cain and Abel*, where such an impression is rightly conveyed, but also in the other pieces. It is as if Titian, in striving to go beyond anything that had hitherto been done of the same kind, had also gone beyond his own artistic convictions, and thus, while compassing a remarkable pictorial achievement, lost his true balance. Tintoretto, creating his own atmosphere, as far outside and above mere physical realities as that of Michelangelo himself, might have succeeded in mitigating this impression, which is, on the whole, a painful one. Take for instance the *Martyrdom of St. Christopher* of the younger painter – not a ceiling picture by the way – in the apse of S. Maria del Orto. Here, too, is depicted, with sweeping and altogether irresistible power, an act of hideous violence. And yet it is not this element of the subject which makes upon the spectator the most profound effect, but the impression of saintly submission, of voluntary self-sacrifice, which is the dominant note of the whole.

It may be convenient to mention here *The Descent of the Holy Spirit*, although in its definitive form, as we see it in its place in the Church of the Salute, it appears markedly more advanced in style than the works of the period at which we have now arrived, giving, both in manner and feeling, a distinct suggestion of the methods and standpoint which mark the later phase of old age. Vasari tells us that the picture, originally painted in 1541, was seriously damaged and subsequently repainted; Crowe and Cavalcaselle state that the work now seen at the Salute was painted to replace an altar-piece which the Brothers of Santo Spirito had declined to accept. Even as the picture now appears, somewhat faded, and moreover seen at a disadvantage amid its cold surroundings of polished white marble, it is a composition of wonderful, of almost febrile animation, and a painting saturated with light, pierced through everywhere with its rays. The effect produced is absolutely that which the mystical subject requires.[*31] Abandoning the passionless serenity which has been the rule in sacred subjects of the middle time, Titian shows himself more stimulated, more moved by his subject.

It was in the spring of 1543 that the master first came into personal contact with Pope Paul III. and the Farnese family. The meeting took place at Ferrara, and our painter then accompanied the papal court to Busseto, and subsequently proceeded to Bologna. Aretino's correspondence proves that Titian must at that time have painted the Pope, and that he must also have refused the sovereign pontiff's offer of the *Piombo*, which was then still, as it had been for years past, in the possession of Sebastiano Luciani. That Titian, with all his eagerness for wealth and position, could not find it in his heart to displace his fellow-countryman, a friend no doubt of the early time, may legitimately excite admiration and sympathy now, as according to Aretino it actually did at the time. The portraits of the Farnese family included that of the Pope, repeated subsequently for Cardinal Santafiore, that of Pier Luigi, then that of Paul III. and this monstrous yet well-loved son together,[*32] and a likeness of Cardinal Alessandro Farnese. Upon the three-quarter length portrait of Paul III. in the Naples Museum, Crowe and Cavalcaselle have lavished their most enthusiastic praise, placing it, indeed, among his masterpieces.

All the same – interesting as the picture undoubtedly is, remarkable in finish, and of undoubtedly Titianesque origin – the writer finds it difficult, nay impossible, to accept this *Paul III.* as a work from the hand of Titian himself. Careful to excess, and for such an original too much wanting in brilliancy and vitality, it is the best of many repetitions and variations; of this particular type the original is not at present forthcoming. Very different is the "Paul III." of the Hermitage, which even in a reproduction loudly proclaims its originality.[*33] This is by no means identical in design with the Naples picture, but appears much less studied, much more directly taken from the life. The astute Farnese Pope has here the same simiesque type, the same furtive distrustful look, as in the great unfinished group now to be described.[*34] This Titian, which doubtless passed into the Hermitage with the rest of the Barbarigo pictures, may have been the first foundation for the series of portraits of the Farnese Pope, and as such would naturally have been retained by the master for his own use. The portrait-group in the Naples Museum, showing, with Paul III., Cardinal Alessandro Farnese and Ottavio Farnese (afterwards Duke of Parma), is, apart from its extraordinary directness and swift technical mastery, of exceptional interest as being unfinished, and thus doubly instructive. The composition, lacking in its unusual momentariness the repose and dignity of Raphael's *Leo X. with Cardinals Giulio de' Medici and de' Rossi* at the Pitti, is not wholly happy. Especially is the action of Ottavio Farnese, as in reverence he bends down to reply to the supreme Pontiff, forced and unconvincing; but the unflattered portrait of the pontiff himself is of a bold and quite unconventional truth, and in movement much happier. The picture may possibly, by reason of this unconventional conception less than perfectly realised, have failed to please the sitters, and thus have been left in its present state.[*35]

Few of Titian's canvases of vast dimensions have enjoyed a higher degree of popularity than the large *Ecce Homo* to which the Viennese proudly point as one of the crowning ornaments of the great Imperial Gallery of their city. Completed in 1543[*36] for Giovanni d'Anna, a son of the Flemish merchant Martin van der Hanna, who had established himself in Venice, it was vainly coveted by Henri III. on the occasion of his memorable visit in 1574, but was in 1620 purchased for the splendid favourite, George Villiers, Duke of Buckingham, by the English envoy Sir Henry Wotton. From him the noblest and most accomplished of English collectors, Thomas, Earl of Arundel, sought to obtain the prize with the unparalleled offer of £7000, yet even thus failed. At the time of the great *débâcle*, in 1648, the guardians and advisers of his youthful son and successor were glad enough to get the splendid gallery over to the Low Countries, and to sell with the rest the *Ecce Homo*, which brought under these circumstances but a tenth part of what Lord Arundel would have given for it. Passing into the collection of the Archduke Leopold William, it was later on finally incorporated with that of the Imperial House of Austria. From the point of view of scenic and decorative magnificence combined with dramatic propriety, though not with any depth or intensity of dramatic passion, the work is undoubtedly imposing. Yet it suffers somewhat, even in this respect, from the fact that the figures are not more than small life-size. With passages of Titianesque splendour there are to be noted others, approaching to the acrid and inharmonious, which one would rather attribute to the master's assistants than to himself. So it is, too, with certain exaggerations of design characteristic rather of the period than the man – notably with the two figures to the left of the foreground. The Christ in His meekness is too little divine, too heavy and inert;[*37] the Pontius Pilate not inappropriately reproduces the features of the worldling and *viveur* Aretino. The mounted warrior to the extreme right, who has been supposed to represent Alfonso d'Este, shows the genial physiognomy made familiar by the Madrid picture so long deemed to be his portrait, but which, as has already been pointed out, represents much more probably his successor Ercole II. d'Este, whom we find again in that superb piece by the master, the so-called *Giorgio Cornaro* of Castle Howard. The *Ecce Homo* of Vienna is another of the works of which both the general *ordonnance* and the truly Venetian splendour must have profoundly influenced Paolo Veronese.

To this period belongs also the *Annunciation of the Virgin* now in the Cathedral of Verona – a rich, harmonious, and appropriate altar-piece, but not one of any special significance in the life-work of the painter.

Shall we not, pretty much in agreement with Vasari, place here, just before the long-delayed visit to Rome, the *Christ with the Pilgrims at Emmaus* of the Louvre? A strong reason for dating this, one of the noblest, one of the most deeply felt of all Titian's works, before rather than after the stay in the Eternal City, is that in its *naïveté*, in its realistic episodes, in its fulness of life, it is so entirely and delightfully Venetian. Here again the colour-harmony in its subdued richness and solemnity has a completeness such as induces the beholder to accept it in its unity rather than to analyse those infinite subtleties of juxtaposition and handling which, avoiding bravura, disdain to show themselves on the surface. The sublime beauty of the landscape, in which, as often elsewhere, the golden radiance of the setting sun is seen battling with masses of azure cloud, has not been exceeded by Titian himself. With all the daring yet perfectly unobtrusive and unconscious realism of certain details, the conception is one of the loftiest, one of the most penetrating in its very simplicity, of Venetian art at its apogee. The divine mansuetude, the human and brotherly sympathy of the Christ, have not been equalled since the early days of the *Cristo della Moneta*. Altogether the *Pilgrims at Emmaus* well marks that higher and more far-reaching conception of sacred art which reveals itself in the productions of Titian's old age, when we compare them with the untroubled serenity and the conventional assumptions of the middle time.[*38]

To the year 1545 belongs the supremely fine *Portrait of Aretino*, which is one of the glories of the Pitti Gallery. This was destined to propitiate the Grand Duke Cosimo of Tuscany, the son of his passionately attached friend of earlier days, Giovanni delle Bande Nere. Aretino, who had particular reasons for desiring to appear before the obdurate Cosimo in all the pomp and opulence of his later years, was obviously wounded that Titian, true to his genius, and to his method at this moment, should have made the keynote of his masterpiece a dignified simplicity. For once unfaithful to his brother Triumvir and friend, he attacks him in the accompanying letter to the Tuscan ruler with the withering sarcasm that "the satins, velvets, and brocades would perhaps have been better if Titian had received a few more scudi for working them out." If Aretino's pique had not caused the momentary clouding over of his artistic vision, he would have owned that the canvas now in the Pitti was one of the happiest achievements of Titian and one of the greatest things in portraiture. There is no flattery here of the "Divine Aretino," as with heroic impudence the notorious publicist styles himself. The sensual type is preserved, but rendered acceptable, and in a sense attractive, by a certain assurance and even dignity of bearing, such as success and a position impregnable of its unique and unenviable kind may well have lent to the adventurer in his maturity. Even Titian's brush has not worked with greater richness and freedom, with an effect broader or more entirely legitimate than in the head with its softly flowing beard and the magnificent yet not too ornate robe and vest of plum-coloured velvet and satin.

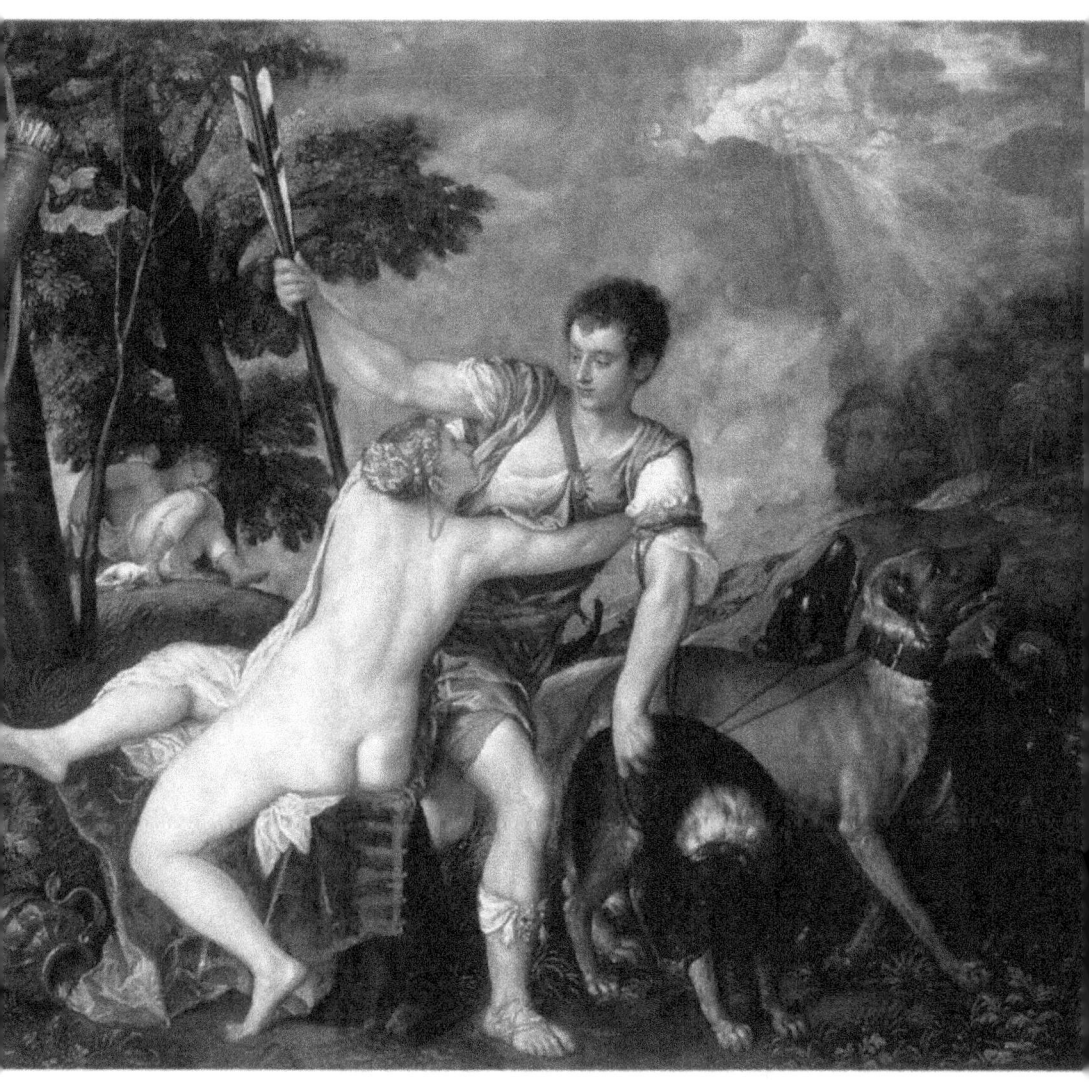

Titian, Venus and Adonis, 1550, Ashmolean, Oxford

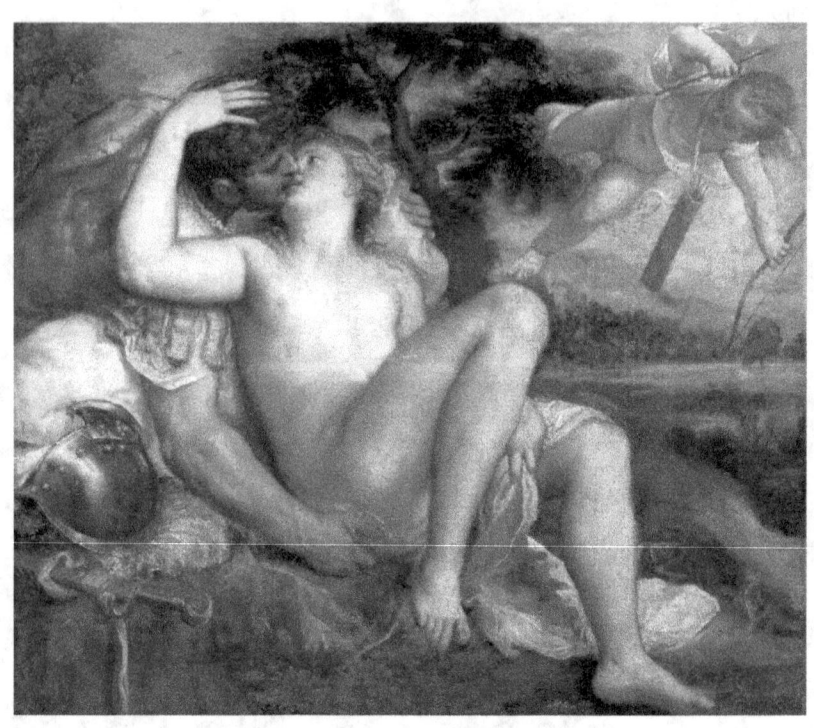

Titian, Venus and Mars and Amor, 1530, Vienna

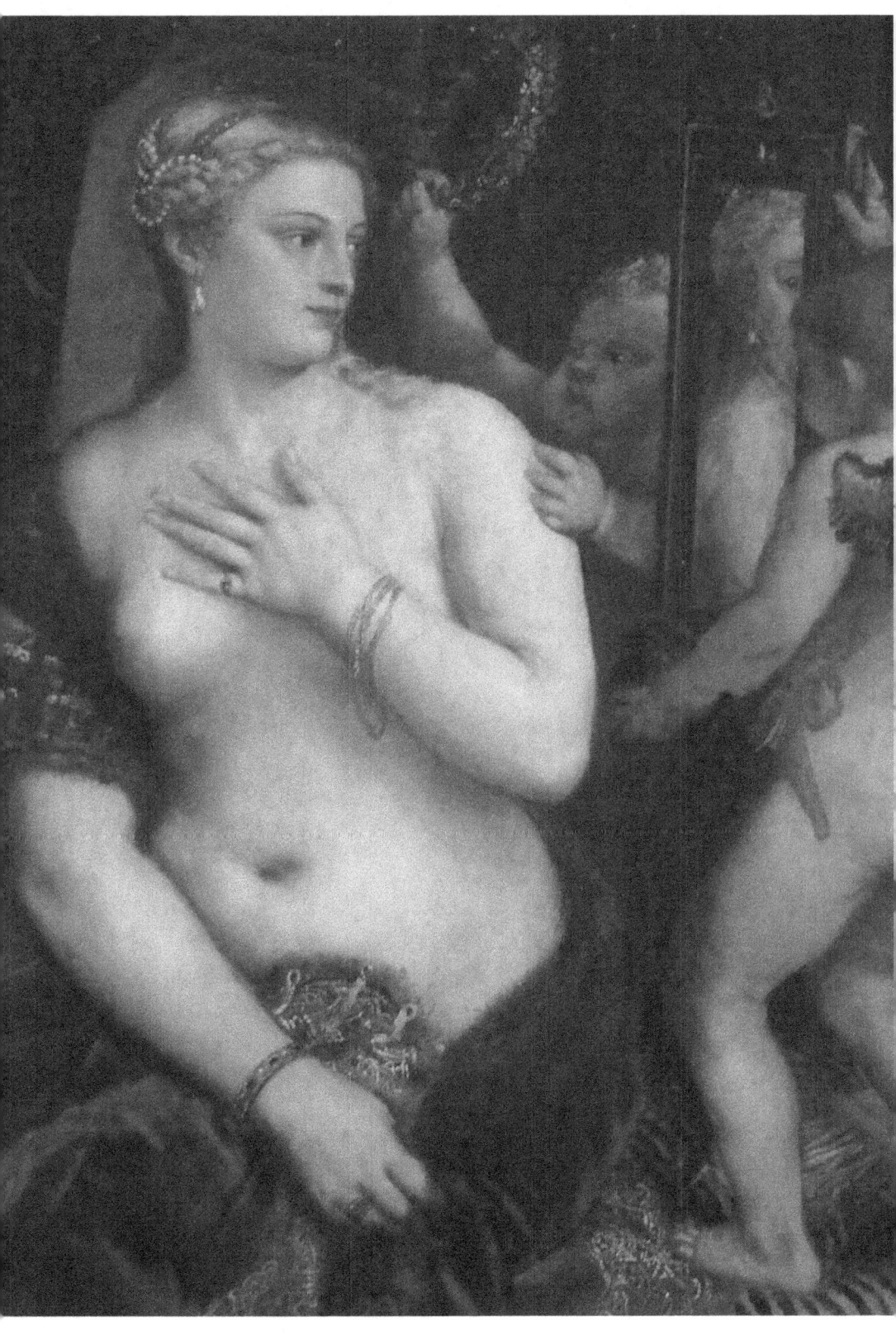

Titian, Venus With a Mirror, 1554-55, Washington, DC

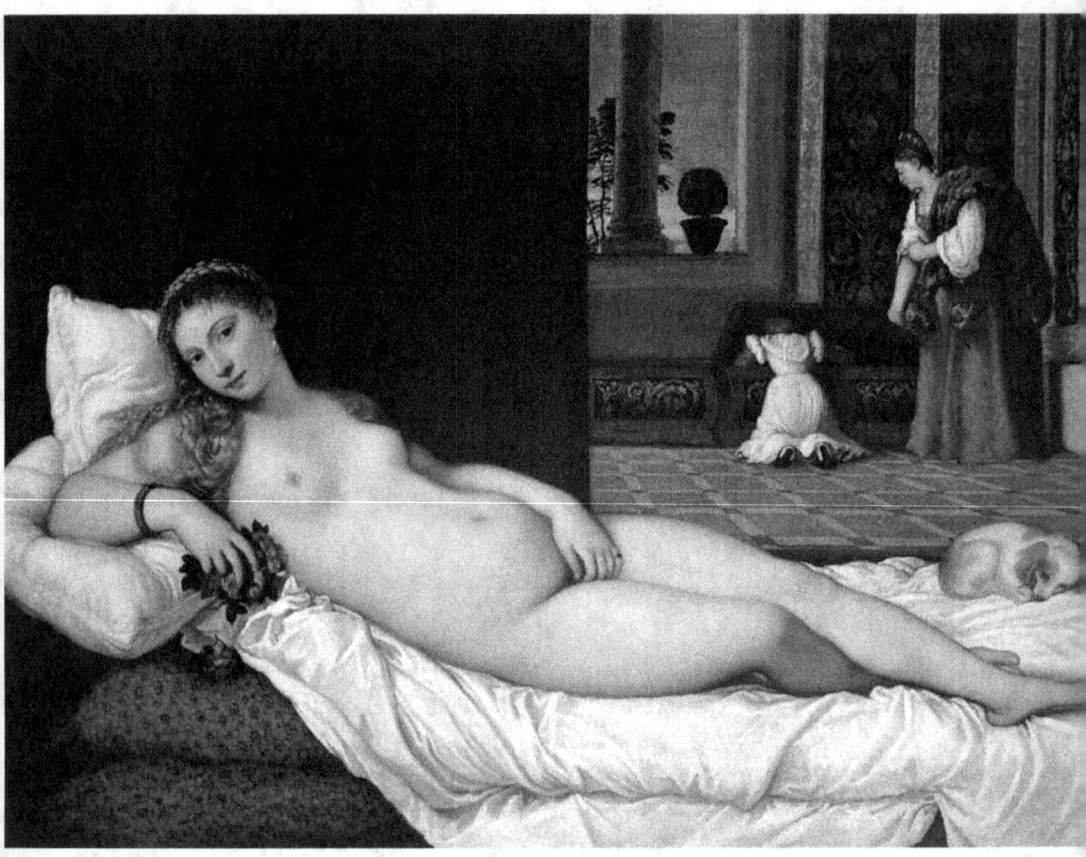

Titian, The Venus of Urbino, 1538, Uffizi, Florence

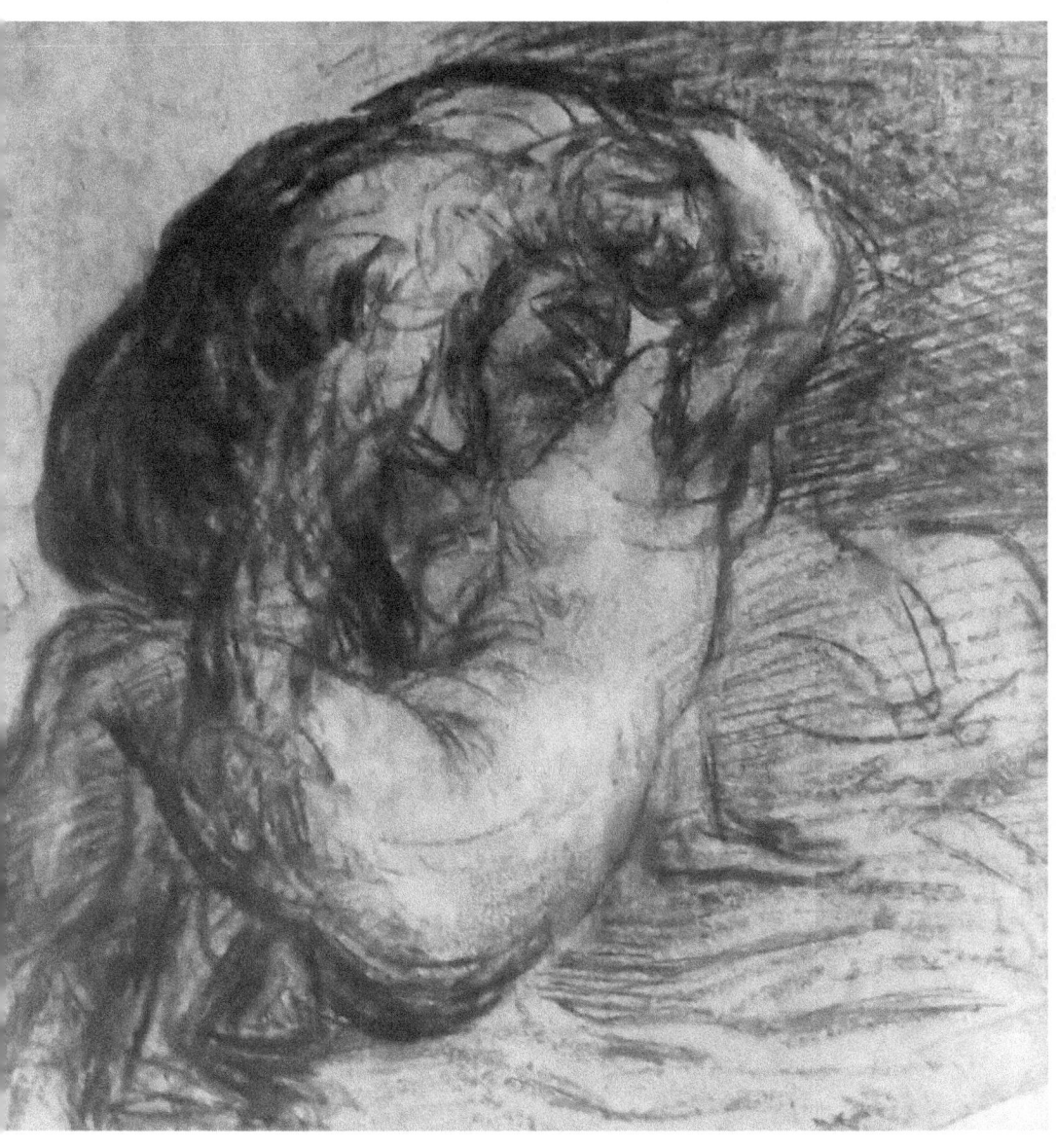

Titian, A Couple, c. 1570, Cambridge

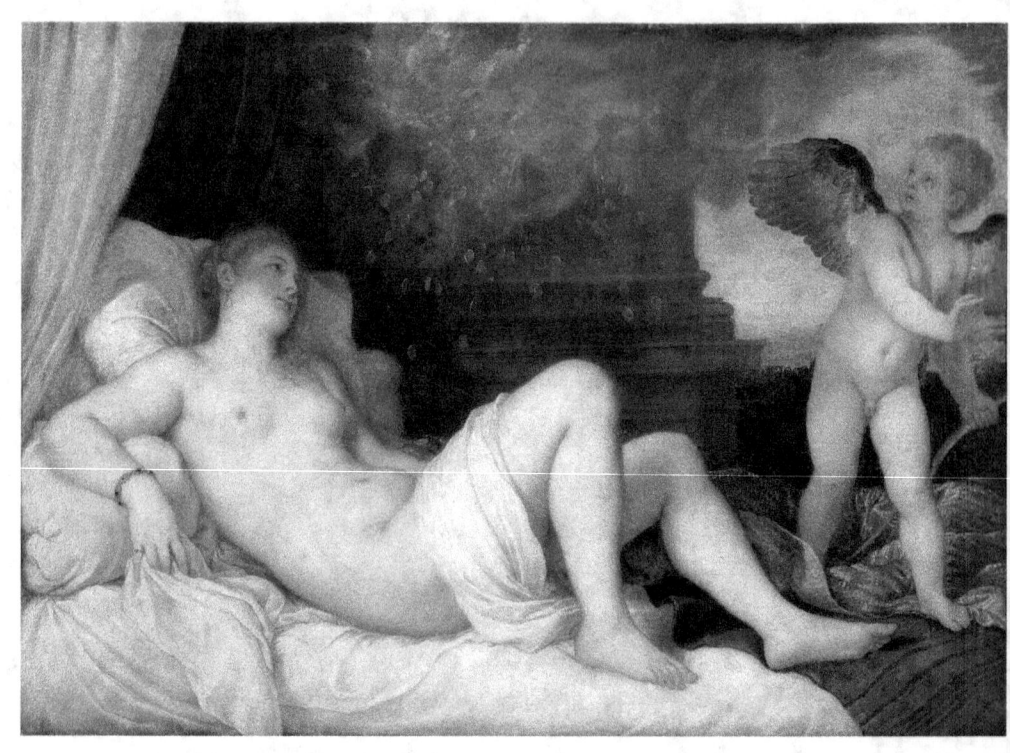

Titian, Danaë, 1544, Naples

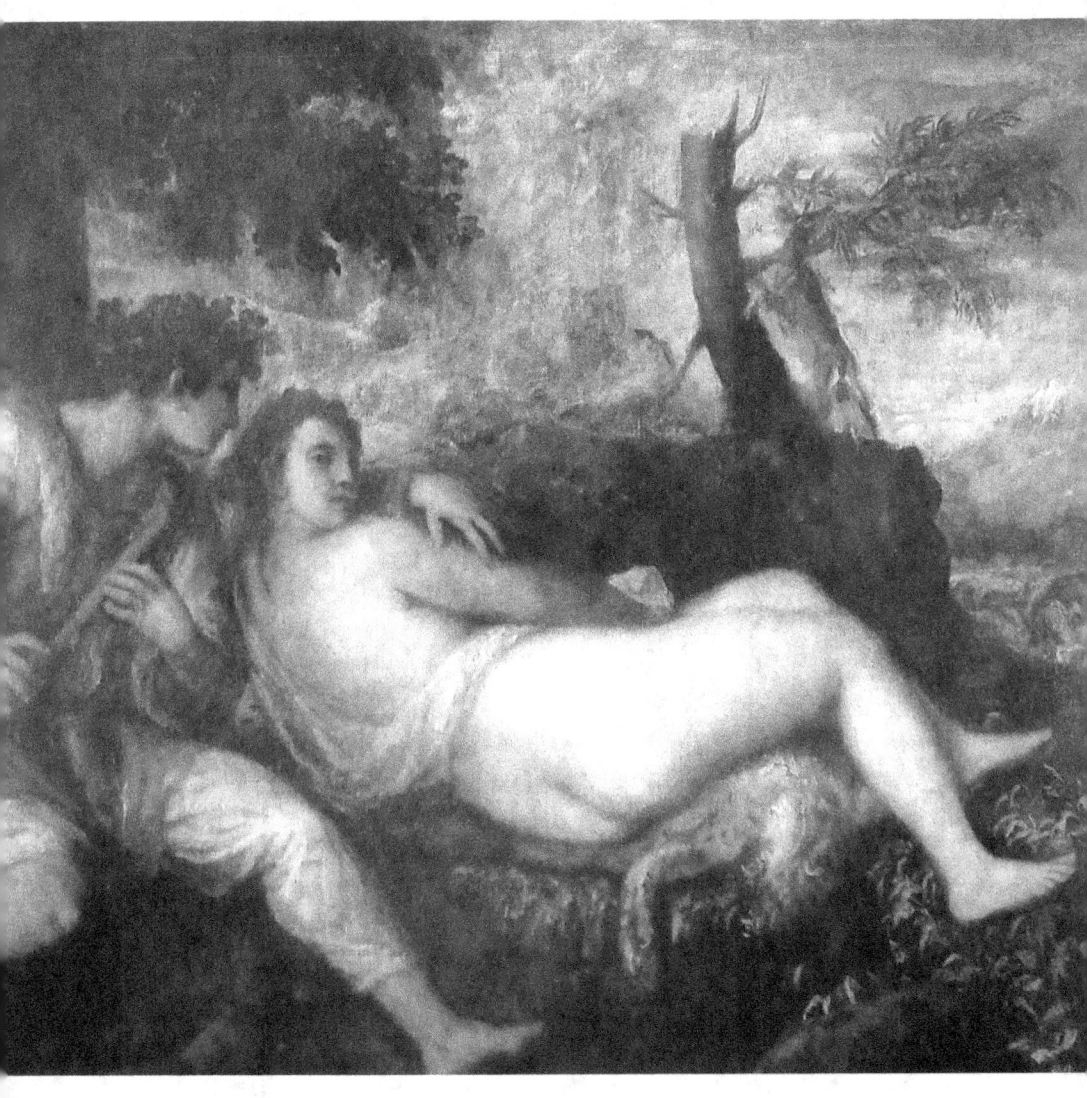

Titian, Nymph and Shepherd, 1575, Vienna

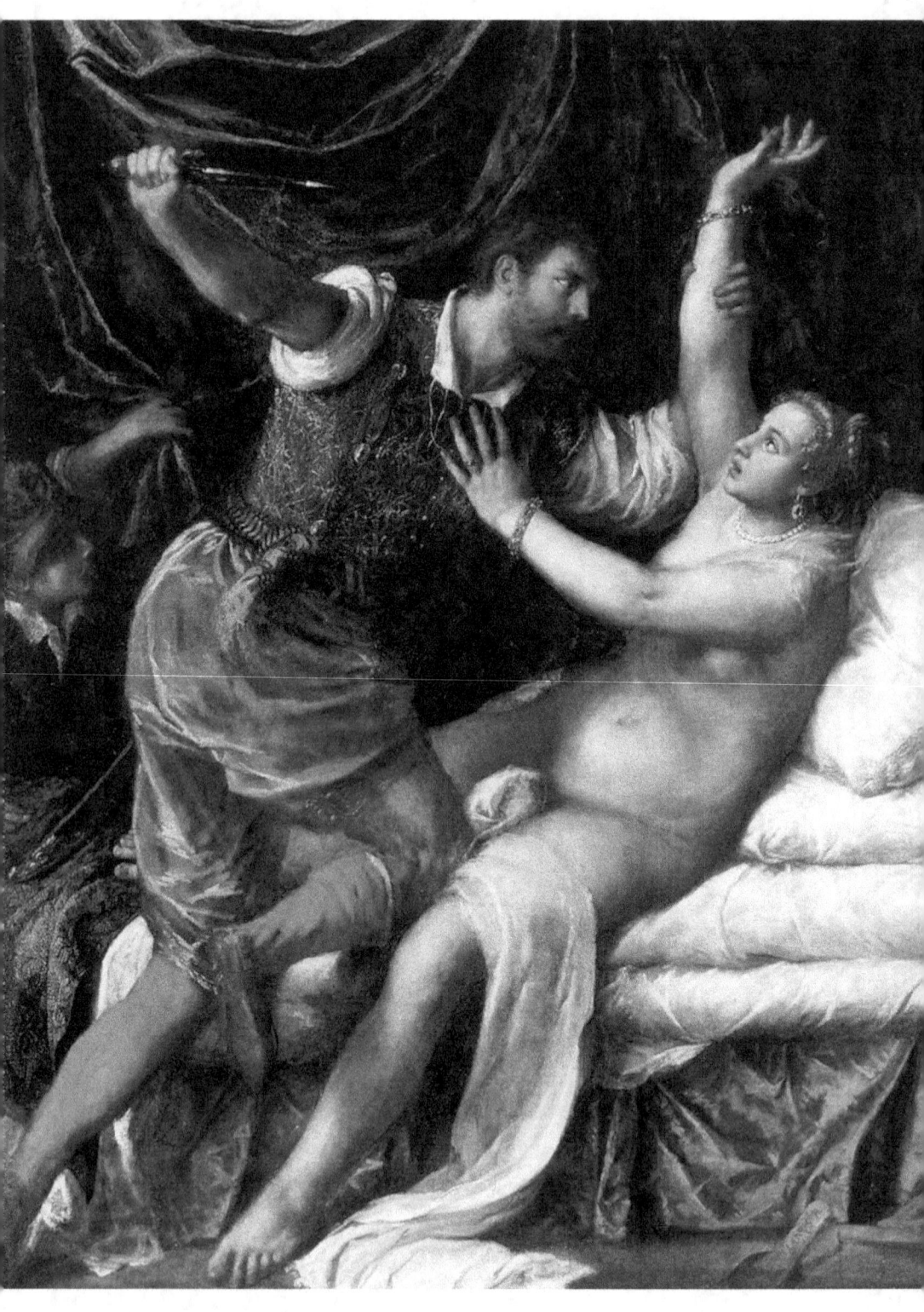

Titian, Tarquin and Lucretia, 1568-71, Cambridge

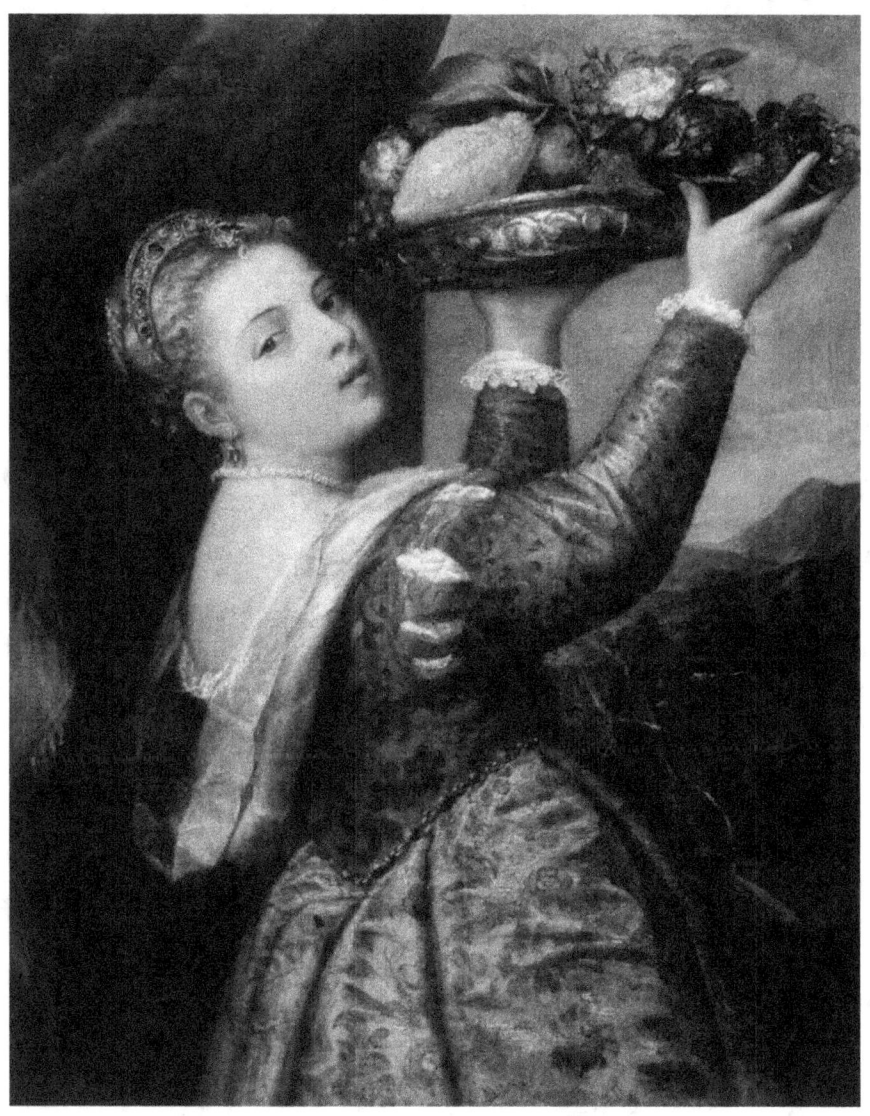

Titian, Girl With a Platter of Fruit, c. 1555, Berlin

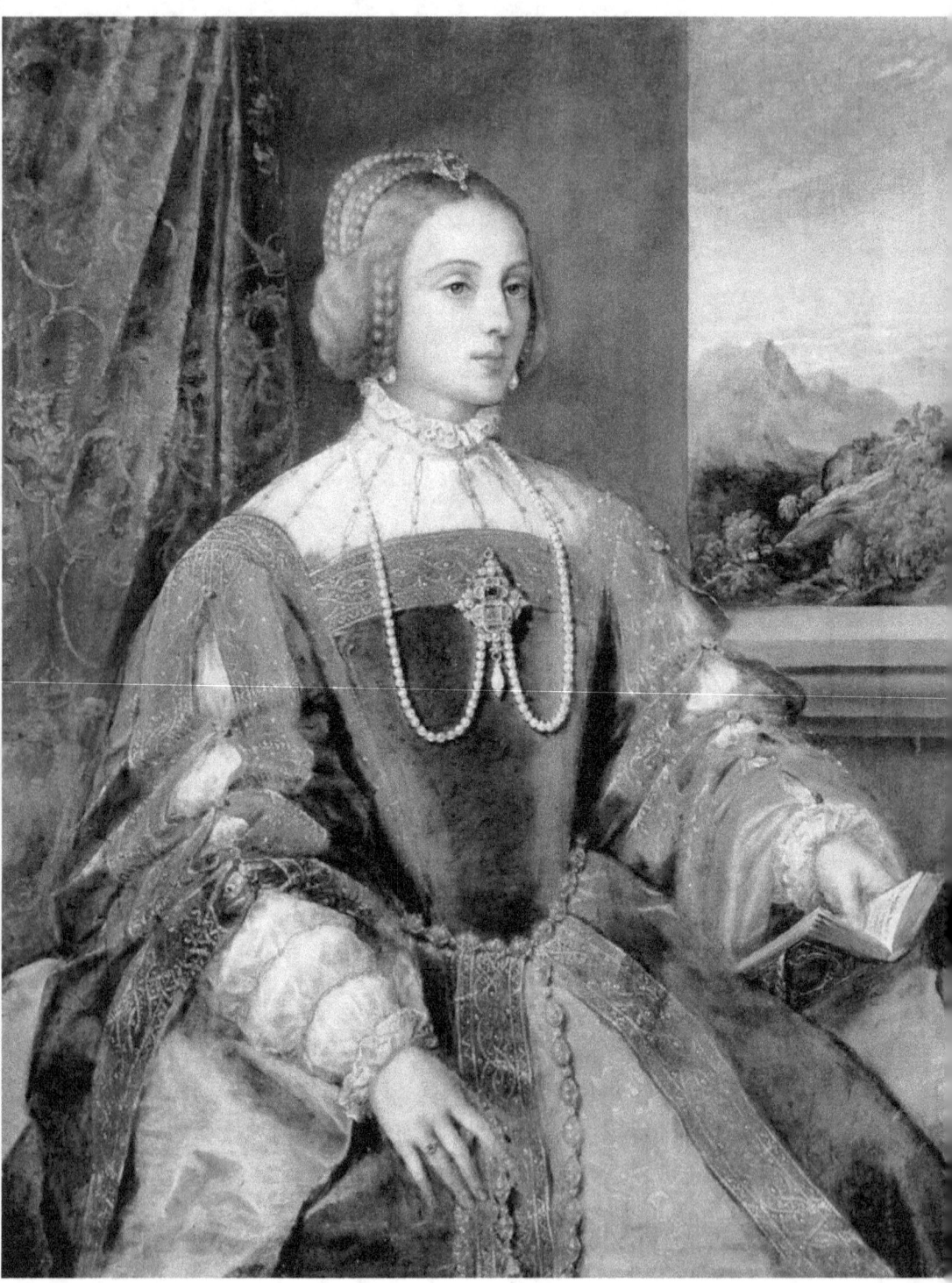

Titian, Portrait of Isabella of Portugal, 1548, Prado

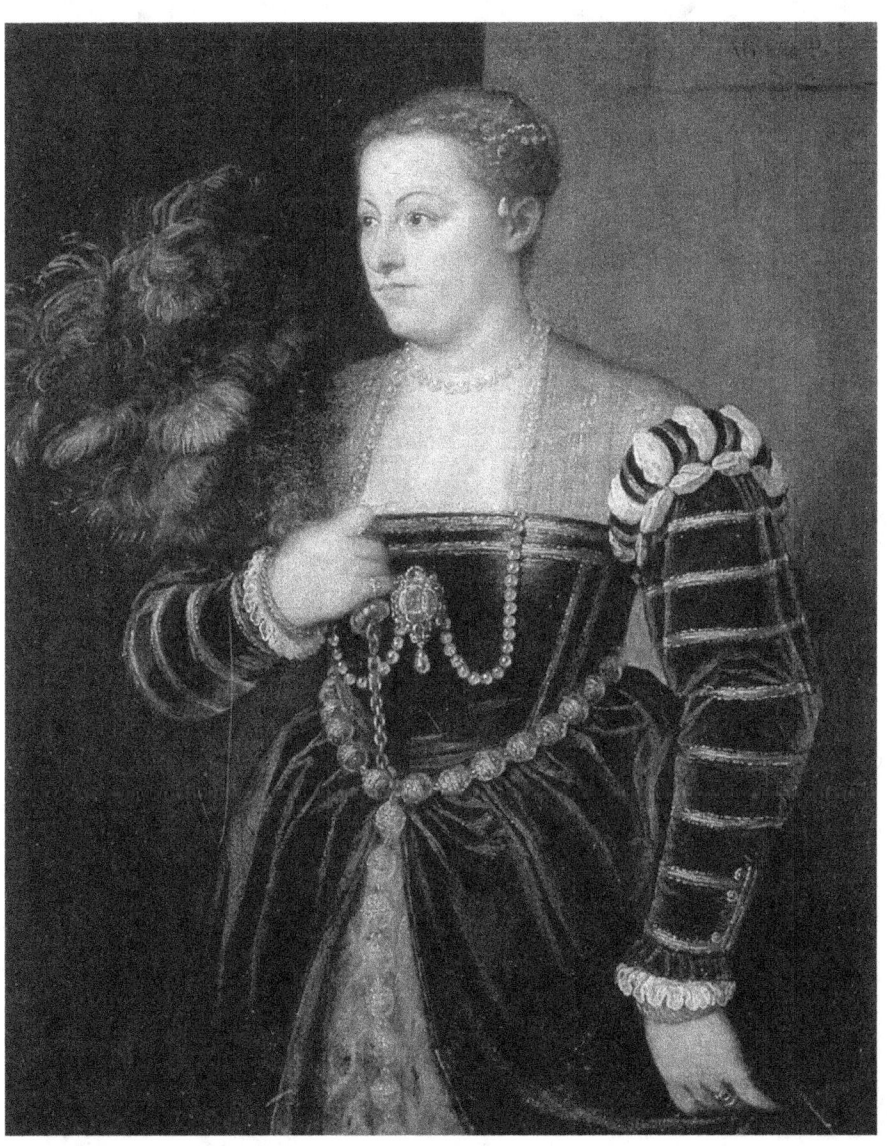

Titian, Lavinia, 1560-65

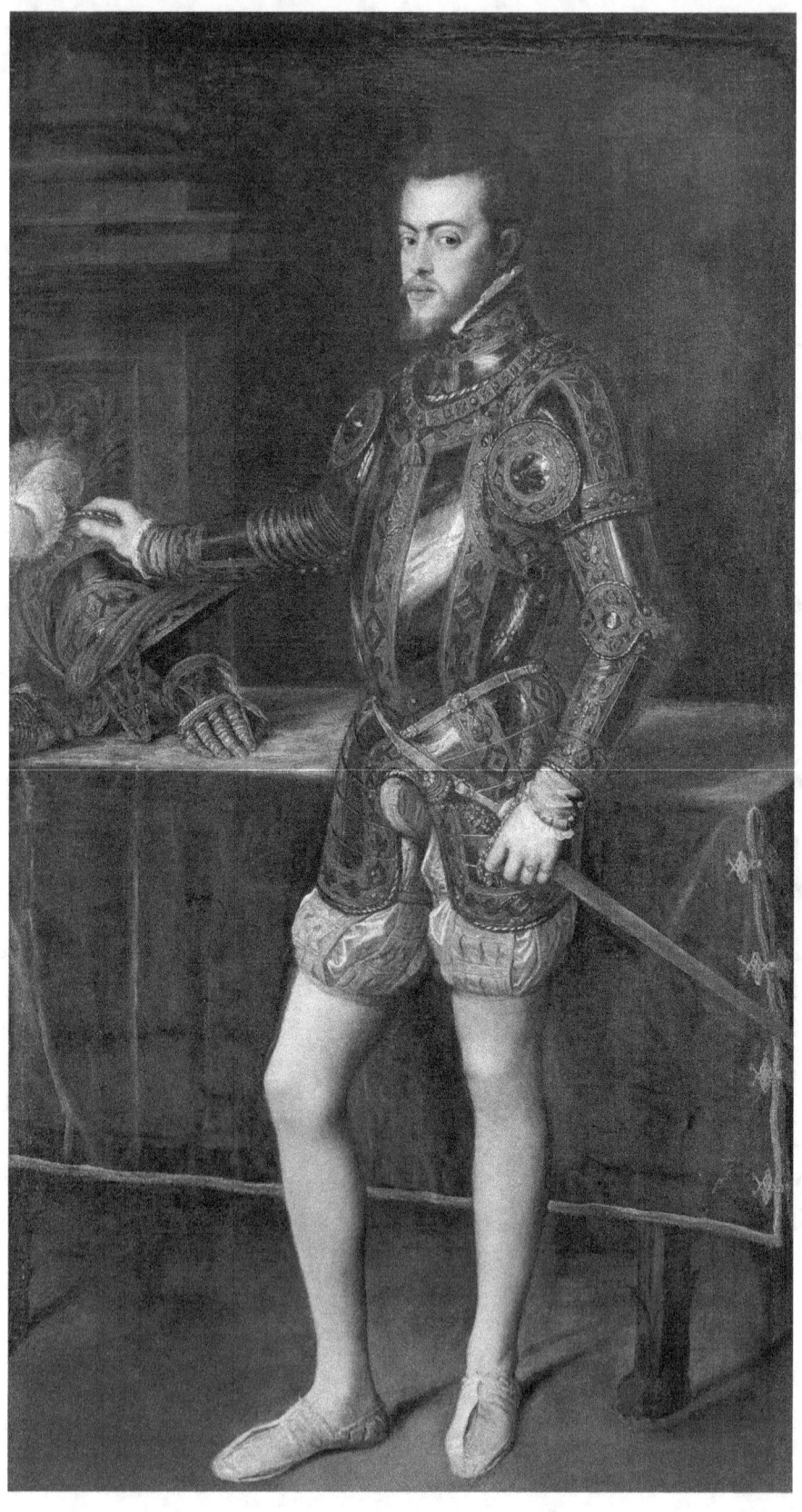

Titian, Philip II, 1551, Prado, Madrid

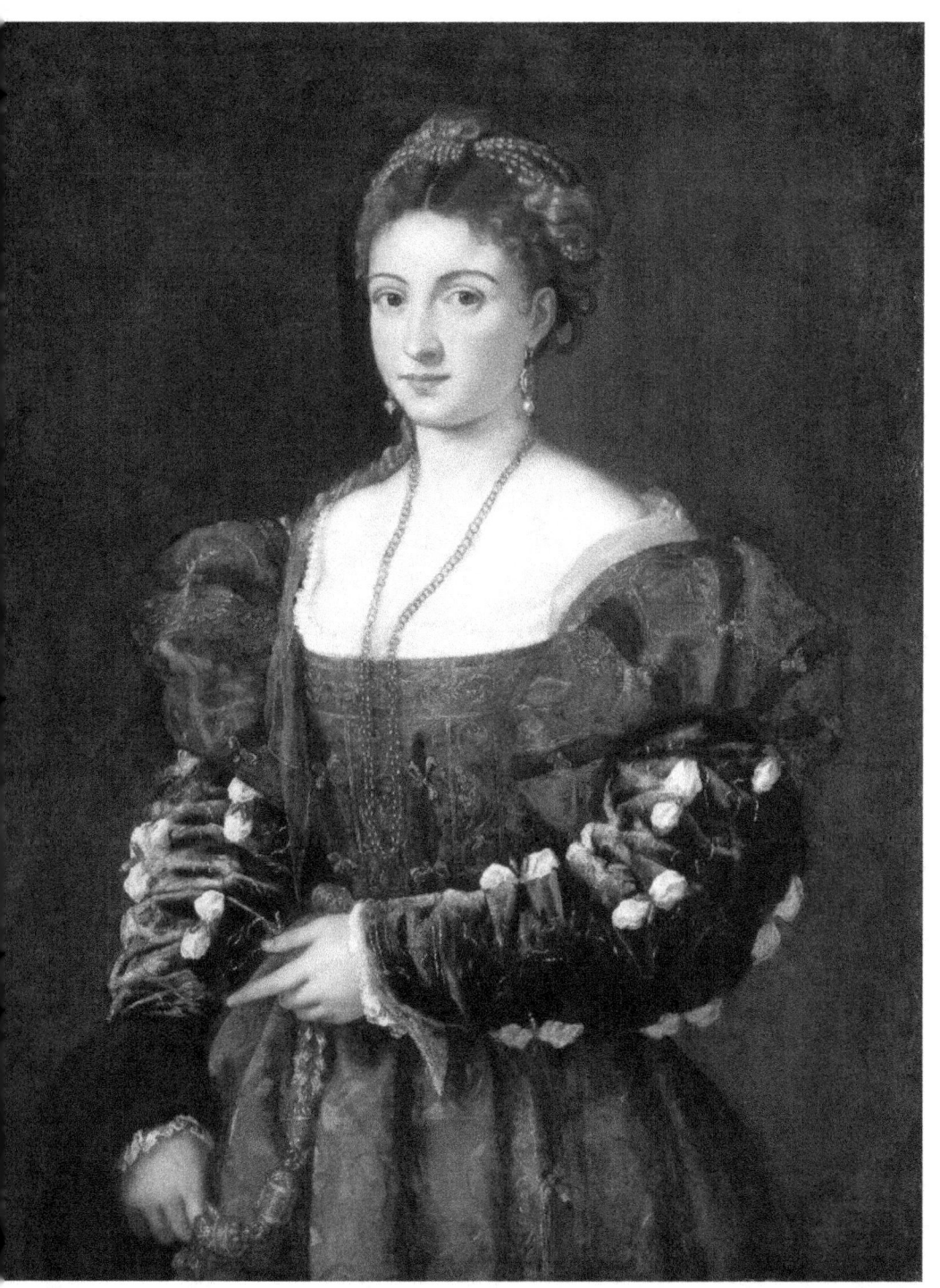

Titian, The Bella, 1536, Pitti Palace

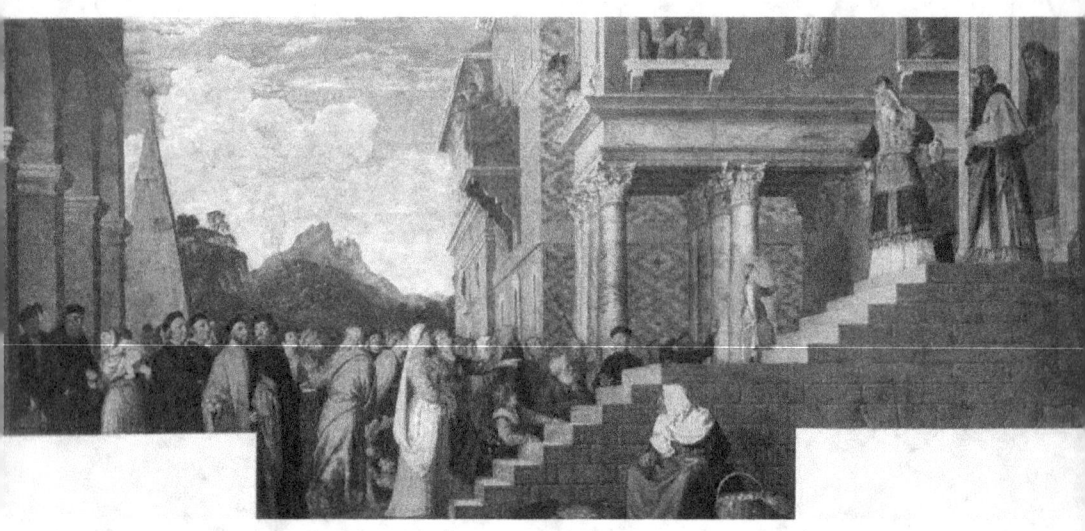

Titian, The Presentation of the Virgin, 1534-38, Venice

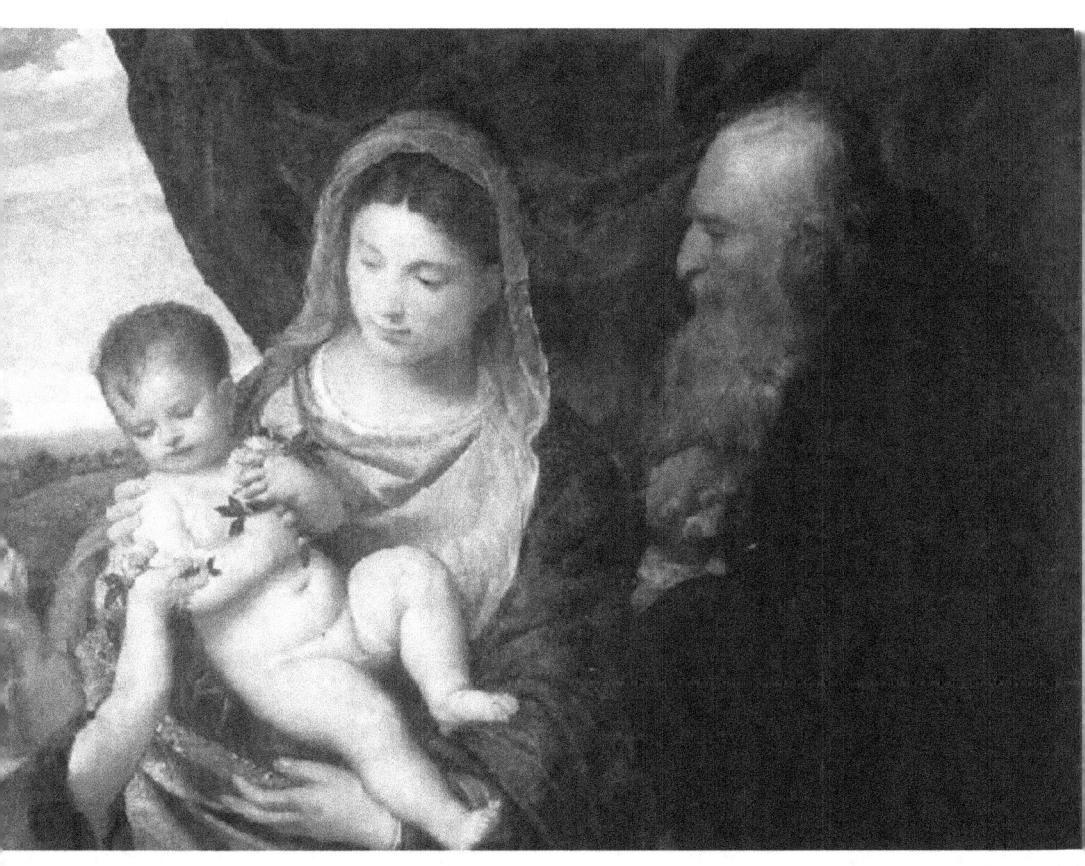

Titian, The Holy Family, 1530s, Uffizi

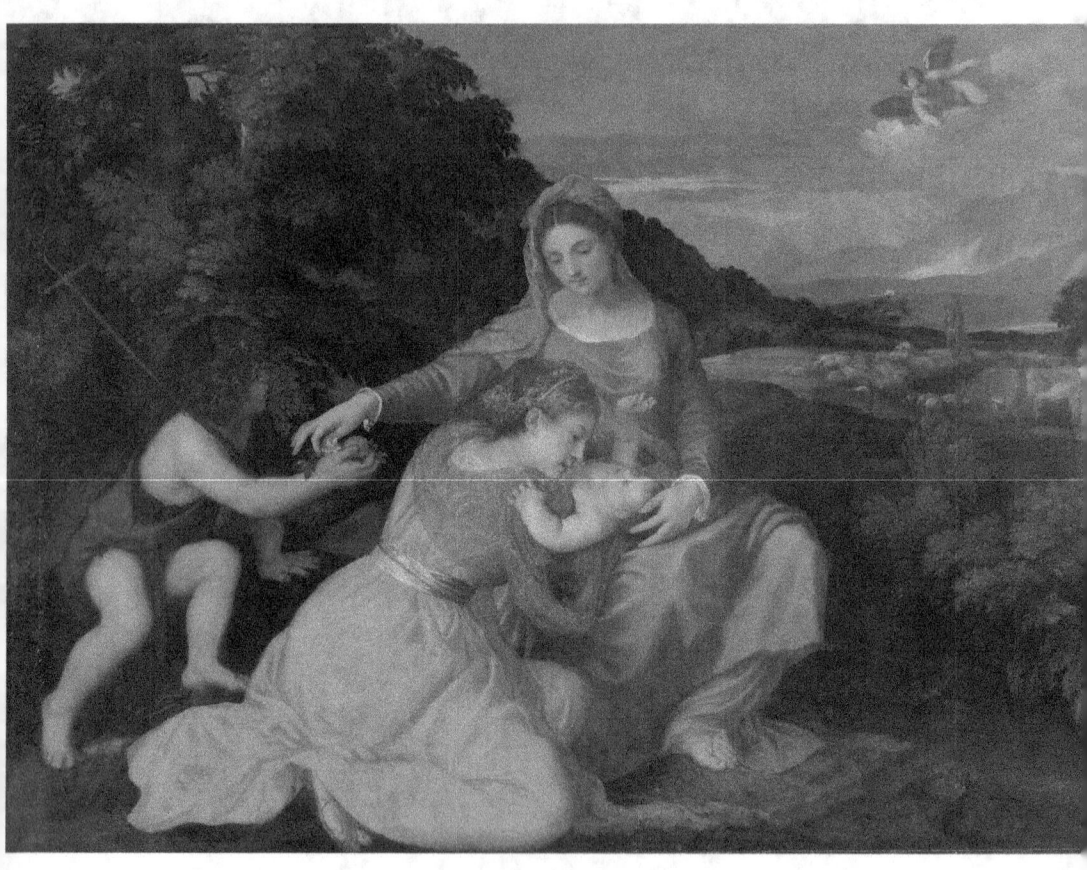

Titian, The Aldobrandini Madonna, National Gallery, London

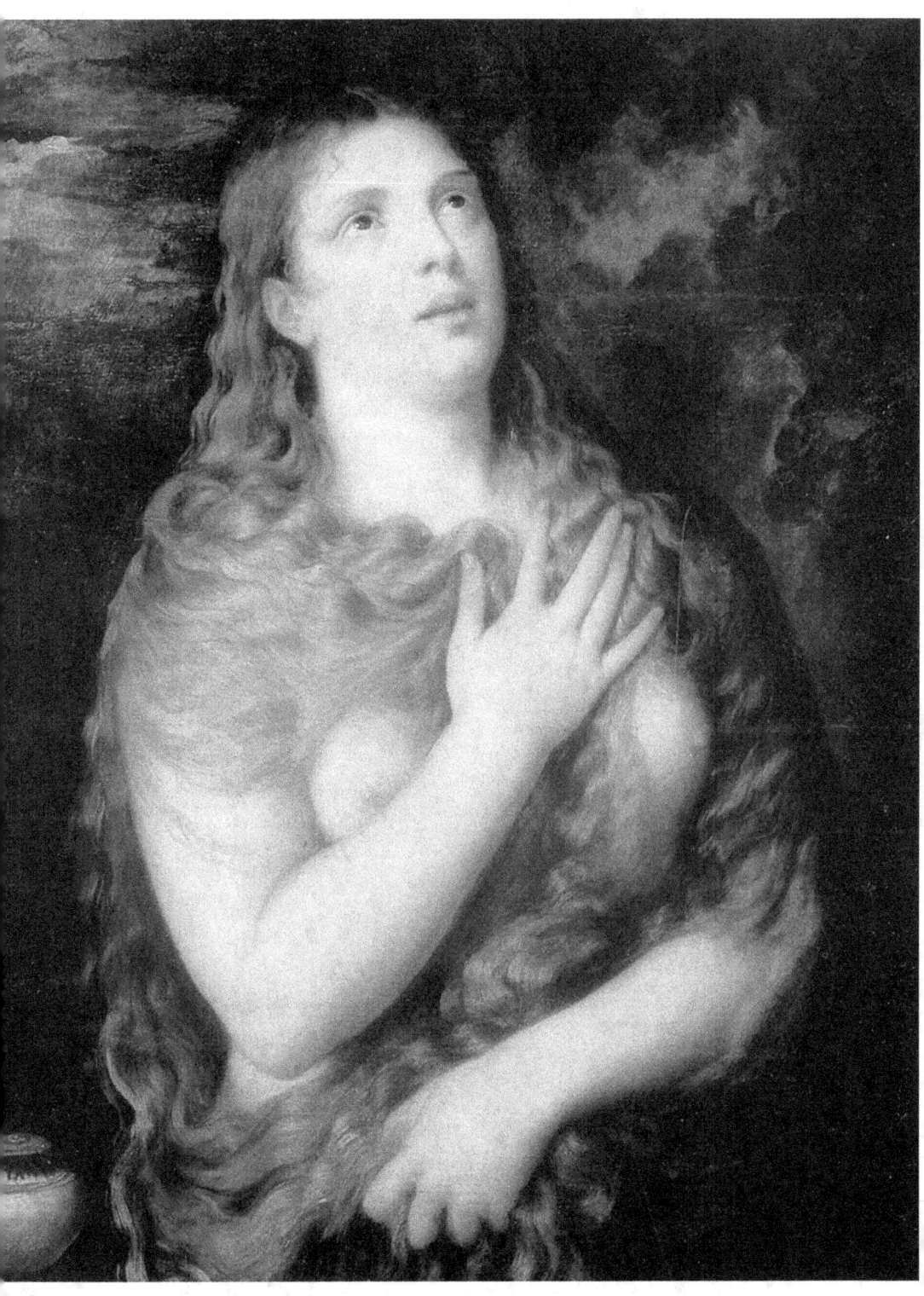

Titian, Mary Magdalene, 1533, Pittit Palace, Florence

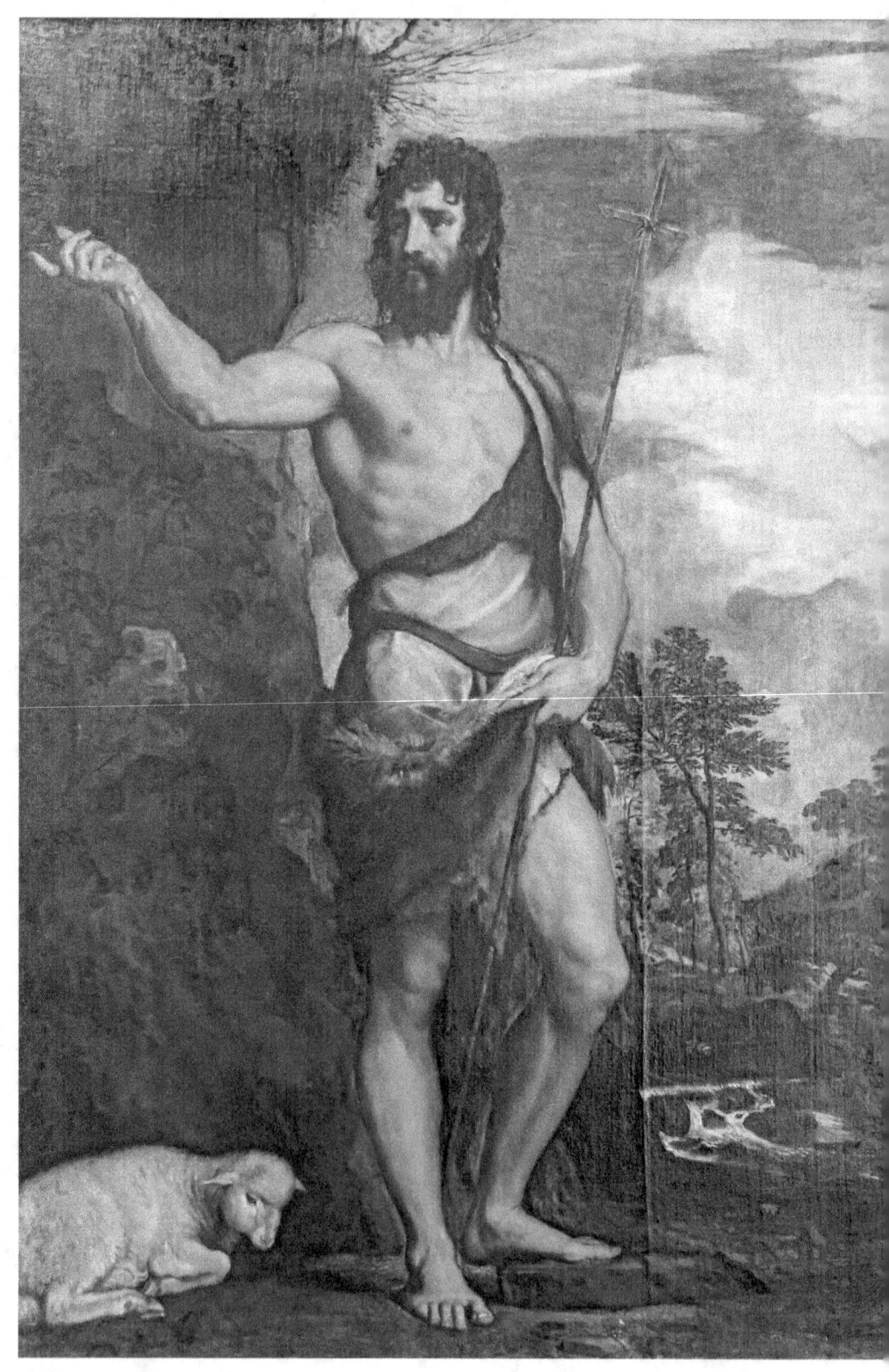

Titian, John the Baptist, 1542, Venice

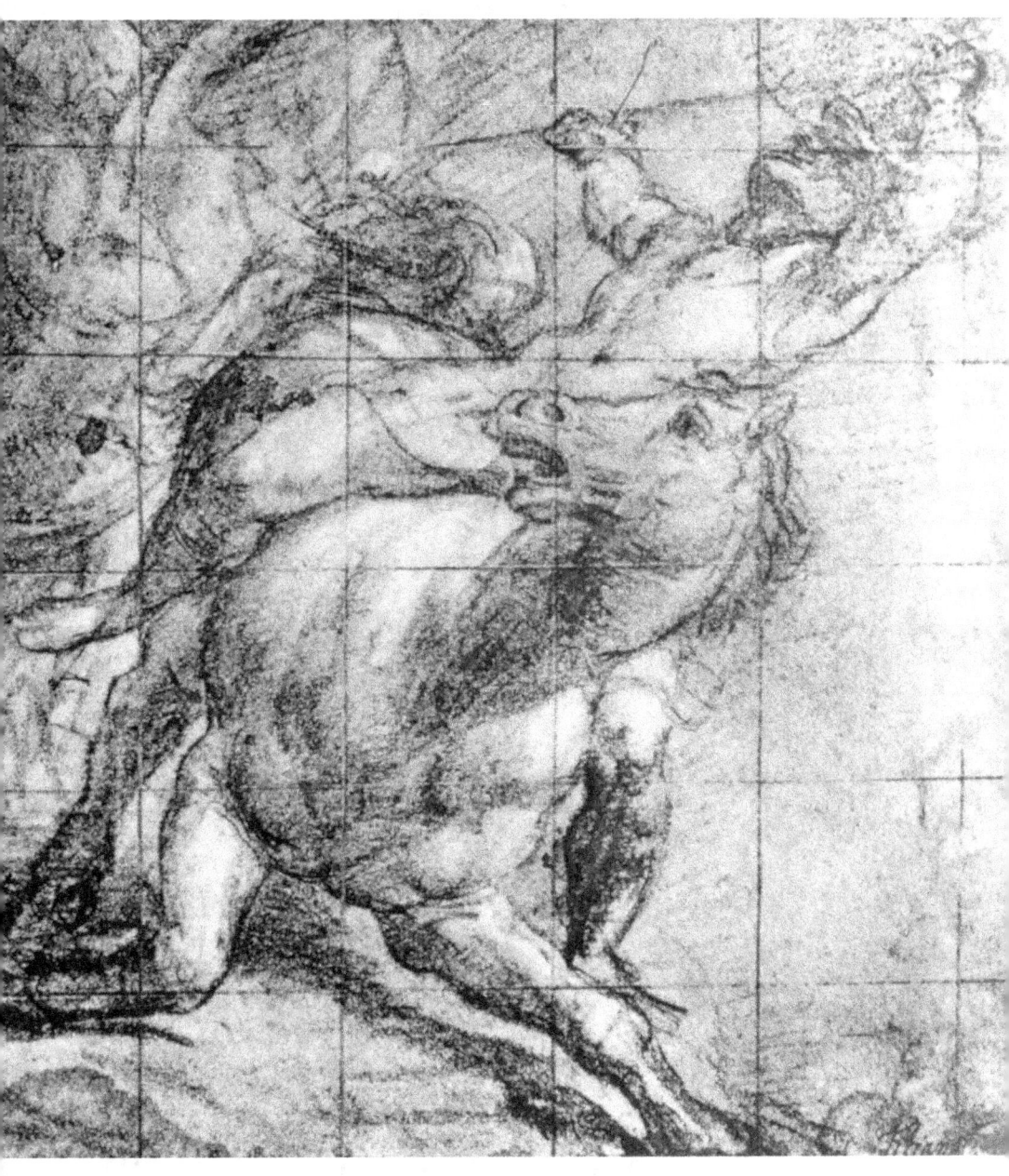

Titian, Studio per cavallo e cavaliere, 1537, Ashmolean Museum, Oxford

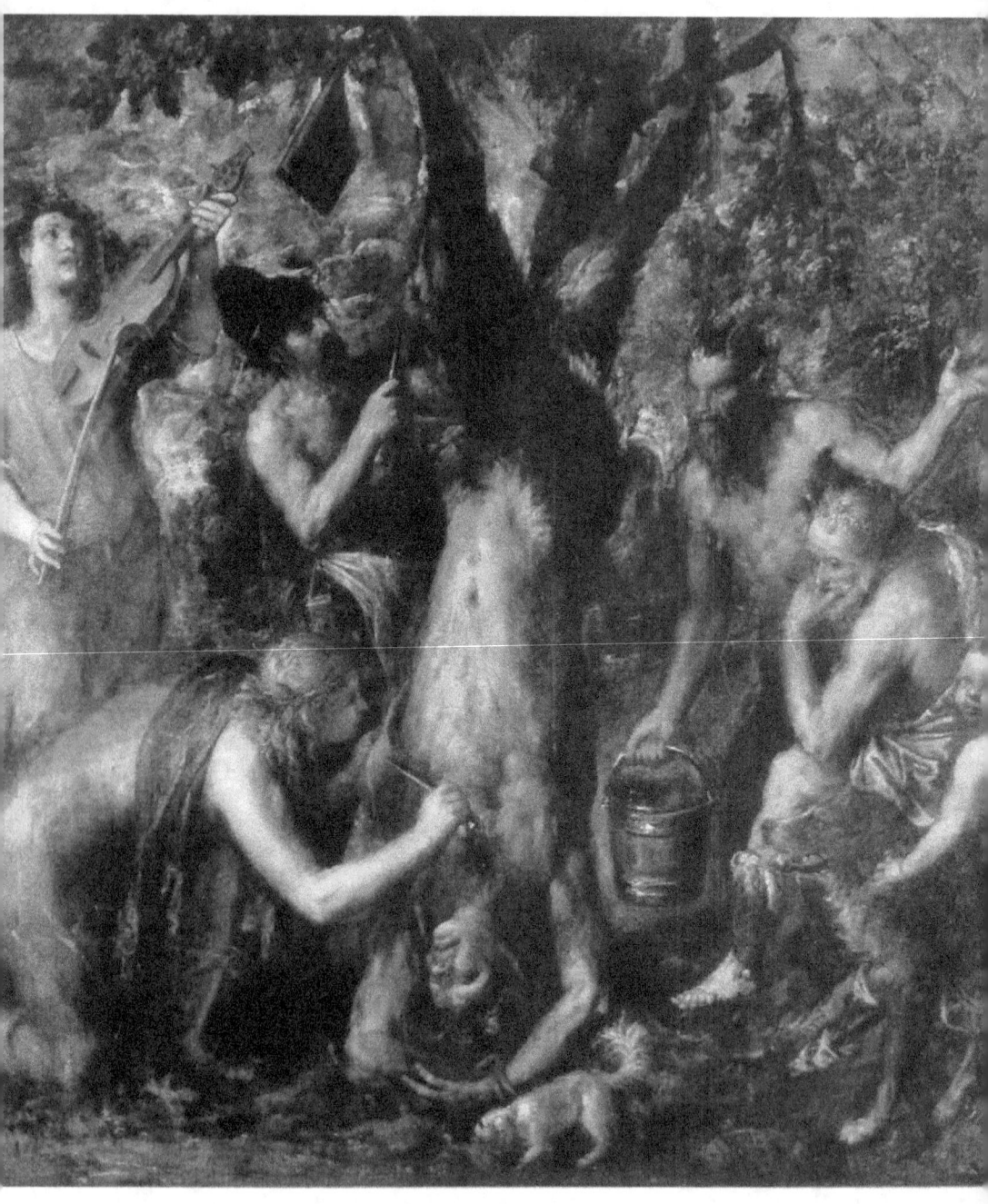

Titian, The Flaying of Marsyas, c. 1570-76, Kromeriz,

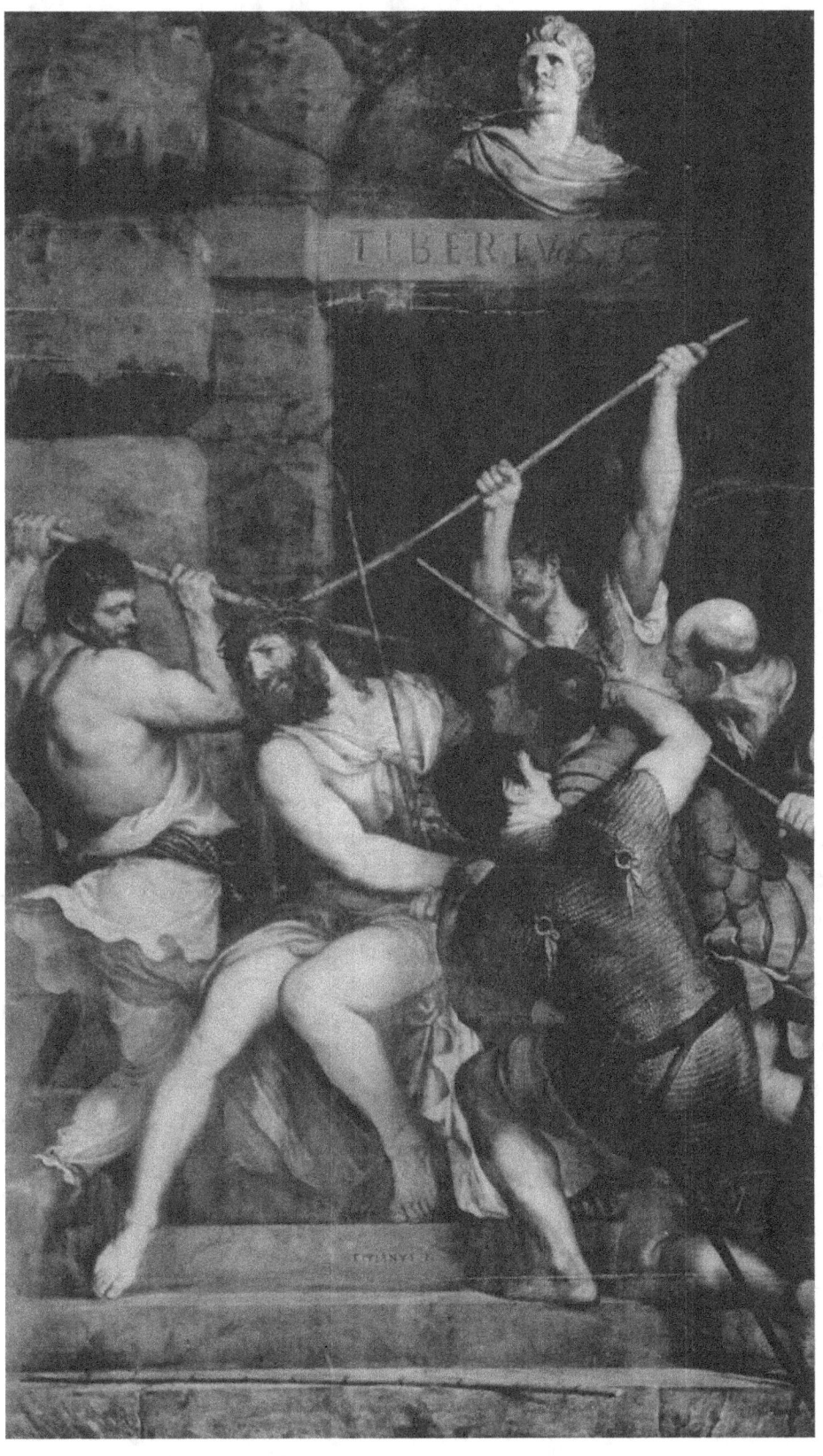

Titian, The Crowning With Thorns, 1572-76, Munich

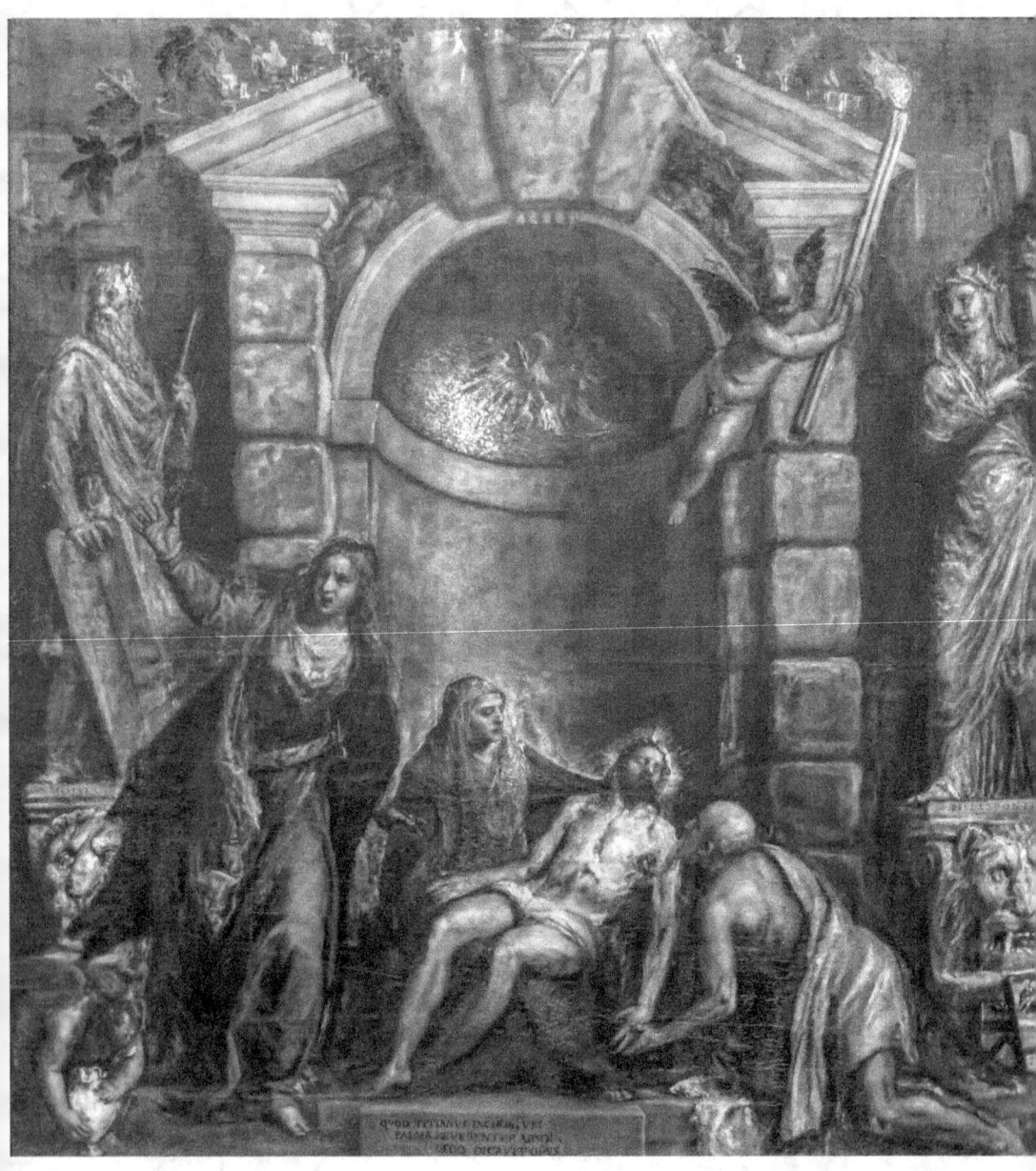

Titian, Pietà, 1576, Venice

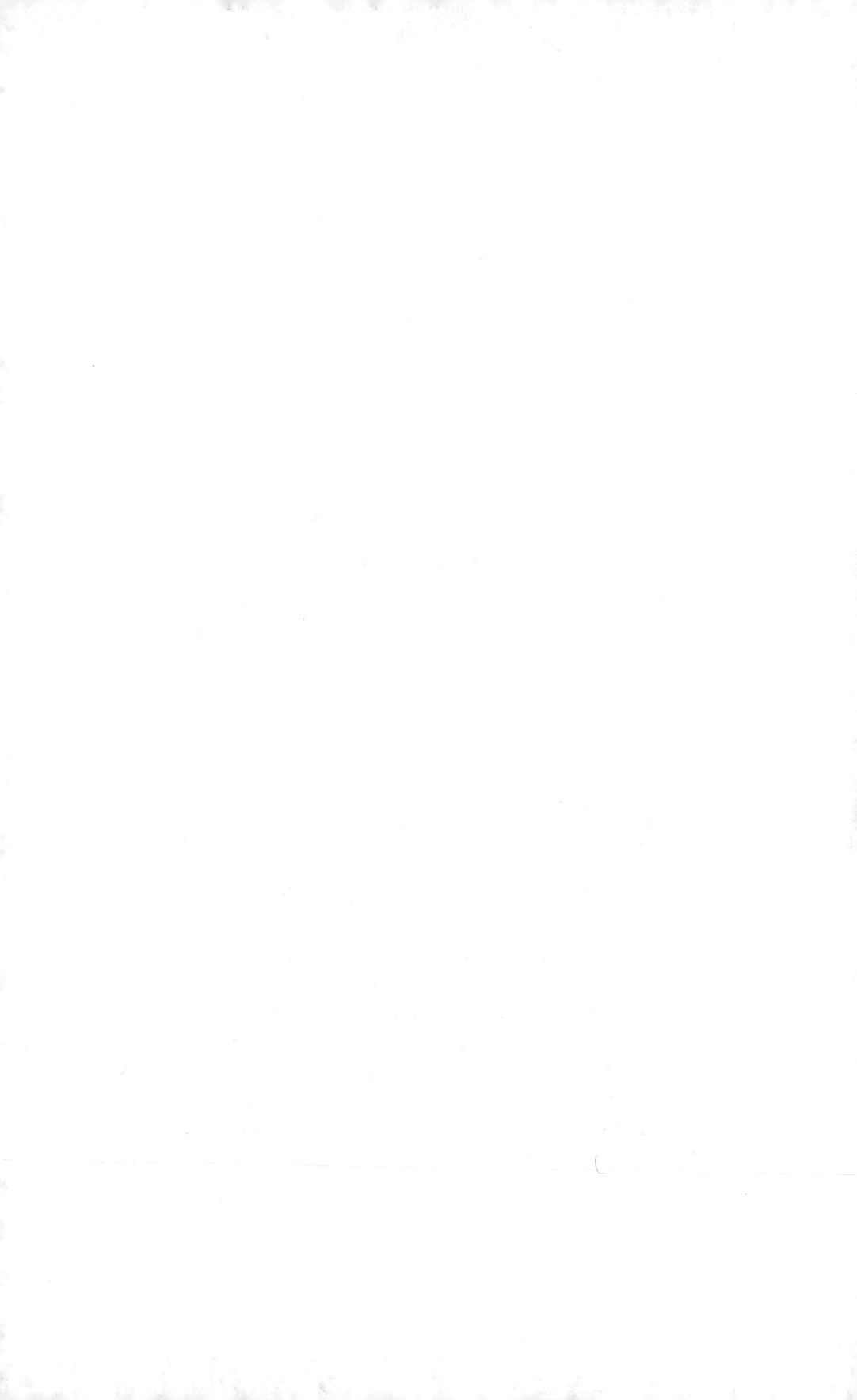

# CHAPTER III

At last, in the autumn of 1545, the master of Cadore, at the age of sixty-eight years, was to see Rome, its ruins, its statues, its antiquities, and what to the painter of the Renaissance must have meant infinitely more, the Sixtine Chapel and the Stanze of the Vatican. Upon nothing in the history of Venetian art have its lovers, and the many who, with profound interest, trace Titian's noble and perfectly consistent career from its commencement to its close, more reason to congratulate themselves than on this circumstance, that in youth and earlier manhood fortune and his own success kept him from visiting Rome. Though his was not the eclectic tendency, the easily impressionable artistic temperament of a Sebastiano Luciani – the only eclectic, perhaps, who managed all the same to prove and to maintain himself an artist of the very first rank – if Titian had in earlier life been lured to the Eternal City, and had there settled, the glamour of the grand style might have permanently and fatally disturbed his balance. Now it was too late for the splendid and gracious master, who even at sixty-eight had still before him nearly thirty fruitful years, to receive any impressions sufficiently deep to penetrate to the root of his art. There is some evidence to show that Titian, deeply impressed with the highest manifestations of the Florentine and Umbro-Florentine art transplanted to Rome, considered that his work had improved after the visit of 1545-1546. If there was such improvement – and certainly in the ultimate phases of his practice there will be evident in some ways a wider view, a higher grasp of essentials, a more responsive sensitiveness in the conceiving anew of the great sacred subjects – it must have come, not from any effort to assimilate the manner or to assume the standpoint which had obtained in Rome, but from the closer contact with a world which at its centre was beginning to take a deeper, a more solemn and gloomy view of religion and life. It should not be forgotten that this was the year when the great Council of Trent first met, and that during the next twenty years or more the whole of Italy, nay, the whole of the Catholic world, was overshadowed by its deliberations.

Titian's friend and patron of that time, Guidobaldo II., Duke of Urbino, had at first opposed Titian's visit to the Roman court, striving to reserve to himself the services of the Venetian master until such time as he should have carried out for him the commissions with which he was charged. Yielding, however, to the inevitable, and yielding, too, with a good grace, he himself escorted his favourite with his son Orazio from Venice through Ferrara to Pesaro, and having detained him a short while there, granted him an escort through the Papal States to Rome. There he was well received by the Farnese Pope, and with much cordiality by Cardinal Bembo. Rooms were accorded to him in the Belvedere section of the Vatican Palace, and there no doubt he painted the unfinished portrait-group *Paul III. with Cardinal*

*Alessandro Farnese and Ottavio Farnese*, which has been already described, and with it other pieces of the same type, and portraits of the Farnese family and circle now no longer to be traced. Vasari, well pleased no doubt to renew his acquaintance with the acknowledged head of the contemporary Venetian painters, acted as his cicerone in the visits to the antiquities of Rome, to the statues and art-treasures of the Vatican, while Titian's fellow-citizen Sebastiano del Piombo was in his company when he studied the Stanze of Raphael.

It was but three years since Michelangelo's *Last Judgment* had been uncovered in the Sixtine, and it would have been in the highest degree interesting to read his comments on this gigantic performance, towards which it was so little likely that his sympathies would spontaneously go out. Memorable is the visit paid by Buonarroti, with an unwonted regard for ceremonious courtesy, to Titian in his apartments at the Belvedere, as it is recalled by Vasari with that naïve touch, that power of suggestion, which gives such delightful colour to his unstudied prose. No *Imaginary Conversation* among those that Walter Savage Landor has devised equals in significance this meeting of the two greatest masters then living, simply as it is sketched in by the Aretine biographer. The noble Venetian representing the alternating radiance and gloom of earth, its fairest pages as they unfold themselves, the joys and sorrows, the teeming life of humanity; the mighty Florentine disdainful of the world, its colours, its pulsations, its pomps and vanities, incurious of mankind save in its great symbolical figures, soaring like the solitary eagle into an atmosphere of his own where the dejected beholder can scarce breathe, and, sick at heart, oppressed with awe, lags far behind!

Titian the gracious, the serene, who throughout a long life of splendid and by comparison effortless achievement has openly and candidly drunk deep of all the joys of life, a man even as others are! Michelangelo the austere, the scornful, to whom the pleasures of the world, the company in well-earned leisure of his fellow-man, suggest but the loss of precious hours which might be devoted to the shaping in solitude of masterpieces; in the very depths of whose nature lurk nevertheless, even in old age, the strangest ardours, the fiercest and most insatiate longings for love and friendship!

Let Vasari himself be heard as to this meeting. "Michelangelo and Vasari going one day to pay a visit to Titian in the Belvedere, saw, in a picture which he had then advanced towards completion, a nude female figure representing *Danaë* as she receives the embrace of Jove transformed into a rain of gold, and, as the fashion is in people's presence, praised it much to him. When they had taken leave, and the discussion was as to the art of Titian, Buonarroti praised it highly, saying that the colour and handling pleased him much, but that it was a subject for regret that at Venice they did not learn from the very beginning to design correctly, and that its painters did not follow a better method in their study of art." It is the battle that will so often be renewed between the artist who looks upon colour as merely a complement and adjunct to design, and the painter who regards it as not only the outer covering, but the body and soul of art. We remember how the stiff-necked Ingres, the greatest Raphaelesque of this century, hurled at Delacroix's head the famous dictum, "Le dessin c'est la probité de l'art," and how his illustrious rival, the chief of a romanticism which he would hardly acknowledge, vindicated by works rather than by words his contention that, if design was indeed art's conscience, colour was its life-blood, its very being.

The *Danaë*, seen and admired with reservations by Buonarroti in the painting-room of Titian at the Belvedere, is now, with its beauty diminished in important particulars, to be found with the rest of the Farnese pictures in the gallery of the Naples Museum. It serves to show that if the artist was far beyond the stage of imitation or even of assimilation on the larger scale, he was, at any rate, affected by the Roman atmosphere in art. For once he here comes nearer to the realisation of Tintoretto's ideal – the colour of Titian and the design of Michelangelo – than his impetuous pupil and rival ever did. While preserving in the *Danaë* his own true warmth and transparency of Venetian colour – now somewhat obscured yet not effaced – he combines unusual weightiness and majesty with voluptuousness in the nude, and successfully strives after a more studied rhythm in the harmony of the composition generally than the art of Venice usually affected.

Titian, in his return from Rome, which he was never to revisit, made a stay at Florence with an eye, as we may guess, both to business and pleasure. There, as Vasari takes care to record, our master visited the artistic sights, and *rimase stupefatto* – remained in breathless astonishment – as he had done when he made himself acquainted with the artistic glories of Rome. This is but vague, and a little too much smacks of self-flattery and adulation of the brother Tuscans. Titian was received by Duke Cosimo at Poggio a Caiano, but his offer to paint the portrait of the Medici ruler was not well received. It may be, as Vasari surmises, that this attitude was taken up by the duke in order not to do wrong to the "many noble craftsmen" then practising in his city and dominion. More probably, however, Cosimo's hatred and contempt of his father's minion Aretino, whose portrait by Titian he had condescended to retain, yet declined to acknowledge, impelled him to show something less than favour to the man who was known to be the closest friend and intimate of this self-styled "Scourge of Princes."

Crowe and Cavalcaselle have placed about the year 1555 the extravagantly lauded *St. John the Baptist in the Desert*, once in the church of S.M. Maria Maggiore at Venice, and now in the Accademia there. To the writer it appears that it would best come in at this stage – that is to say in or about 1545 – not only because the firm close handling in the nude would be less explicable ten years later on, but because the conception of the majestic St. John is for once not pictorial but purely sculptural. Leaving Rome, and immediately afterwards coming into contact for the first time with the wonders of the earlier Florentine art, Titian might well have conceived, might well have painted thus. Strange to say, the influence is not that of Michelangelo, but, unless the writer is greatly deceived, that of Donatello, whose noble ascetic type of the *Precursor* is here modernised, and in the process deprived of some of its austerity. The glorious mountain landscape, with its brawling stream, fresher and truer than any torrent of Ruysdael's, is all Titian. It makes the striking figure of St. John, for all its majesty, appear not a little artificial.

The little town of Serravalle, still so captivatingly Venetian in its general aspect, holds one of the most magnificent works of Titian's late time, a vast *Virgin and Child with St. Peter and St. Andrew*. This hangs – or did when last seen by the writer – in the choir of the Church of St. Andrew; there is evidence in Titian's correspondence that it was finished in 1547, so that it must have been undertaken soon after the return from Rome. In the distance between the two majestic figures of the saints is a prospect of landscape with a lake, upon which Titian has shown on a reduced scale Christ calling Peter and Andrew from their nets; an undisguised adaptation this, by the veteran master, of the divine Urbinate's *Miraculous Draught of Fishes*, but one which made of the borrowed motive a new thing, no excrescence but an integral part of the conception. In this great work, which to be more universally celebrated requires only to be better known to those who do not come within the narrow circle of students, there is evidence that while Titian, after his stay at the Papal court, remained firm as a rock in his style and general principles – luckily a Venetian and no pseudo-Roman, – his imagination became more intense in its glow, gloomier but grander, than it had been in middle age – his horizon altogether vaster. To a grand if sometimes too unruffled placidity succeeded a physical and psychical perturbation which belonged both to the man in advanced years and to the particular moment in the century. Even in his treatment of classic myth, of the nude in goddess and woman, there was, as we shall see presently, a greater unrest and a more poignant sensuality – there was evidence of a mind and temperament troubled anew instead of being tranquillised by the oncoming of old age.

Are we to place here, as Crowe and Cavalcaselle do, the *Venus and Cupid* of the Tribuna and the *Venus with the Organ Player* of the Prado? The technical execution of these canvases, the treatment of landscape in the former, would lead the writer to place them some years farther on still in the *oeuvre* of the master. There are, however, certain reasons for following them in this chronological arrangement. The *Venus and Cupid* which hangs in the Tribuna of the Uffizi, as the pendant to the more resplendent but more realistic *Venus of Urbino*, is a darker and less well-preserved picture than its present companion, but a grander if a more audacious presentment of the love-goddess. Yet even here she is not so much the Cytherean as an embodiment of the Venetian ideal of the later time, an exemplification of the undisguised worship of fleshly loveliness which then existed in Venice. It has been pointed out that the later Venus has the features of Titian's fair daughter Lavinia, and this is no doubt to a certain extent true. The goddesses, nymphs, and women of this time bear a sort of general family resemblance to her and to each other. This piece illustrates the preferred type of Titian's old age, as the *Vanitas, Herodias,* and *Flora* illustrate the preferred type of his youth; as the paintings which we have learnt to associate with the Duchess of Urbino illustrate that of his middle time. The dignity and rhythmic outline of Eros in the *Danaë* of Naples have been given up in favour of a more naturalistic conception of the insinuating urchin, who is in this *Venus and Cupid* the successor of those much earlier *amorini* in the *Worship of Venus* at Madrid. The landscape in its sweeping breadth is very characteristic of the late time, and would give good reason for placing the picture later than it here appears. The difficulty is this. The *Venus with the Organ Player*[*39] of Madrid, which in many essential points is an inferior repetition of the later Venus of the Tribuna, contains the portrait of Ottavio Farnese, much as we see him in the unfinished group painted, as has been recorded, at Rome in 1546. This being the case, it is not easy to place the *Venus and Cupid*, or its subsequent adaptation, much later than just before the journey to Augsburg. The *Venus with the Organ Player* has been overrated; there are things in this canvas which we cannot without offence to Titian ascribe to his own brush. Among these are the tiresome, formal landscape, the wooden little dog petted by Venus, and perhaps some other passages. The goddess herself and the amorous Ottavio, though this last is not a very striking or successful portrait, may perhaps be left to the master. He vindicates himself more completely than in any other passage of the work when he depicts the youthful, supple form of the Venetian courtesan, as in a merely passive pose she personates the goddess whose insignificant votary she really is. It cannot be denied that he touches here the lowest level reached by him in such delineations. What offends in this *Venus with the Organ Player*, or rather *Ottavio Farnese with his Beloved*, is that its informing sentiment is not love, or indeed any community of sentiment, but an ostentatious pride in the possession of covetable beauty subdued like that of Danaë herself by gold.

If we are to assume with Crowe and Cavalcaselle that the single figure *Ecce Homo* of the Prado Gallery was the piece taken by the master to Charles V. when, at the bidding of the Emperor, he journeyed to Augsburg, we can only conclude that his design was carried out by pupils or assistants. The execution is not such as we can ascribe to the brush which is so shortly to realise for the monarch a group of masterpieces.

It was in January 1548 that Titian set forth to obey the command of the Emperor, "per far qualche opera," as Count Girolamo della Torre has it in a letter of recommendation given to Titian for the Cardinal of Trent at Augsburg. It is significant to find the writer mentioning the painter, not by any of the styles and titles which he had a right to bear, especially at the court of Charles V., but extolling him as "Messer Titiano Pittore et il primo huomo della Christianita."[*40]

It might be imagined that it would be a terrible wrench for Titian, at the age of seventy, to transplant himself suddenly, and for the first time, into a foreign land. But then he was not as other men of seventy are. The final years of his unexampled career will conclusively show that he preserved his mental and physical vigour to the end. Further, the imperial court with its Spanish etiquette, its Spanish language and manners, was much the same at Augsburg as he had known it on previous occasions at Bologna. Moreover, Augsburg and Nuremberg[*41] had, during the last fifty years, been in close touch with Venice in all matters appertaining to art and commerce. Especially the great banking house of the Fuggers had the most intimate relations with the queen-city of the Adriatic. Yet art of the two great German cities would doubtless appeal less to the Venetian who had arrived at the zenith of his development than it would and did to the Bellinis and their school at the beginning of the century. The gulf had become a far wider one, and the points of contact were fewer.

The trusted Orazio had been left behind, notwithstanding the success which he had achieved during the Roman tour, and it may be assumed that he presided over the studio and workshop at Biri Grande during his father's absence. Titian was accompanied to Augsburg by his second cousin, Cesare Vecellio,[*42] who no doubt had a minor share in very many of the canvases belonging to the period of residence at Augsburg. Our master's first and most grateful task must have been the painting of the great equestrian portrait of the Emperor at the Battle of Mühlberg, which now hangs in the Long Gallery of the Prado at Madrid. It suffered much injury in the fire of the Pardo Palace, which annihilated so many masterpieces, but is yet very far from being the "wreck" which, with an exaggeration not easily pardonable under the circumstances, Crowe and Cavalcaselle have described it. In the presence of one of the world's masterpieces criticism may for once remain silent, willingly renouncing all its rights. No purpose would be served here by recording how much paint has been abraded in one corner, how much added in another. A deep sense of thankfulness should possess us that the highest manifestation of Titian's genius has been preserved, even though it be shorn of some of its original beauty. Splendidly armed in steel from head to foot, and holding firmly grasped in his hand the spear, emblem of command in this instance rather than of combat, Cæsar advances with a mien impassive yet of irresistible domination. He bestrides with ease his splendid dark-brown charger, caparisoned in crimson, and heavily weighted like himself with the full panoply of battle, a perfect harmony being here subtly suggested between man and beast. The rich landscape, with a gleam of the Elbe in the distance, is still in the half gloom of earliest day; but on the horizon, and in the clouds overhead, glows the red ominous light of sunrise, colouring the veils of the morning mist. The Emperor is alone – alone as he must be in life and in death – a man, yet lifted so high above other men that the world stretches far below at his feet, while above him this ruler knows no power but that of God. It is not even the sneer of cold command, but a majesty far higher and more absolutely convinced of its divine origin, that awes the beholder as he gazes. In comparison with the supreme dignity of this ugly, pallid Hapsburger, upon whom disease and death have already laid a shadowy finger, how artificial appear the divine assumptions of an Alexander, how theatrical the Olympian airs of an Augustus, how merely vulgar and ill-worn the imperial poses of a Napoleon.

No veracious biographer of Titian could pretend that he is always thus imaginative, that coming in contact with a commanding human individuality he always thus unfolds the outer wrappings to reveal the soul within. Indeed, especially in the middle time just past, he not infrequently contents himself with the splendid outsides of splendid things. To interpret this masterpiece as the writer has ventured to do, it is not necessary to assume that Titian reasoned out the poetic vision, which was at the same time an absolutely veracious presentment, argument-atively with himself, as the painter of such a portrait in words might have done. Pictorial genius of the creative order does not proceed by such methods, but sees its subject as a whole, leaving to others the task of probing and unravelling. It should be borne in mind, too, that this is the first in order, as it is infinitely the greatest and the most significant among the vast equestrian portraits of monarchs by court painters. Velazquez on the one hand, and Van Dyck on the other, have worked wonders in the same field. Yet their finest productions, even the *Philip IV.*, the *Conde Duque Olivarez*, the *Don Balthasar Carlos* of the Spaniard, even the two equestrian portraits of Charles I., the *Francisco de Moncada*, the *Prince Thomas of Savoy* of the Fleming, are in comparison but magnificent show pieces aiming above all at decorative pomp and an imposing general effect.

We come to earth and every-day weariness again with the full-length of Charles V., which is now in the Alte Pinakothek of Munich. Here the monarch, dressed in black and seated in a well-worn crimson velvet chair, shows without disguise how profoundly he is ravaged by ill-health and *ennui*. Fine as the portrait still appears notwithstanding its bad condition, one feels somehow that Titian is not in this instance, as he is in most others, perfect master of his material, of the main elements of his picture. The problem of relieving the legs cased in black against a relatively light background, and yet allowing to them their full plastic form, is not perfectly solved. Neither is it, by the way, as a rule in the canvases of those admirable painters of men, the quasi-Venetians, Moretto of Brescia and Moroni of Bergamo. The Northerners – among them Holbein and Lucidel – came nearer to perfect success in this particular matter. The splendidly brushed-in prospect of cloudy sky and far-stretching country recalls, as Morelli has observed, the landscapes of Rubens, and suggests that he underwent the influence of the Cadorine in this respect as in many others, especially after his journey as ambassador to Madrid.

Another portrait, dating from the first visit to Augsburg, is the half-length of the Elector John Frederick of Saxony, now in the Imperial Gallery at Vienna. He sits obese and stolid, yet not without the dignity that belongs to absolute simplicity, showing on his left cheek the wound received at the battle of Mühlberg. The picture has, as a portrait by Titian, no very commanding merit, no seduction of technique, and it is easy to imagine that Cesare Vecellio may have had a share in it. Singular is the absence of all pose, of all attempt to harmonise the main lines of the design or give pictorial elegance to the naïve directness of the presentment. This mode of conception may well have been dictated to the courtly Venetian by sturdy John Frederick himself.

The master painted for Mary, Queen Dowager of Hungary, four canvases specially mentioned by Vasari, *Prometheus Bound to the Rock, Ixion, Tantalus,* and *Sisyphus,* which were taken to Spain at the moment of the definitive migration of the court in 1556. Crowe and Cavalcaselle state that the whole four perished in the all-devouring conflagration of the Pardo Palace, and put down the *Prometheus* a n d *Sisyphus* of the Prado Gallery as copies by Sanchez Coello. It is difficult to form a definite judgment on canvases so badly hung, so darkened and injured. They certainly look much more like Venetian originals than Spanish copies. These mythological subjects may very properly be classed with the all too energetic ceiling-pictures now in the Sacristy of the Salute. Here again the master, in the effort to be grandiose in a style not properly his, overreaches himself and becomes artificial. He must have left Augsburg this time in the autumn of 1548, since in the month of October of that year we find him at Innsbruck making a family picture of the children of King Ferdinand, the Emperor's brother. That monarch himself, his two sons and five daughters, he had already portrayed.

Much feasting, much rejoicing, in the brilliant and jovial circle presided over by Aretino and the brother Triumvirs, followed upon our master's return to Venice. Aretino, who after all was not so much the scourge as the screw of princes, would be sure to think the more highly of the friend whom he really cherished in all sincerity, when he returned from close and confidential intercourse with the mightiest ruler of the age, the source not only of honour but of advantages which the Aretine, like Falstaff, held more covetable because more substantial. To the year 1549 belongs the gigantic woodcut *The Destruction of Pharaoh's Host*, designed, according to the inscription on the print, by "the great and immortal Titian," and engraved by Domenico delle Greche, who, notwithstanding his name, calls himself "depentore Venetiano." He is not, as need hardly be pointed out, to be confounded with the famous Veneto-Spanish painter, Domenico Theotocopuli, Il Greco, whose date of birth is just about this time (1548).

Titian, specially summoned by the Emperor, travelled back to Augsburg in November 1550. Charles had returned thither with Prince Philip, the heir-presumptive of the Spanish throne, and it can hardly be open to question that one of the main objects for which the court painter was made to undertake once more the arduous journey across the Alps was to depict the son upon whom all the monarch's hopes and plans were centred. Charles, whose health had still further declined, was now, under an accumulation of political misfortune, gloomier than ever before, more completely detached from the things of the world. Barely over fifty at this moment, he seemed already, and, in truth, was an old man, while the master of Cadore at seventy-three shone in the splendid autumn of his genius, which even then had not reached its final period of expansion. Titian enjoyed the confidence of his imperial master during this second visit in a degree which excited surprise at the time; the intercourse with Charles at this tragic moment of his career, when, sick and disappointed, he aspired only to the consolations of faith, seeing his sovereign remedy in the soothing balm of utter peace, may have worked to deepen the gloom which was overspreading the painter's art if not his soul. It is not to be believed, all the same, that this atmosphere of unrest and misgiving, of faith coloured by an element of terror, in itself operated so strongly as unaided to give a final form to Titian's sacred works. There was in this respect kinship of spirit between the mighty ruler and his servant; Titian's art had already become sadder and more solemn, had already shown a more sombre passion. The tragic gloom is now to become more and more intense, until we come to the climax in the astonishing *Pietà* left unfinished when the end comes a quarter of a century later still.

And with this change in the whole atmosphere of the sacred art comes another in the inverse sense, which, being an essential trait, must be described, though to do so is not quite easy. Titian becomes more and more merely sensuous in his conception of the beauty of women. He betrays in his loss of serenity that he is less than heretofore impervious to the stings of an invading sensuality, which serves to make of his mythological and erotic scenes belonging to this late time a tribute to the glories of the flesh unennobled by the gilding touch of the purer flame. And the painter who, when Charles V. retired into his solitude, had suffered the feeble flame of his life to die slowly out, was to go on working for King Philip, as fierce in the intensity of his physical passion as in the fervour of his faith, would receive encourage-ment to develop to the full these seemingly conflicting tendencies of sacred and amorous passion.

The Spanish prince whom it was the master's most important task on this occasion to portray was then but twenty-four years of age, and youth served not indeed to hide, but in a slight measure to attenuate, some of his most characteristic physical defects. His unattractive person even then, however, showed some of the most repellent peculiarities of his father and his race. He had the supreme distinction of Charles but not his majesty, more than his haughty reserve, even less than his power of enlisting sympathy. In this most difficult of tasks – the portrayal that should be at one and the same time true in its essence, distinguished, and as sympathetic as might be under the circumstances, of so unlovable a personage – Titian won a new victory. His *Prince Philip of Austria in Armour* at the Prado is one of his most complete and satisfying achievements, from every point of view. A veritable triumph of art, but as usual a triumph to which the master himself disdains to call attention, is the rendering of the damascened armour, the puffed hose, and the white silk stockings and shoes.

The two most important variations executed by the master, or under his immediate direction, are the full-lengths of the Pitti Palace and the Naples Museum, in both of which sumptuous court-dress replaces the gala military costume. They are practically identical, both in the design and the working out, save that in the Florence example Philip stands on a grass plot in front of a colonnade, while in that of Naples the background is featureless. As the pictures are now seen, that in the Pitti is marked by greater subtlety in the characterisation of the head, while the Naples canvas appears the more brilliant as regards the working out of the costume and accessories.

To the period of Titian's return from the second visit to Augsburg belongs a very remarkable portrait which of late years there has been some disinclination to admit as his own work. This is the imposing full-length portrait which stands forth as the crowning decoration of the beautiful and well-ordered gallery at Cassel. In the days when it was sought to obtain *quand même* a striking designation for a great picture, it was christened *Alfonso d'Avalos, Marqués del Vasto*. More recently, with some greater show of probability, it has been called *Guidobaldo II., Duke of Urbino*. In the *Jahrbuch der königlich-preussischen Kunstsammlungen,*[*43] Herr Carl Justi, ever bold and ingenious in hypothesis, strives, with the support of a mass of corroborative evidence that cannot be here quoted, to prove that the splendid personage presented is a Neapolitan nobleman of the highest rank, Giovan Francesco Acquaviva, Duke of Atri. There is the more reason to accept his conjecture since it helps us to cope with certain difficulties presented by the picture itself. It may be conceded at the outset that there are disturbing elements in it, well calculated to give pause to the student of Titian. The handsome patrician, a little too proud of his rank, his magnificent garments and accoutrements, his virile beauty, stands fronting the spectator in a dress of crimson and gold, wearing a plumed and jewelled hat, which in its elaboration closely borders on the grotesque, and holding a hunting-spear. Still more astonishing in its exaggeration of a

Venetian mode in portraiture[*44] is the great crimson, dragon-crowned helmet which, on the left of the canvas, Cupid himself supports. To the right, a rival even of Love in the affections of our enigmatical personage, a noble hound rubs himself affectionately against the stalwart legs of his master. Far back stretches a prospect singularly unlike those rich-toned studies of sub-Alpine regions in which Titian as a rule revels. It has an august but more colourless beauty recalling the middle Apennines; one might almost say that it prefigures those prospects of inhospitable Sierra which, with their light, delicate tonality, so admirably relieve and support the portraits of Velazquez. All this is unusual, and still more so is the want of that aristocratic gravity, of that subordination of mere outward splendour to inborn dignity, which mark Titian's greatest portraits throughout his career. The splendid materials for the picture are not as absolutely digested, as absolutely welded into one consistent and harmonious whole, as with such authorship one would expect. But then, on the other hand, take the magnificent execution in the most important passages: the distinguished silvery tone obtained notwithstanding the complete red-and-gold costume and the portentous crimson helmet; the masterly brush-work in these last particulars, in the handsome virile head of the model and the delicate flesh of the *amorino*. The dog might without exaggeration be pronounced the best, the truest in movement, to be found in Venetian art – indeed, in art generally, until Velazquez appears. Herr Carl Justi's happy conjecture helps us, if we accept it, to get over some of these difficulties and seeming contradictions. The Duke of Atri belonged to a great Neapolitan family, exiled and living at the French court under royal countenance and protection. The portrait was painted to be sent back to France, to which, indeed, its whole subsequent history belongs. Under such circumstances the young nobleman would naturally desire to affirm his rank and pretensions as emphatically as might be; to outdo in splendour and *prestance* all previous sitters to Titian; to record himself apt in war, in the chase, in love, and more choice in the fashion of his appointments than any of his compeers in France or Italy.

An importance to which it is surely not entitled in the life-work of the master is given to the portrait of the Legate Beccadelli, executed in the month of July 1552, and included among the real and fancied masterpieces of the Tribuna in the Uffizi. To the writer it has always appeared the most nearly tiresome and perfunctory of Titian's more important works belonging to the same class. Perhaps the elaborate legend inscribed on the paper held by the prelate, including the unusual form of signature "Titianus Vecellius faciebat Venetiis MDLII, mense Julii," may have been the cause that the canvas has attracted an undue share of attention.[*45] At p. 218 of Crowe and Cavalcaselle's second volume we get, under date the 11th of October 1552, Titian's first letter to Philip of Spain. There is mention in it of a *Queen of Persia*, which the artist does not expressly declare to be his own work, a n d o f a *Landscape* a n d *St. Margaret* previously sent by Ambassador Vargas ("… il Paesaggio et il ritratto di Sta. Margarita mandatovi per avanti"). The comment of the biographers on this is that "for the first time in the annals of Italian painting we hear of a picture which claims to be nothing more than a landscape, etc." Remembering, however, that when in 1574, at the end of his life, our master sent in to Philip's secretary, Antonio Perez, a list of paintings delivered from time to time, but not paid for, he described the *Venere del Pardo*, or *Jupiter and Antiope*, as "La nuda con il paese con el satiro," would it not be fair to assume that the description *Il Paesaggio et il ritratto di Sta. Margarita* means one and the same canvas – *The Figure of St. Margaret in a Landscape?* Thus should we be relieved from the duty of searching among the authentic works of the master of Cadore for a landscape pure and simple, and in the process stumbling across a number of spurious and doubtful things. The *St. Margaret* is evidently the picture which, having been many years at the Escorial, now hangs in the Prado Gallery. Obscured and darkened though it is by the irreparable outrages of time, it may be taken as a very characteristic example of Titian's late but not latest manner in sacred art. In the most striking fashion does it exhibit that peculiar gloom and agitation of the artist face to face with religious subjects which at an earlier period would have left his serenity undisturbed. The saint, uncertain of her triumph, armed though she is with the Cross, flees in affright from the monster whose huge bulk looms, terrible even in overthrow, in the darkness of the foreground. To the impression of terror communicated by the whole conception the distance of the lurid landscape – a city in flames – contributes much.

In the spring and summer of 1554 were finished for Philip of Spain the *Danaë* of Madrid; for Mary, Queen of Hungary, a *Madonna Addolorata*; for Charles V. the *Trinity*, to which he had with Titian devoted so much anxious thought. The *Danaë* of the Prado, less grandiose, less careful in finish than the Naples picture, is painted with greater spontaneity and *élan* than its predecessor, and vibrates with an undisguisedly fleshly passion. Is it to the taste of Philip or to a momentary touch of cynicism in Titian himself that we owe the deliberate dragging down of the conception until it becomes symbolical of the lowest and most venal form of love? In the Naples version Amor, a fairly-fashioned divinity of more or less classic aspect, presides; in the Madrid and subsequent interpretations of the legend, a grasping hag, the attendant of Danaë, holds out a cloth, eager to catch her share of the golden rain. In the St. Petersburg version, which cannot be accounted more than an atelier piece, there is, with some slight yet appreciable variations, a substantial agreement with the Madrid picture. Of this Hermitage *Danaë* there is a replica in the collection of the Duke of Wellington at Apsley House. In yet another version (also a contemporary atelier piece), which is in the Imperial Gallery at Vienna, and has for that reason acquired a certain celebrity, the greedy duenna is depicted in full face, and holds aloft a chased metal dish.

Satisfaction of a very different kind was afforded to Queen Mary of Hungary and Charles V. The lady obtained a *Christ appearing to the Magdalen*, which was for a long time preserved at the Escorial, where there is still to be found a bad copy of it. A mere fragment of the original, showing a head and bust of Christ holding a hoe in his left hand, has been preserved, and is now No. 489 in the gallery of the Prado. Even this does not convince the student that Titian's own brush had a predominant share in the performance. The letter to Charles V., dated from Venice the 10th of September 1554, records the sending of a *Madonna Addolorata* and the great *Trinity*. These, together with another *Virgen de los Dolores* ostensibly by Titian, and the *Ecce Homo* already mentioned, formed afterwards part of the small collection of devotional paintings taken by Charles to his monastic retreat at Yuste, and appropriated after his death by Philip. If the picture styled *La Dolorosa*, and now No. 468 in the gallery of the Prado, is indeed the one painted for the great monarch who was so sick in body and spirit, so fast declining to his end, the suspicion is aroused that the courtly Venetian must have acted with something less than fairness towards his great patron, since the *Addolorata* cannot be acknowledged as his own work. Still less can we accept as his own that other *Virgen de los Dolores*, now No. 475 in the same gallery.

It is very different with the *Trinity*, called in Spain *La Gloria*, and now No. 462 in the same gallery. Though the master must have been hampered by the express command that the Emperor should be portrayed as newly arisen from the grave and adoring the *Trinity* in an agony of prayer, and with him the deceased Empress Isabel, Queen Mary of Hungary, and Prince Philip, also as suppliants, he succeeded in bringing forth not indeed a complete masterpiece, but a picture all aspiration and fervent prayer – just the work to satisfy the yearnings of the man who, once the mightiest, was then the loneliest and saddest of mortals on earth. The crown and climax of the whole is the group of the Trinity itself, awful in majesty, dazzling in the golden radiance of its environment, and, beautifully linking it with mortality, the blue-robed figure of the Virgin, who stands on a lower eminence of cloud as she intercedes for the human race, towards whom her pitying gaze is directed. It would be absurd to pretend that we have here a work entitled, in virtue of the perfect achievement of all that has been sought for, to rank with such earlier masterpieces as the *Assunta* or the *St. Peter Martyr*. Yet it represents in one way sacred art of a higher, a more inspired order, and contains some pictorial beauties – such as the great central group – of which Titian would not in those earlier days have been equally capable.

There is another descent, though not so marked a one as in the case of the *Danaë*, with the *Venus and Adonis* painted for Philip, the new King-Consort of England, and forwarded by the artist to London in the autumn of 1554. That the picture now in the *Sala de la Reina Isabel* at Madrid is this original is proved, in the first place, by the quality of the flesh-painting, the silvery shimmer, the vibration of the whole, the subordination of local colour to general tone, yet by no means to the point of extinction – all these being distinctive qualities of this late time. It is further proved by the fact that it still shows traces of the injury of which Philip complained when he received the picture in London. A long horizontal furrow is clearly to be seen running right across the canvas. Apart from the consideration that pupils no doubt had a hand in the work, it lacks, with all its decorative elegance and felicity of movement, the charm with which Titian, both much earlier in his career and later on towards the end, could invest such mythological subjects.[*46] That the aim of the artist was not a very high one, or this *poesia* very near to his heart, is demonstrated by the amusingly material fashion in which he recommends it to his royal patron. He says that "if in the *Danaë* the forms were to be seen front-wise, here was occasion to look at them from a contrary direction – a pleasant variety for the ornament of a *Camerino*." Our worldly-wise painter evidently knew that material allurements as well as supreme art were necessary to captivate Philip. It cannot be alleged, all the same, that this purely sensuous mode of conception was not perfectly in consonance with his own temperament, with his own point of view, at this particular stage in his life and practice.

The new Doge Francesco Venier had, upon his accession in 1554, called upon Titian to paint, besides his own portrait, the orthodox votive picture of his predecessor Marcantonio Trevisan, and this official performance was duly completed in January 1555, and hung in the Sala de' Pregadi. At the same time Venier determined that thus tardily the memory of a long – deceased Doge, Antonio Grimani, should be rehabilitated by the dedication to him of a similar but more dramatic and allusive composition. The commission for this piece also was given to Titian, who made good progress with it, yet for reasons unexplained never carried the important undertaking to completion. It remained in the workshop at the time of his death, and was completed – with what divergence from the original design we cannot authoritatively say – by assistants. Antonio Grimani, supported by members of his house, or officers attached to his person, kneels in adoration before an emblematic figure of Faith which appears in the clouds holding the cross and chalice, which winged child-angels help to support, and haloed round with an oval glory of cherubim – a conception, by the way, quite new and not at all orthodox. To the left appears a majestic figure of St. Mark, while the clouds upon which Faith is upborne, rise just sufficiently to show a very realistic prospect of Venice. There is not to be found in the whole life-work of Titian a clumsier or more disjointed composition as a whole, even making the necessary allowances for alterations, additions, and restorations. Though the figure of Faith is a sufficiently noble conception in itself, the group which it makes with the attendant angels is inexplicably heavy and awkward in arrangement; the flying *pulli* have none of the audacious grace and buoyancy that Lotto or Correggio would have imparted to them, none of the rush of Tintoretto. The noble figure of St. Mark must be of Titian's designing, but is certainly not of his painting, while the corresponding figure on the other side is neither the one nor the other. Some consolation is afforded by the figure of the kneeling Doge himself, which is a masterpiece – not less in the happy expression of naïve adoration than in the rendering, with matchless breadth and certainty of brush, of burnished armour in which is mirrored the glow of the Doge's magnificent state robes.

# CHAPTER IV

*Portraits of Titian's daughter Lavinia – Death of Aretino – "Martyrdom of St. Lawrence" – Death of Charles V. – Attempted assassination of Orazio Vecellio – "Diana and Actaeon" and "Diana and Calisto" – The "Comoro Family" – The "Magdalen" of the Hermitage – The "Jupiter and Antiope" and "Rape of Europa" – Vasari defines Titian's latest manner – "St. Jerome" of the Brera – "Education of Cupid" – "Jacopo da Strada" – Impressionistic manner of the end – "Ecce Homo" of Munich – "Nymph and Shepherd" of Vienna – The unfinished "Pietà" – Death of Titian.*

It was in the month of March 1555 that Titian married his only daughter Lavinia to Cornelio Sarcinelli of Serravalle, thus leaving the pleasant home at Biri Grande without a mistress; for his sister Orsa had been dead since 1549.[*47] It may be convenient to treat here of the various portraits and more or less idealised portrait-pieces in which Titian has immortalised the thoroughly Venetian beauty of his daughter. First we have in the great *Ecce Homo* of Vienna the graceful white-robed figure of a young girl of some fourteen years, placed, with the boy whom she guards, on the steps of Pilate's palace. Then there is the famous piece *Lavinia with a Dish of Fruit*, dating according to Morelli from about 1549, and painted for the master's friend Argentina Pallavicino of Reggio.

This last-named work passed in 1821 from the Solly Collection into the Berlin Gallery. Though its general aspect is splendidly decorative, though it is accounted one of the most popular of all Titian's works, the Berlin picture cannot be allowed to take the highest rank among his performances of the same class. Its fascinations are of the obvious and rather superficial kind, its execution is not equal in vigour, freedom, and accent to the best that the master did about the same time. It is pretty obvious here that only the head is adapted from that of Lavinia, the full-blown voluptuous form not being that of the youthful maiden, who could not moreover have worn this sumptuous and fanciful costume except in the studio. In the strongest contrast to the conscious allurement of this showpiece is the demure simplicity of mien in the avowed portrait *Lavinia as a Bride* in the Dresden Gallery. In this last she wears a costume of warm white satin and a splendid necklace and earrings of pearls. Morelli has pointed out that the fan, in the form of a little flag which she holds, was only used in Venice by newly betrothed ladies; and this fixes the time of the portrait as 1555, the date of the marriage contract. The execution is beyond all comparison finer here, the colour more transparent in its warmth, than in the more celebrated Berlin piece. Quite eight or ten years later than this must date the *Salome* of the Prado Gallery, which is in general design a variation of the *Lavinia* of Berlin. The figure holding up – a grim substitute for the salver of fruit – the head of St. John on a charger has probably been painted without any fresh reference to the model. The writer is unable to agree with Crowe and Cavalcaselle when they affirm that this *Salome* is certainly painted by one of the master's followers. The touch is assuredly Titian's own in the very late time, and the canvas, though much slighter and less deliberate in execution than its predecessors, is in some respects more spontaneous, more vibrant in touch. Second to none as a work of art – indeed more striking than any in the naïve and fearless truth of the rendering – is the *Lavinia Sarcinelli as a Matron* in the Dresden Gallery. Morelli surely exaggerates a little when he describes Lavinia here as a woman of forty. Though the demure, bright-eyed maiden has grown into a self-possessed Venetian dame of portentous dimensions, Sarcinelli's spouse is fresh still, and cannot be more than two-or three-and-thirty. This assumption, if accepted, would fix the time of origin of the picture at about 1565, and, reasoning from analogies of technique, this appears to be a more acceptable date than the year 1570-72, at which Morelli would place it.

One of the most important chapters in our master's life closed with the death of Aretino, which took place suddenly on the 21st of October 1556. He had been sitting at table with friends far into the night or morning. One of them, describing to him a farcical incident of Rabelaisian quality, he threw himself back in his chair in a fit of laughter, and slipping on the polished floor, was thrown with great force on his head and killed almost instantaneously. This was indeed the violent and sudden death of the strong, licentious man; poetic justice could have devised no more fitting end to such a life.

In the year 1558 Crowe and Cavalcaselle, for very sufficient reasons, place the *Martyrdom of St. Lawrence*, now preserved in the hideously over-ornate Church of the Jesuits at Venice. To the very remarkable analysis which they furnish of this work, the writer feels unable to add anything appreciable by way of comment, for the simple reason that though he has seen it many times, on no occasion has he been fortunate enough to obtain such a light as would enable him to judge the picture on its own merits as it now stands.[*48] Of a design more studied in its rhythm, more akin to the Florentine and Roman schools, than anything that has appeared since the *St. Peter Martyr*, with a *mise-en-scène* more classical than anything else from Titian's hand that can be pointed to, the picture may be guessed, rather than seen, to be also a curious and subtle study of conflicting lights. On the one hand we have that of the gruesome martyrdom itself, and of a huge torch fastened to the carved shaft of a pedestal; on the other, that of an effulgence from the skies, celestial in brightness, shedding its consoling beams on the victim.

The *Christ crowned with Thorns*, which long adorned the church of S. Maria delle Grazie at Milan, and is now in the Long Gallery of the Louvre, may belong to about this time, but is painted with a larger and more generous brush, with a more spontaneous energy, than the carefully studied piece at the Gesuiti. The tawny harmonies finely express in their calculated absence of freshness the scene of brutal and unholy violence so dramatically enacted before our eyes. The rendering of muscle, supple and strong under the living epidermis, the glow of the flesh, the dramatic momentariness of the whole, have not been surpassed even by Titian. Of the true elevation, of the spiritual dignity that the subject calls for, there is, however, little or nothing. The finely limbed Christ is as coarse in type and as violent in action as his executioners; sublimity is reached, strange to say, only in the bust of Tiberius, which crowns the rude archway through which the figures have issued into the open space. Titian is here the precursor of the *Naturalisti* – of Caravaggio and his school. Yet, all the same, how immeasurable is the distance between the two!

On the 21st of September 1558 died the imperial recluse of Yuste, once Charles V., and it is said his last looks were steadfastly directed towards that great canvas *The Trinity*, which to devise with Titian had been one of his greatest consolations at a moment when already earthly glories held him no more. Philip, on the news of his father's death, retired for some weeks to the monastery of Groenendale, and thence sent a despatch to the Governor of Milan, directing payment of all the arrears of the pensions "granted to Titian by Charles his father (now in glory)," adding by way of unusual favour a postscript in his own hand.[*49] Orazio Vecellio, despatched by his father in the spring of 1559 to Milan to receive the arrears of pension, accepted the hospitality of the sculptor Leone Leoni, who was then living in splendid style in a palace which he had built and adorned for himself in the Lombard city. He was the rival in art as well as the mortal enemy of Benvenuto Cellini, and as great a ruffian as he, though one less picturesque in blackguardism. One day early in June, when Orazio, having left Leoni's house, had returned to superintend the removal of certain property, he was set upon, and murderously assaulted by the perfidious host and his servants. The whole affair is wrapped in obscurity. It remains uncertain whether vengeance, or hunger after the arrears of Titian's pension, or both, were the motives which incited Leoni to attempt the crime. Titian's passionate reclamations, addressed immediately to Philip II., met with but partial success, since the sculptor, himself a great favourite with the court of Spain, was punished only with fine and banishment, and the affair was afterwards compromised by the payment of a sum of money.

Titian's letter of September 22, 1559, to Philip II. announces the despatch of the companion pieces *Diana and Calisto* and *Diana and Actæon*, as well as of an *Entombment* intended to replace a painting of the same subject which had been lost on the way. The two celebrated canvases,[*50] now in the Bridgewater Gallery, are so familiar that they need no new description. Judging by the repetitions, reductions, and copies that exist in the Imperial Gallery of Vienna, the Prado Gallery, the Yarborough Collection, and elsewhere, these mythological *poesie* have captivated the world far more than the fresher and lovelier painted poems of the earlier time – the *Worship of Venus*, the *Bacchanal*, the *Bacchus and Ariadne*. At no previous period has Titian wielded the brush with greater *maestria* and ease than here, or united a richer or more transparent glow with greater dignity of colour. About the compositions themselves, if we are to take them as the *poesie* that Titian loved to call them, there is a certain want of significance, neither the divine nor the human note being struck with any depth or intensity of vibration. The glamour, the mystery, the intimate charm of the early pieces is lost, and there is felt, enwrapping the whole, that sultry atmosphere of untempered sensuousness which has already, upon more than one occasion, been commented upon. That this should be so is only natural when creative power is not extinguished by old age, but is on the contrary coloured with its passion, so different in quality from that of youth.

The *Entombment*, which went to Madrid with the mythological pieces just now discussed, serves to show how vivid was Titian's imagination at this point, when he touched upon a sacred theme, and how little dependent he was in this field on the conceptions of his earlier prime. A more living passion informs the scene, a more intimate sympathy colours it, than we find in the noble *Entombment* of the Louvre, much as the picture which preceded it by so many years excels the Madrid example in fineness of balance, in dignity, in splendour and charm of colour. Here the personages are set free by the master from all academic trammels, and express themselves with a greater spontaneity in grief. The colour, too, of which the general scheme is far less attractive to the eye than in the Louvre picture, blazes forth in one note of lurid splendour in the red robe of the saint who supports the feet of the dead Christ.

In this same year Titian painted on the ceiling of the ante-chamber to Sansovino's great Library in the Piazzetta the allegorical figure *Wisdom*, thus entering into direct competition with young Paolo Veronese, Schiavone, and the other painters who, striving in friendly rivalry, had been engaged a short time before on the ceiling of the great hall in the same building. This noble design contains a pronounced reminiscence of Raphael's incomparable allegorical figures in the Camera della Segnatura, but excels them as much in decorative splendour and facile breadth of execution as it falls behind them in sublimity of inspiration.

Crowe and Cavalcaselle are probably right in assigning the great *Cornaro Family* in the collection of the Duke of Northumberland to the year 1560 or thereabouts. Little seen of late years, and like most Venetian pictures of the sixteenth century shorn of some of its glory by time and the restorer, this family picture appears to the writer to rank among Titian's masterpieces in the domain of portraiture, and to be indeed the finest portrait-group of this special type that Venice has produced. In the simplicity and fervour of the conception Titian rises to heights which he did not reach in the *Madonna di Casa Pesaro,* where he is hampered by the necessity for combining a votive picture with a series of avowed portraits. It is pretty clear that this *Cornaro* picture, like the Pesaro altar-piece, must have been commissioned to commemorate a victory or important political event in the annals of the illustrious family. Search among their archives and papers, if they still exist, might throw light upon this point, and fix more accurately the date of the magnificent work. In the open air – it may be outside some great Venetian church – an altar has been erected, and upon it is placed a crucifix, on either side of which are church candles, blown this way and the other by the wind. Three generations of patricians kneel in prayer and thanksgiving, taking precedence according to age, six handsome boys, arranged in groups of three on either side of the canvas, furnishing an element of great pictorial attractiveness but no vital significance. The act of worship acquires here more reality and a profounder meaning than it can have in those vast altar-pieces in which the divine favour is symbolised by the actual presence of the Madonna and Child. An open-air effect has been deliberately aimed at and attained, the splendid series of portraits being relieved against the cloud-flecked blue sky with a less sculptural plasticity than the master would have given to them in an indoor scheme. This is another admirable example of the dignity and reserve which Titian combines with sumptuous colour at this stage of his practice. His mastery is not less but greater, subtler, than that of his more showy and brilliant contemporaries of the younger generation; the result is something that appears as if it must inevitably have been so and not otherwise. The central figure of the patriarch is robed in deep crimson with grayish fur, rather black in shadow; the man in the prime of manhood wears a more positive crimson, trimmed with tawnier fur, browner in shadow; a lighter sheen is on the brocaded mantle of yet another

shade of crimson worn by the most youthful of the three
patricians. Just the stimulating note to break up a harmony which
might otherwise have been of a richness too cloying is furnished –
in the master's own peculiar way – by the scarlet stockings of one
boy in the right hand group, by the cinnamon sleeve of
another.[*51]

To the year 1561 belongs, according to the elaborate
inscription on the picture, the magnificent *Portrait of a Man* which
is No. 172 in the Dresden Gallery. It presents a Venetian
gentleman in his usual habit, but bearing a palm branch such as
we associate with saints who have endured martyrdom. Strangely
sombre and melancholy in its very reserve is this sensitive face,
and the tone of the landscape echoes the pathetic note of disquiet.
The canvas bears the signature "Titianus Pictor et Aeques (sic)
Caesaris." There group very well with this Dresden picture,
though the writer will not venture to assert positively that they
belong to exactly the same period, the *St. Dominic* of the Borghese
Gallery and the *Knight of Malta* of the Prado Gallery. In all three –
in the two secular portraits as in the sacred piece which is also a
portrait – the expression given, and doubtless intended, is that of
a man who has withdrawn himself in his time of fullest physical
vigour from the pomps and vanities of the world, and sadly
concentrates his thoughts on matters of higher import.

On the 1st of December 1561 Titian wrote to the king to
announce the despatch of a *Magdalen*, which had already been
mentioned more than once in the correspondence. According to
Vasari and subsequent authorities, Silvio Badoer, a Venetian
patrician, saw the masterpiece on the painter's easel, and took it
away for a hundred scudi, leaving the master to paint another for
Philip. This last has disappeared, while the canvas which
remained in Venice cannot be identified with any certainty. The
finest extant example of this type of *Magdalen* is undoubtedly that
which from Titian's ne'er-do-well son, Pompinio, passed to the
Barbarigo family, and ultimately, with the group of Titians
forming part of the Barbarigo collection, found its way into the

Imperial Gallery of the Hermitage at St. Petersburg. This answers in every respect to Vasari's eloquent description of the *magna peccatrix*, lovely still in her penitence. It is an embodiment of the favourite subject, infinitely finer and more moving than the much earlier *Magdalen* of the Pitti, in which the artist's sole preoccupation has been the alluring portraiture of exuberant feminine charms. This later *Magdalen*, as Vasari says, "ancorchè che sia bellissima, non muove a lascivia, ma a commiserazione," and the contrary might, without exaggeration, be said of the Pitti picture.[*52] Another of the Barbarigo heirlooms which so passed into the Hermitage is the ever-popular *Venus with the Mirror*, the original of many repetitions and variations. Here, while one winged love holds the mirror, the other proffers a crown of flowers, not to the goddess, but to the fairest of women. The rich mantle of Venetian fashion, the jewels, the coiffure, all show that an idealised portrait of some lovely Cytherean of Venice, and no true mythological piece, has been intended.

At this date, or thereabouts, is very generally placed, with the *Rape of Europa* presently to be discussed, the *Jupiter and Antiope* of the Louvre, more popularly known as the *Venere del Pardo*.[*53] Seeing that the picture is included in the list[*54] sent by Titian to Antonio Perez in 1574, setting forth the titles of canvases delivered during the last twenty-five years, and then still unpaid for, it may well have been completed somewhere about the time at which we have arrived. To the writer it appears nevertheless that it is in essentials the work of an earlier period, taken up and finished thus late in the day for the delectation of the Spanish king. Seeing that the *Venere del Pardo* has gone through two fires – those of the Pardo and the Louvre – besides cleanings, restorations, and repaintings, even more disfiguring, it would be very unsafe to lay undue stress on technique alone. Yet compare the close, sculptural modelling in the figure of Antiope with the broader, looser handling in the figure of Europa; compare the two landscapes, which are even more divergent in style. The glorious sylvan prospect, which adds so much freshness and beauty to the

*Venere del Pardo*, is conspicuously earlier in manner than, for instance, the backgrounds to the *Diana and Actæon* and *Diana and Calisto* of Bridgewater House. The captivating work is not without its faults, chief among which is the curious awkwardness of design which makes of the composition, cut in two by a central tree, two pictures instead of one. Undeniably, too, there is a certain meanness and triviality in the little nymph or mortal of the foreground, which may, however, be due to the intervention of an assistant. But then, with an elasticity truly astounding in a man of his great age, the master has momentarily regained the poetry of his youthful prime, and with it a measure of that Giorgionesque fragrance which was evaporating already at the close of the early time, when the *Bacchanals* were brought forth. The Antiope herself far transcends in the sovereign charm of her beauty – divine in the truer sense of the word – all Titian's Venuses, save the one in the *Sacred and Profane Love*. The figure comes in some ways nearer even in design, and infinitely nearer in feeling, to Giorgione's *Venus* at Dresden than does the *Venus of Urbino* in the Tribuna, which was closely modelled upon it. And the aged Titian had gone back even a step farther than Giorgione; the group of Antiope with Jupiter in the guise of a Satyr is clearly a reminiscence of a *Nymph surprised by a Satyr* – one of the engravings in the *Hypnerotomachia Poliphili* first published in 1499, but republished with the same illustrations in 1545.[*55]

According to the correspondence published by Crowe and Cavalcaselle there were completed for the Spanish King in April 1562 the *Poesy of Europa carried by the Bull*, and the *Christ praying in the Garden*, while a *Virgin and Child* was announced as in progress.

These paintings, widely divergent as they are in subject, answer very well to each other in technical execution, while in both they differ very materially from the *Venere del Pardo*. The *Rape of Europa*, which has retained very much of its blond brilliancy and charm of colour, affords convincing proof of the unrivalled power with which Titian still wielded the brush at this stage which precedes that of his very last and most impressionistic style. For decorative effect, for "go," for frankness and breadth of execution, it could not be surpassed. Yet hardly elsewhere has the great master approached so near to positive vulgarity as here in the conception of the fair Europa as a strapping wench who, with ample limbs outstretched, complacently allows herself to be carried off by the Bull, making her appeal for succour merely *pour la forme*. What gulfs divide this conception from that of the Antiope, from Titian's earlier renderings of female loveliness, from Giorgione's supreme Venus![*56]

The *Agony in the Garden*, which is still to be found in one of the halls of the Escorial, even now in its faded state serves to evidence the intensity of religious fervour which possessed Titian when, so late in life, he successfully strove to renew the sacred subjects. If the composition – as Crowe and Cavalcaselle assert – does more or less resemble that of the famous *Agony* by Correggio now at Apsley House, nothing could differ more absolutely from the Parmese master's amiable virtuosity than the aged Titian's deep conviction.[*57]

To the year 1562 belongs the nearly profile portrait of the artist, painted by himself with a subtler refinement and a truer revelation of self than is to be found in those earlier canvases of Berlin and the Uffizi in which his late prime still shows as a green and vigorous manhood. This is now in the *Sala de la Reina Isabel* of the Prado. The pale noble head, refined by old age to a solemn beauty, is that of one brought face to face with the world beyond; it is the face of the man who could conceive and paint the sacred pieces of the end, the *Ecce Homo* of Munich and the last *Pietà*, with an awe such as we here read in his eyes. Much less easy is it to connect this likeness with the artist who went on concurrently producing his Venuses, mythological pieces, and pastorals, and joying as much as ever in their production.

Vasari, who, as will be seen, visited Venice in 1566, when he was preparing that new and enlarged edition of the *Lives* which was to appear in 1568, had then an opportunity of renewing his friendly acquaintance with the splendid old man whom he had last seen, already well stricken in years, twenty-one years before in Rome. It must have been at this stage that he formed the judgment as to the latest manner of Titian which is so admirably expressed in his biography of the master. Speaking especially of the *Diana and Actæon*, the *Rape of Europa*, and the *Deliverance of Andromeda*,[*58] he delivers himself as follows: – "It is indeed true that his technical manner in these last is very different from that of his youth. The first works are, be it remembered, carried out with incredible delicacy and pains, so that they can be looked at both at close quarters and from afar. These last ones are done with broad coarse strokes and blots of colour, in such wise that they cannot be appreciated near at hand, but from afar look perfect. This style has been the cause that many, thinking therein to play the imitators and to make a display of practical skill, have produced clumsy, bad pictures. This is so, because, notwithstanding that to many it may seem that Titian's works are done without labour, this is not so in truth, and they who think so deceive themselves. It is, on the contrary, to be perceived that they are painted at many sittings, that they have been worked upon with the colours so many times as to make the labour evident; and this method of execution is judicious, beautiful, astonishing, because it makes the pictures seem living."

No better proof could be given of Vasari's genuine *flair* and intuition as a critic of art than this passage. We seem to hear, not the Tuscan painter bred to regard the style of Michelangelo as an article of faith, to imitate his sculptural smoothness of finish and that of Angelo Bronzino, but some intelligent exponent of impressionistic methods, defending both from attack and from superficial imitation one of the most advanced of modernists.

Among the sacred works produced in this late time is a *Crucifixion*, still preserved in a damaged state in the church of S. Domenico at Ancona. To a period somewhat earlier than that at which we have arrived may belong the late *Madonna and Child in a Landscape* which is No. 1113 in the Alte Pinakothek of Munich.

The writer follows Giovanni Morelli in believing that this is a studio picture touched by the master, and that the splendidly toned evening landscape is all his. He cannot surely be made wholly responsible for the overgrown and inflated figure of the divine *Bambino,* so disproportionate, so entirely wanting in tenderness and charm.

The power of vivid conception, the spontaneous fervour which mark Titian's latest efforts in the domain of sacred art, are very evident in the great *St. Jerome* of the Brera here reproduced. Cima, Basaiti, and most of the Bellinesques had shown an especial affection for the subject, and it had been treated too by Lotto, by Giorgione, by Titian himself; but this is surely as noble and fervent a rendering as Venetian art in its prime has brought forth. Of extraordinary majesty and beauty is the landscape, with its mighty trees growing out of the abrupt mountain slope, close to the naked rock.

In the autumn of 1564 we actually find the venerable master, then about eighty-seven years of age, taking a journey to Brescia in connection with an important commission given to him for the decoration of the great hall in the Palazzo Pubblico at Brescia, to which the Vicentine artist Righetto had supplied the ceiling, and Palladio had added columns and interior wall-decorations. The three great ceiling-pictures, which were afterwards, as a consequence of the contract then entered upon, executed by the master, or rather by his assistants, endured only until 1575, when in the penultimate year of Titian's life they perished in a great fire.

The correspondence shows that the vast *Last Supper* painted for the Refectory of the Escorial, and still to be found there, was finished in October 1564, and that there was much haggling and finessing on the part of the artist before it was despatched to Spain, the object being to secure payment of the arrears of pension still withheld by the Milanese officials. When the huge work did arrive at the Escorial the monks perpetrated upon it one of those acts of vandalism of which Titian was in more than one instance the victim. Finding that the picture would not fit the particular wall of their refectory for which it had been destined, they ruthlessly cut it down, slicing off a large piece of the upper part, and throwing the composition out of balance by the mutilation of the architectural background.

Passing over the *Transfiguration* on the high altar of San Salvatore at Venice, we come to the *Annunciation* in the same church with the signature "Titianus fecit fecit," added by the master, if we are to credit the legend, in indignation that those who commissioned the canvas should have shown themselves dissatisfied even to the point of expressing incredulity as to his share in the performance. Some doubt has been cast upon this story, which may possibly have been evolved on the basis of the peculiar signature. It is at variance with Vasari's statement that Titian held the picture in slight esteem in comparison with his other works. It is not to be contested that for all the fine passages of colour and execution, the general tone is paler in its silveriness, less vibrant and effective on the whole, than in many of the masterpieces which have been mentioned in their turn. But the conception is a novel and magnificent one, contrasting instructively in its weightiness and majesty with the more naïve and pathetic renderings of an earlier time.

The *Education of Cupid*, popularly but erroneously known as *The Three Graces*[*59] is one of the pearls of the Borghese Gallery. It is clearly built in essentials on the master's own *d'Avalos Allegory*, painted many years before. This later allegory shows Venus binding the eyes of Love ere he sallies forth into the world, while his bow and his quiver well-stocked with arrows are brought forward by two of the Graces. In its conception there is no great freshness or buoyancy, no pretence at invention. The aged magician of the brush has interested himself more in the execution than in the imagining of his picture. It is a fine and typical specimen of the painting *di macchia*, which Vasari has praised in a passage already quoted. A work such as this bears in technique much the same relation to the productions of Titian's first period that the great *Family Picture* of Rembrandt at Brunswick does to his work done some thirty-five or forty years before. In both instances it is a life-time of legitimate practice that has permitted the old man to indulge without danger in an abridgment of labour, a synthetic presentment of fact, which means no abatement, but in some ways an enhancement of life, breadth, and pictorial effect. To much about the same time, judging from the handling and the types, belongs the curious allegory, *Religion succoured by Spain* – otherwise *La Fé* – now No. 476 in the gallery of the Prado. This canvas, notwithstanding a marked superficiality of invention as well as of execution, is in essentials the master's own; moreover it can boast its own special decorative qualities, void though it is of any deep significance. The showy figure of Spain holding aloft in one hand a standard, and with the other supporting a shield emblazoned with the arms of the realm, recalls the similar creations of Paolo Veronese. Titian has rarely been less happily inspired than in the figure of Religion, represented as a naked female slave newly released from bondage.

When Vasari in 1566 paid the visit to Venice, of which a word has already been said, he noted, among a good many other things then in progress, the *Martyrdom of St. Lawrence*, based upon that now at the Gesuiti in Venice. This was despatched nearly two years later to the Escorial, where it still occupies its place on the high altar of the mighty church dedicated to St. Lawrence. The Brescian ceiling canvases appeared, too, in his list as unfinished. They were sent to their destination early in 1568, to be utterly destroyed, as has been told, by fire in 1575.

The best proof we have that Titian's artistic power was in many respects at its highest in 1566, is afforded by the magnificent portrait of the Mantuan painter and antiquary Jacopo da Strada, now in the Imperial Gallery at Vienna. It bears, besides the usual late signature of the master, the description of the personage with all his styles and titles, and the date MDLXVI. The execution is again *di macchia*, but magnificent in vitality, as in impressiveness of general effect, swift but not hasty or superficial. The reserve and dignity of former male portraits is exchanged for a more febrile vivacity, akin to that which Lotto had in so many of his finest works displayed. His peculiar style is further recalled in the rather abrupt inclination of the figure and the parallel position of the statuette which it holds. But none other than Titian himself could have painted the superb head, which he himself has hardly surpassed.

It is curious and instructive to find the artist, in a letter addressed to Philip on the 2nd of December 1567, announcing the despatch, together with the just now described altar-piece, *The Martyrdom of St. Lawrence*, of "una pittura d'una Venere ignuda" – the painting of a nude Venus. Thus is the peculiar double current of the aged painter's genius maintained by the demand for both classes of work. He well knows that to the Most Catholic Majesty very secular pieces indeed will be not less acceptable than those much-desired sacred works in which now Titian's power of invention is greatest.

Our master, in his dealings with the Brescians, after the completion of the extensive decorations for the Palazzo Pubblico, was to have proof that Italian citizens were better judges of art than the King of Spain, and more grudging if prompter paymasters. They declared, not without some foundation in fact, that the canvases were not really from the hand of Titian, and refused to pay more than one thousand ducats for them. The negotiation was conducted – as were most others at that time – by the trusty Orazio, who after much show of indignation was compelled at last to accept the proffered payment.

The great victory of Lepanto, gained by the united fleets of Spain and Venice over the Turk on the 7th of October 1571, gave fitting occasion for one of Paolo Veronese's most radiant masterpieces, the celebrated votive picture of the Sala del Collegio, for Tintoretto's *Battle of Lepanto*, but also for one of Titian's feeblest works, the allegory *Philip II. offering to Heaven his Son, the Infant Don Ferdinand*, now No. 470 in the gallery of the

Prado. That Sanchez Coello, under special directions from the king, prepared the sketch which was to serve as the basis for the definitive picture may well have hampered and annoyed the aged master. Still this is but an insufficient excuse for the absurdities of the design, culminating in the figure of the descending angel, who is represented in one of those strained, over-bold attitudes, in which Titian, even at his best, never achieved complete success. That he was not, all the same, a stranger to the work, is proved by some flashes of splendid colour, some fine passages of execution.

In the four pieces now to be shortly described, the very latest and most impressionistic form of Titian's method as a painter is to be observed; all of them are in the highest degree characteristic of this ultimate phase. In the beautiful *Madonna and Child* here reproduced,[*60] the hand, though it no longer works with all trenchant vigour of earlier times, produces a magical effect by means of unerring science and a certainty of touch justifying such economy of mere labour as is by the system of execution suggested to the eye. And then this pathetic motive, the simple realism, the unconventional treatment of which are spiritualised by infinite tenderness, is a new thing in Venetian, nay in Italian art. Precisely similar in execution, and equally restrained in the scheme of colour adopted, is the *Christ crowned with Thorns* of the Alte Pinakothek at Munich, a reproduction with important variations of the better-known picture in the Long Gallery of the Louvre. Less demonstratively and obviously dramatic than its predecessor, the Munich example is, as a realisation of the scene, far truer and more profound in pathos. Nobler beyond compare in His unresisting acceptance of insult and suffering is the Munich Christ than the corresponding figure, so violent in its instinctive recoil from pain, of the Louvre picture.

It is nothing short of startling at the very end of Titian's career to meet with a work which, expressed in this masterly late technique of his, vies in freshness of inspiration with the finest of his early *poesie*. This is the *Nymph and Shepherd*[*61] of the

Imperial Gallery at Vienna, a picture which the world had forgotten until it was added, or rather restored, to the State collection on its transference from the Belvedere to the gorgeous palace which it now occupies. In its almost monochromatic harmony of embrowned silver the canvas embodies more absolutely than any other, save perhaps the final *Pietà*, the ideal of tone-harmony towards which the master in his late time had been steadily tending. Richness and brilliancy of local colour are subordinated, and this time up to the point of effacement, to this luminous monotone, so mysteriously effective in the hands of a master such as Titian. In the solemn twilight which descends from the heavens, just faintly flushed with rose, an amorous shepherd, flower-crowned, pipes to a nude nymph, who, half-won by the appealing strain, turns her head as she lies luxuriously extended on a wild beast's hide, covering the grassy knoll; in the distance a strayed goat browses on the leafage of a projecting branch. It may not be concealed that a note of ardent sensuousness still makes itself felt, as it does in most of the later pieces of the same class. But here, transfigured by a freshness of poetic inspiration hardly to be traced in the master's work in pieces of this order, since those early Giorgionesque days when the sixteenth century was in its youth, it offends no more than does an idyll of Theocritus. Since the *Three Ages* of Bridgewater House, divided from the *Nymph and Shepherd* by nearly seventy years of life and labour, Titian had produced nothing which, apart from the question of technical execution, might so nearly be paralleled with that exquisite pastoral. The early *poesia* gives, wrapped in clear even daylight, the perfect moment of trusting, satisfied love; the late one, with less purity, but, strange to say, with a higher passion, renders, beautified by an evening light more solemn and suggestive, the divine ardours fanned by solitude and opportunity.

And now we come to the *Pietà*,[*62] which so nobly and appropriately closes a career unexampled for duration and sustained achievement. Titian had bargained with the Franciscan monks of the Frari, which contained already the *Assunta* and the *Madonna di Casa Pesaro*, for a grave in the Cappella del Crocifisso, offering in payment a *Pietà*, and this offer had been accepted. But some misunderstanding and consequent quarrel having been the ultimate outcome of the proposed arrangements, he left his great canvas unfinished, and willed that his body should be taken to Cadore, and there buried in the chapel of the Vecelli.

The well-known inscription on the base of the monumental niche which occupies the centre of the *Pietà*, "Quod Titianus inchoatum reliquit, Palma reverenter absolvit, Deoque dicavit opus," records how what Titian had left undone was completed as reverently as might be by Palma Giovine. At this stage – the question being much complicated by subsequent restorations – the effort to draw the line accurately between the work of the master on one hand and that of his able and pious assistant on the other, would be unprofitable. Let us rather strive to appreciate what is left of a creation unique in the life-work of Titian, and in some ways his most sublime invention. Genius alone could have triumphed over the heterogeneous and fantastic surroundings in which he has chosen to enframe his great central group. And yet even these – the great rusticated niche with the gold mosaic of the pelican feeding its young, the statues of Moses on one side and of the Hellespontic Sibyl on the other – but serve to heighten the awe of the spectator. The artificial light is obtained in part from a row of crystal lamps on the cornice of the niche, in part, too, from the torch borne by the beautiful boy-angel who hovers in mid-air, yet another focus of illumination being the body of the dead Christ. This system of lighting furnishes just the luminous half-gloom, the deeply significant chiaroscuro, that the painter requires in order to give the most poignant effect to his last and most thrilling conception of the world's tragedy. As is often the case with Tintoretto, but more seldom with Titian, the eloquent passion breathed forth in this *Pietà* is not to be accounted for by any element or elements of the composition taken separately; it depends to so great an extent on the poetic suggestiveness of the illumination, on the strange and indefinable power of evocation that the aged master here exceptionally commands.

Wonderfully does the terrible figure of the Magdalen contrast in its excess of passion with the sculptural repose, the permanence of the main group. As she starts forward, almost menacing in her grief, her loud and bitter cry seems to ring through space, accusing all mankind of its great crime. It is with a conviction far more intense than has ever possessed him in his prime, with an awe nearly akin to terror, that Titian, himself trembling on the verge of eternity, and painting, too, that which shall purchase his own grave, has produced this profoundly moving work. No more fitting end and crown to the great achievements of the master's old age could well be imagined.

There is no temptation to dwell unnecessarily upon the short period of horror and calamity with which this glorious life came to an end. If Titian had died a year earlier, his biographer might still have wound up with those beautiful words of Vasari's peroration: "E stato Tiziano sanissimo et fortunate quant' alcun altro suo pari sia stato ancor mai; e non ha mai avuto dai cieli se non favori e felicità." Too true it is, alas, that no man's life may be counted happy until its close! Now comes upon the great city this all-enveloping horror of the plague, beginning in 1575, but in 1576 attaining to such vast proportions as to sweep away more than a quarter of the whole population of 190,000 inhabitants. On the 17th of August, 1576, old Titian is attacked and swept away – surprised, as one would like to believe, while still at work on his *Pietà*. Even at such a moment, when panic reigns supreme, and the most honoured, the most dearly beloved are left untended, he is not to be hurried into an unmarked grave. Notwithstanding the sanitary law which forbids the burial of one who has succumbed to the plague in any of the city churches, he receives the supreme and at this awful moment unique honour of solemn obsequies. The body is taken with all due observance to the great church of the Frari, and there interred in the Cappella del Crocifisso, which Titian has already, before the quarrel with the Franciscans, designated as his final resting-place. He is spared the grief of knowing that the favourite son, Orazio, for whom all these years he has laboured and schemed, is to follow him immediately, dying also of the plague, and not even at Biri Grande, but in the Lazzaretto Vecchio, near the Lido; that the incorrigible Pomponio is to succeed and enjoy the inheritance after his own unworthy fashion. He is spared the knowledge of the great calamity of 1577, the destruction by fire of the Sala del Gran Consiglio, and with it, of the *Battle of Cadore*, and most of the noble work done officially for the Doges and the Signoria. One would like to think that this catastrophe of the end must have come suddenly upon the venerable master like a hideous dream, appearing to him, as death often does to those upon whom it descends, less significant than it does to us who read. Instead of remaining fixed in sad contemplation of this short final moment when the radiant orb goes suddenly down below the horizon in storm and cloud, let us keep steadily in view the light as, serene in its far-reaching radiance, it illuminated the world for eighty splendid years. Let us think of Titian as the greatest painter, if not the greatest genius in art, that the world has produced; as, what Vasari with such conviction described him to be, "the man as highly favoured by fortune as any of his kind had ever been before him."[*63]

On the following pages are illustrations of some of the contemporaries of Titian.

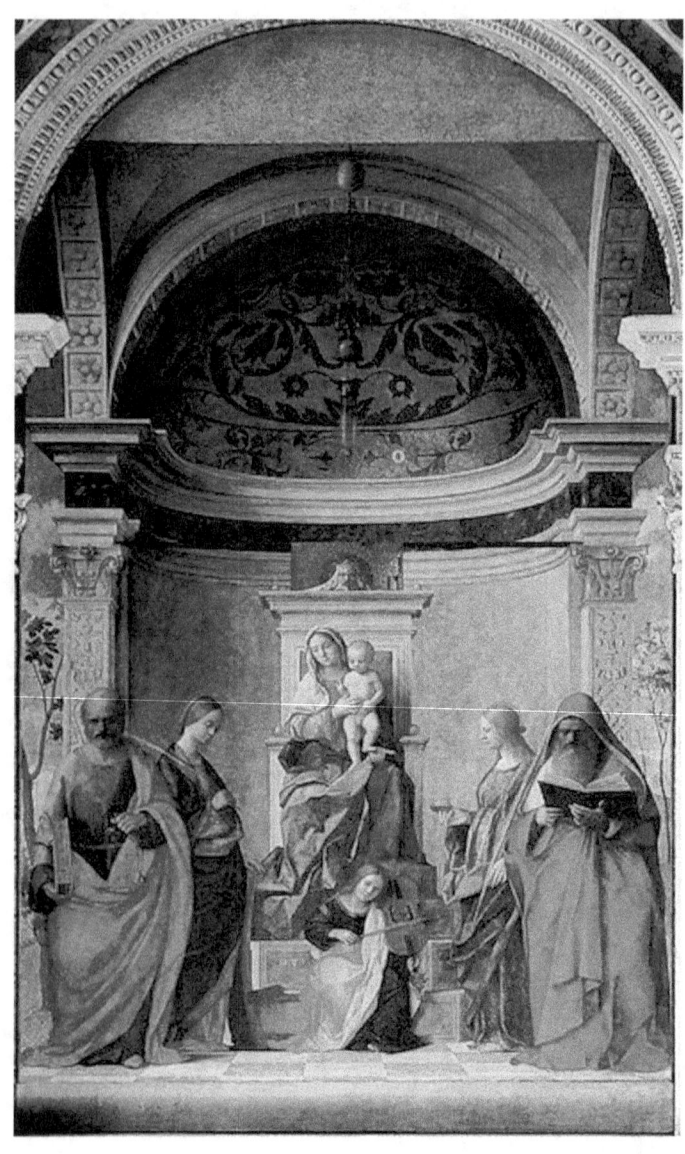

Giovanni Bellini, San Zaccaria Altarpiece

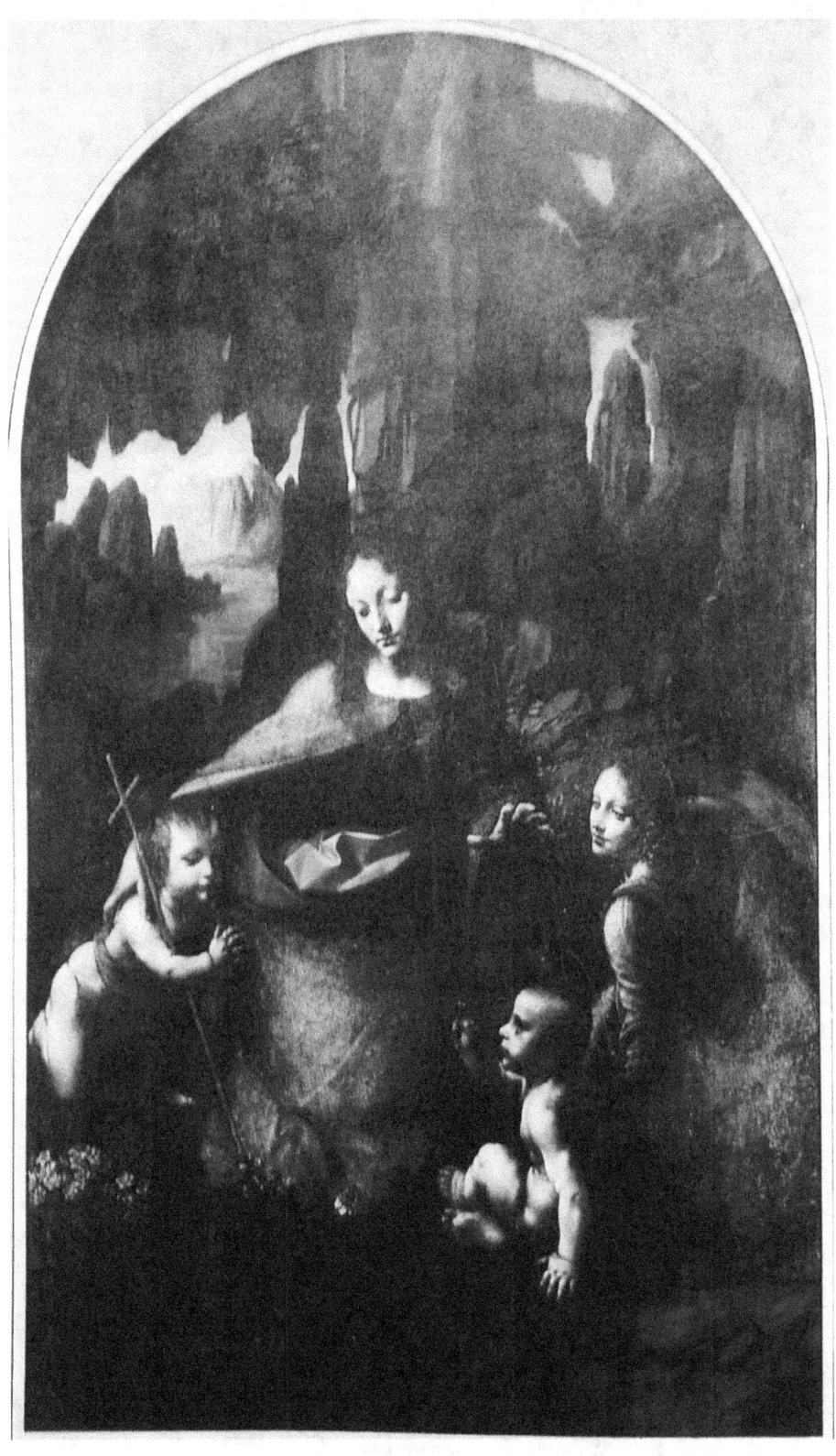

Leonardo da Vinci, *The Virgin of the Rocks*, National Gallery, London

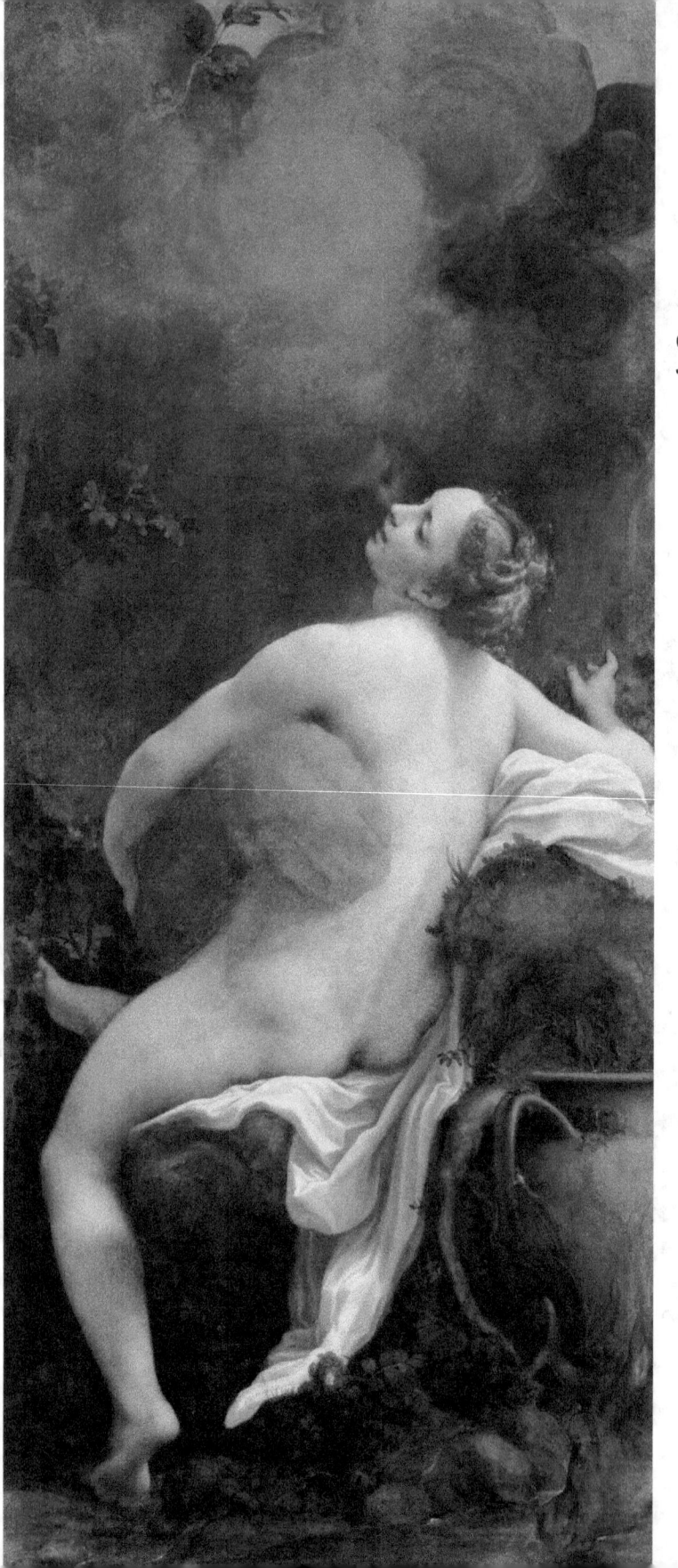

Correggio,
Jupiter and Antiope

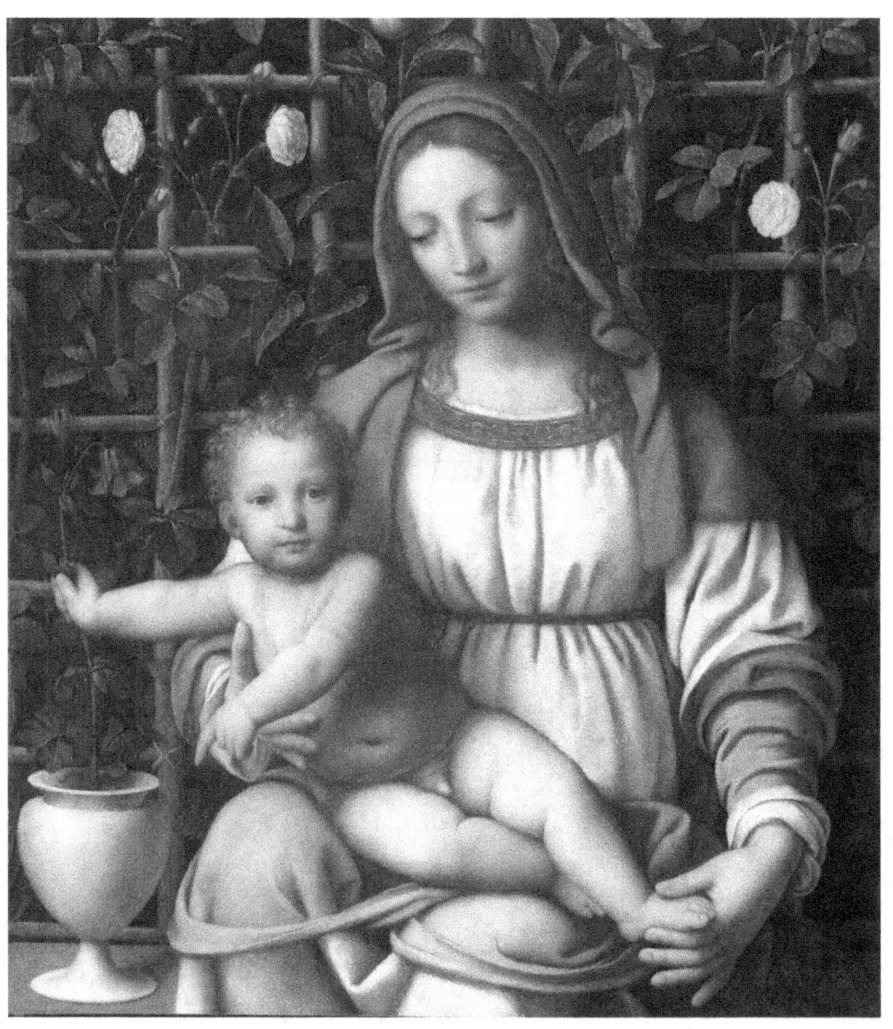

Bernardino Luini, Madonna and Child, Milan

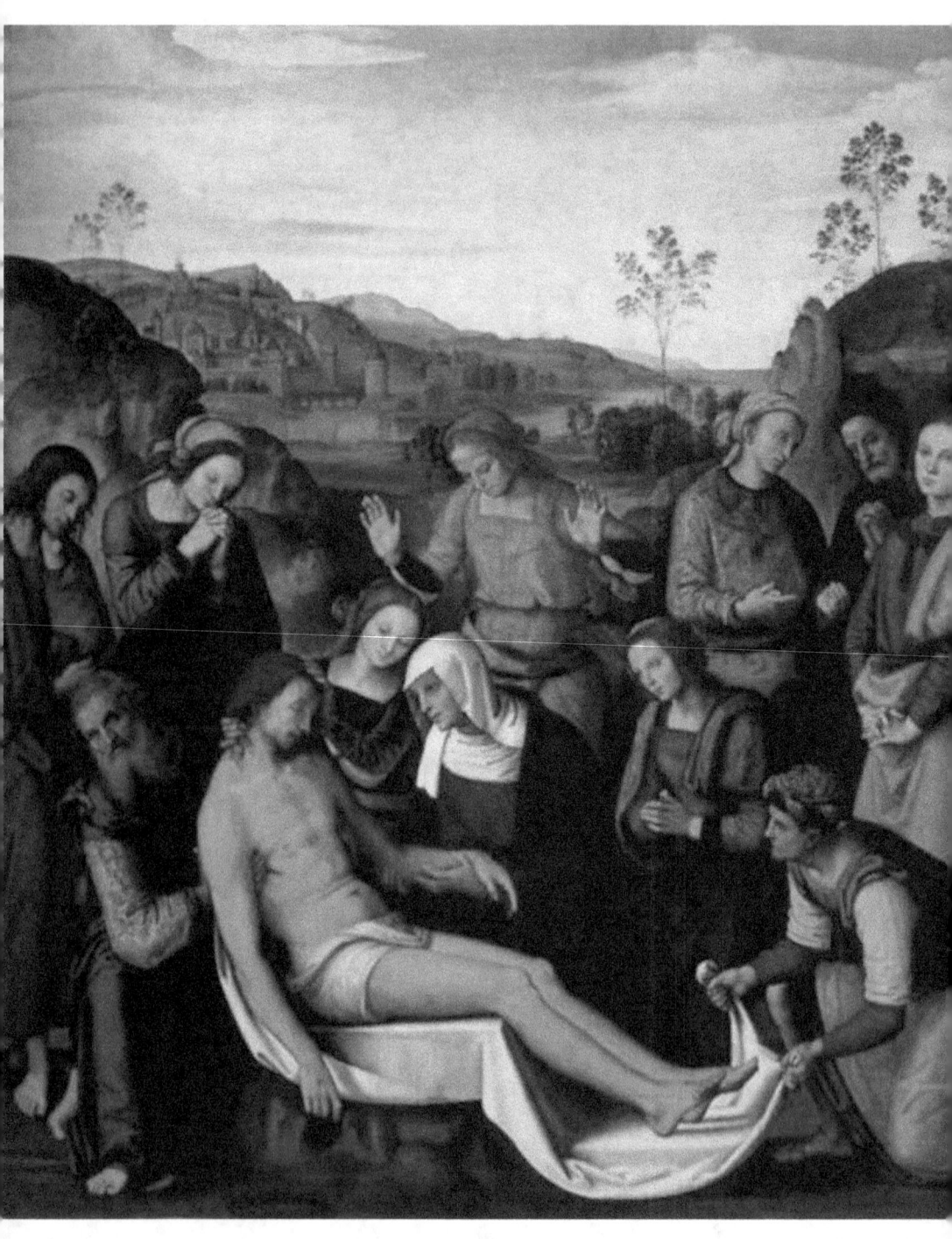

Perugino, The Mourning of the Dead Christ, 1495

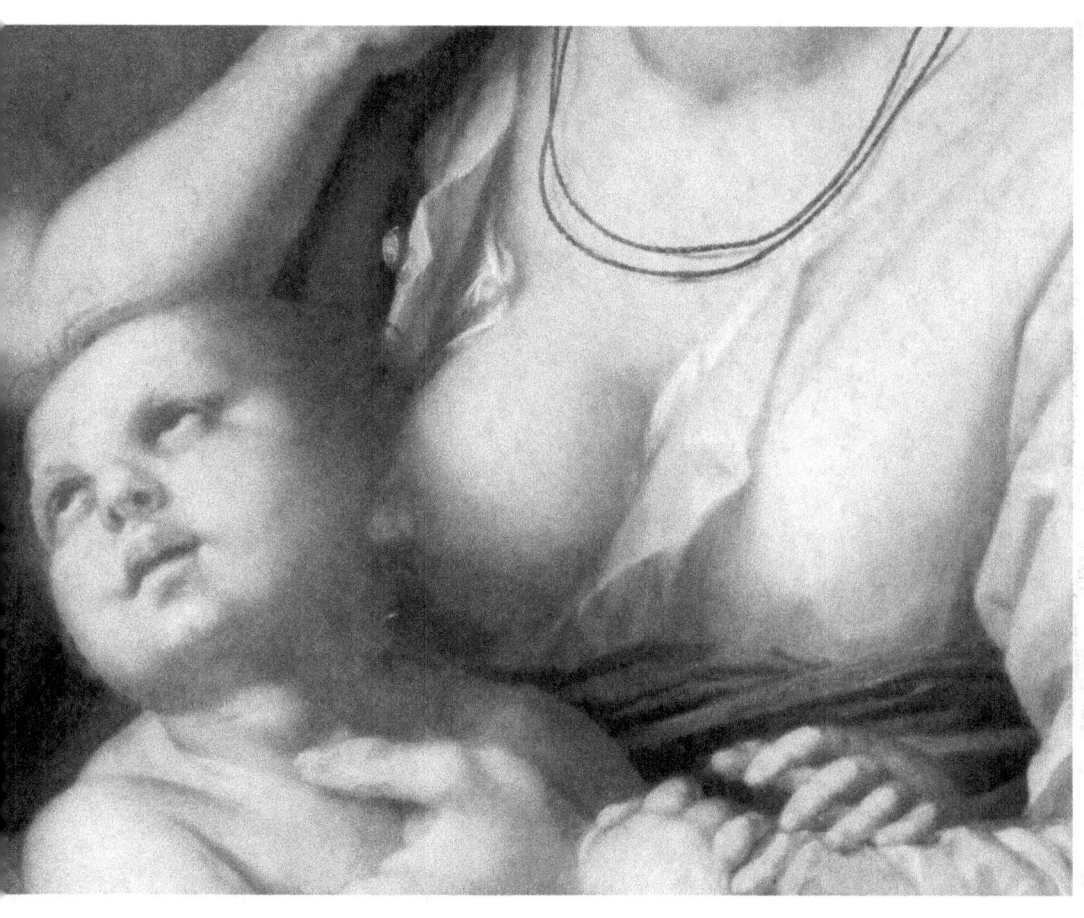

Andrea del Sarto, Madonna and Child, detail

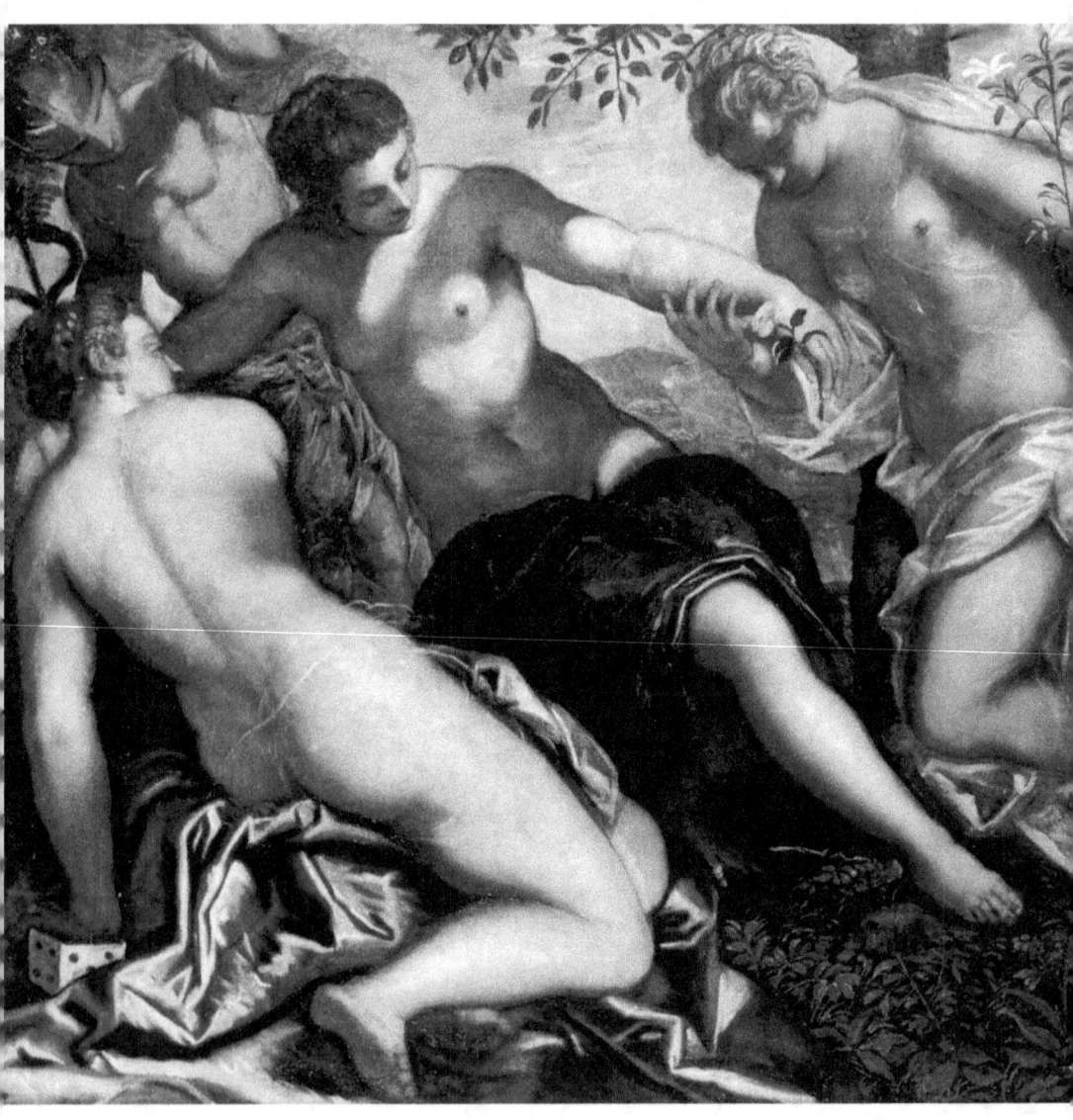

Jacopo Tintoretto, Mercury and the Graces, 1577

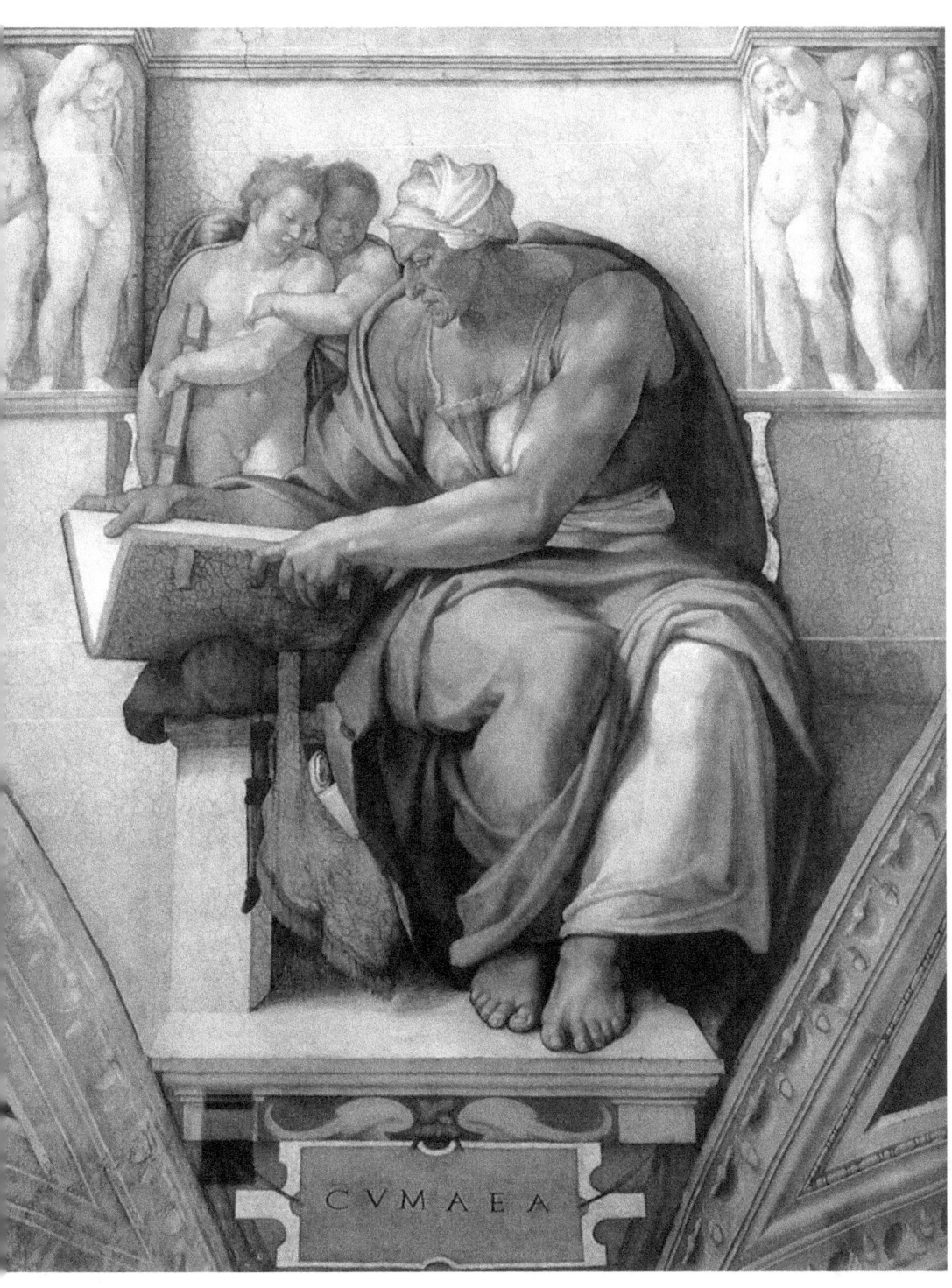

Michelangelo, Cumaean Sibyle, Sistine Chapel.

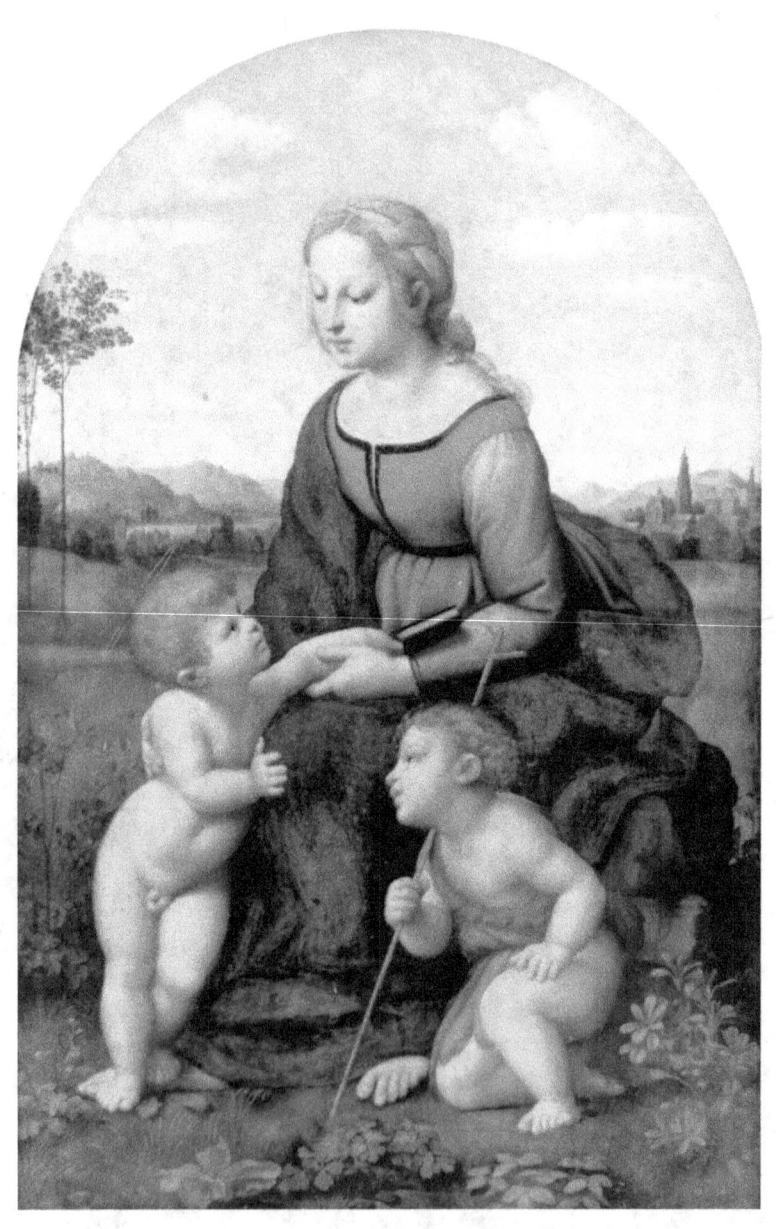

Raphael, La Belle Jardiniere, 1507, Louvre

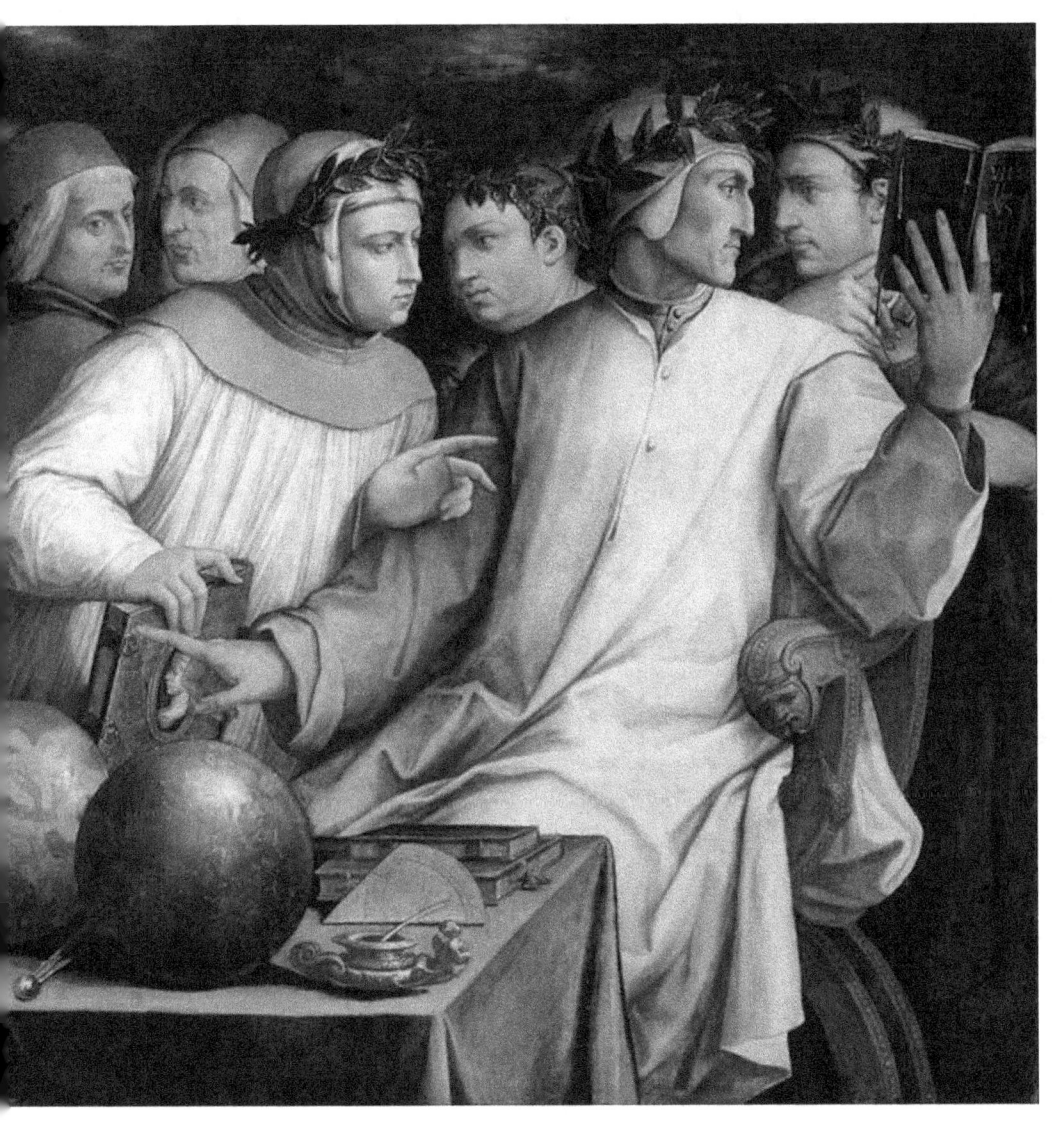

Giorgio Vasari, Six Tuscan Poets, 1544, Minneapolis

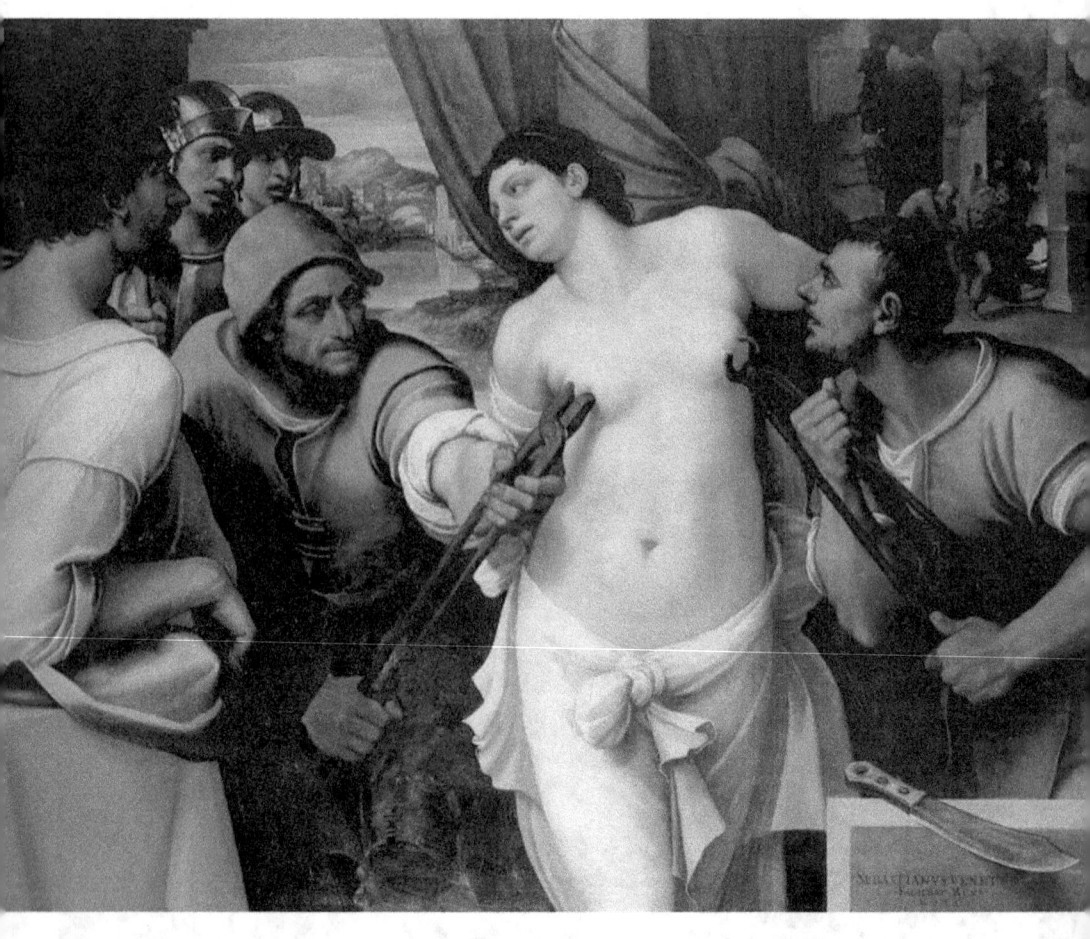

Sebastiano del Piombo, The Martyrdom of St Agatha, 1520,
Pitti Palace, Florence

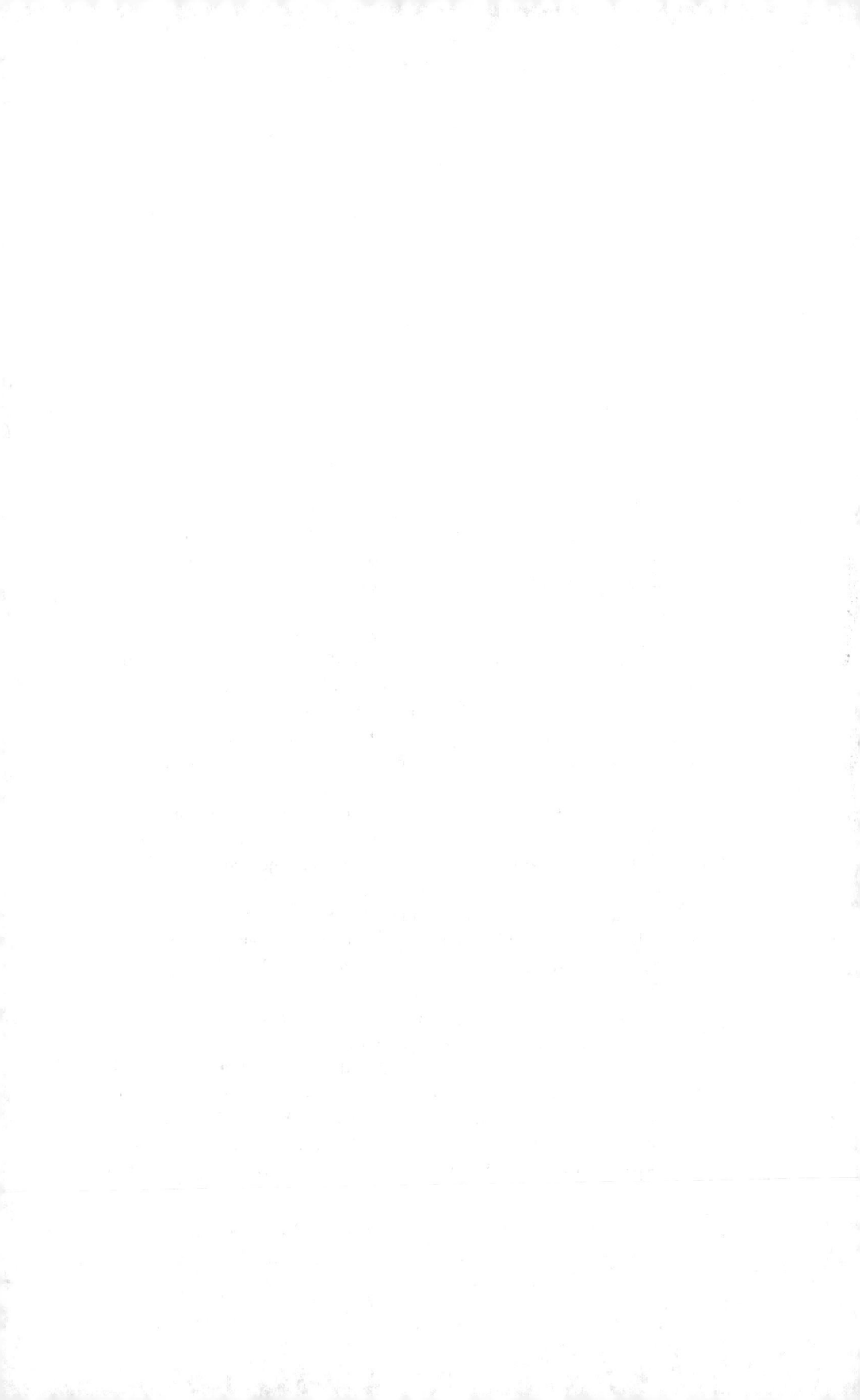

# NOTES

1. "The Earlier Work of Titian," *Portfolio*, October 1897.

2. According to the catalogue of 1892, this picture was formerly in the sacristy of the Escorial in Spain. It can only be by an oversight that it is therein described as "possibly painted there," since Titian never was in Spain.

3. It is especially to be noted that there is not a trace of red in the picture, save for the modest crimson waistband of the St. Catherine. Contrary to almost universal usage, it might almost be said to orthodoxy, the entire draperies of the Virgin are of one intense blue. Her veil-like head-gear is of a brownish gray, while the St. Catherine wears a golden-brown scarf, continuing the glories of her elaborately dressed hair. The audacity of the colour-scheme is only equalled by its success; no calculated effort at anything unusual being apparent. The beautiful naked *putto* who appears in the sky, arresting the progress of the shepherds, is too trivial in conception for the occasion. A similar incident is depicted in the background of the much earlier *Holy Family*, No. 4. at the National Gallery, but there the messenger angel is more appropriately and more reverently depicted as full-grown and in flowing garments.

4. Crowe and Cavalcaselle, vol. i. pp. 396, 397; *Tizian*, von H. Knackfuss, p. 55.

5. Crowe and Cavalcaselle, Appendix to vol. i. p. 448.

6. No. 1288 in the Long Gallery of the Louvre.

7. See the canvas No. 163 in the Imperial Gallery of Vienna. The want of life and of a definite personal character makes it almost repellent, notwithstanding the breadth and easy mastery of the technique. Rubens's copy of a lost or unidentified Titian, No. 845 in the same gallery, shows that he painted Isabella from life in mature middle age, and with a

truthfulness omitting no sign of over-ripeness. This portrait may very possibly have been done in 1522, when Titian appeared at the court of the Gonzagas. Its realism, even allowing for Rubens's unconscious exaggeration, might well have deterred the Gonzaga princess from being limned from life some twelve years later still.

8. Crowe and Cavalcaselle, vol. i., Appendix, p. 451.

9. The idea of painting St. Jerome by moonlight was not a new one. In the house at Venice of Andrea Odoni, the dilettante whose famous portrait by Lotto is at Hampton Court, the Anonimo (Marcantonio Michiel) saw, in 1532, "St. Jerome seated naked in a desert landscape by moonlight, by – – (sic), copied from a canvas by Zorzi da Castelfranco (Giorgione)."

10. See "The Picture Gallery of Charles I.," *The Portfolio*, January 1896, pp. 49 and 99.

11. The somewhat similar *Allegories* No. 173 and No. 187 in the Imperial Gallery at Vienna (New Catalogue, 1895), both classed as by Titian, cannot take rank as more than atelier works. Still farther from the master is the *Initiation of a Bacchante*, No. 1116 (Cat. 1891), in the Alte Pinakothek of Munich. This is a piece too cold and hard, too opaque, to have come even from his studio. It is a *pasticcio* made up in a curiously mechanical way, from the Louvre *Allegory* and the quite late *Education of Cupid* in the Borghese Gallery; the latter composition having been manifestly based by Titian himself, according to what became something like a custom in old age, upon the earlier *Allegory*.

12. A rather tiresome and lifeless portrait of Ippolito is that to be found in the picture No. 20 in the National Gallery, in which it has been assumed that his companion is his favourite painter, Sebastiano del Piombo, to whom the picture is, not without some misgivings, attributed.

13. It has been photographed under this name by Anderson of Rome.

14. In much the same position, since it hardly enjoys the celebrity to which it is entitled, is another masterpiece of portraiture from the brush of Titian, which, as belonging to his earlier middle time, should more properly have been mentioned in the first section of this monograph. This is the great *Portrait of a Man in Black*, No. 1591 in the Louvre. It shows a man of some forty years, of simple mien yet of indefinably tragic aspect; he wears moderately long hair, is clothed entirely in black, and rests his right hand on his hip, while passing the left through his belt. The dimensions of the canvas are more imposing than those of the *Jeune Homme au Gant*. No example in the Louvre, even though it competes with Madrid for the honour of possessing the greatest Titians in the world, is of finer quality than this picture. Near this – No. 1592 in the same great gallery – hangs another *Portrait of a Man in Black* by Titian, and belonging

to his middle time. The personage presented, though of high breeding, is cynical and repellent of aspect. The strong right hand rests quietly yet menacingly on a poniard, this attitude serving to give a peculiarly aggressive character to the whole conception. In the present state of this fine and striking picture the yellowness and want of transparency of the flesh-tones, both in the head and hands, gives rise to certain doubts as to the correctness of the ascription. Yet this peculiarity may well arise from injury; it would at any rate be hazardous to put forward any other name than that of Titian, to whom we must be content to leave the portrait.

15. This is the exceedingly mannered yet all the same rich and beautiful *St. Catherine, St. Roch, with a boy angel, and St. Sebastian.*

16. See Giorgione's *Adrastus and Hypsipyle (Landscape with the Soldier and the Gipsy)* of the Giovanelli Palace, the *Venus* of Dresden, the *Concert Champêtre* of the Louvre.

17. It is unnecessary in this connection to speak of the Darmstadt *Venus* invented by Crowe and Cavalcaselle, and to which as a type they so constantly refer. Giovanni Morelli has demonstrated with very general acceptance that this is only a late adaptation of the exquisite *Venus* of Dresden, which it is his greatest glory to have restored to Barbarelli and to the world.

18. *Die Galerien zu München und Dresden von Ivan Lermolieff,* p. 290.

19. Palma Vecchio, in his presentments of ripe Venetian beauty, was, we have seen, much more literal than Giorgione, more literal, too, less the poet-painter, than the young Titian. Yet in the great *Venus* of the Fitzwilliam Museum, Cambridge – not, indeed, in that of Dresden – his ideal is a higher one than Titian's in such pieces as the *Venus of Urbino* and the later *Venus*, its companion, in the Tribuna. The two Bonifazi of Verona followed Palma, giving, however, to the loveliness of their women not, indeed, a more exalted character, but a less pronounced sensuousness – an added refinement but a weaker personality. Paris Bordone took the note from Titian, but being less a great artist than a fine painter, descended a step lower in the scale. Paolo Veronese unaffectedly joys in the beauty of woman, in the sheen of fair flesh, without any under-current of deeper meaning. Tintoretto, though like his brother Venetians he delights in the rendering of the human form unveiled, is but little disquieted by the fascinating problem which now occupies us. He is by nature strangely spiritual, though he is far from indulging in any false idealisation, though he shrinks not at all from the statement of the truth as it presents itself to him. Let his famous pictures in the Anticollegio of the Doges' Palace, his *Muses* at Hampton Court, and above all that unique painted poem, *The Rescue,* in the Dresden Gallery, serve to support this

view of his art.

20. Crowe and Cavalcaselle, *Life of Titian*, vol. i. p. 420.

21. Two of these have survived in the *Roman Emperor on Horseback*, No. 257, and the similarly named picture, No. 290, at Hampton Court Palace. These panels were among the Mantua pieces purchased for Charles I. by Daniel Nys from Duke Vincenzo in 1628-29. If the Hampton Court pieces are indeed, as there appears no valid reason to doubt, two of the canvases mentioned by Vasari, we must assume that though they bore Giulio's name as *chef d'atelier*, he did little work on them himself. In the Mantuan catalogue contained in d'Arco's *Notizie* they were entered thus: – "Dieci altri quadri, dipintovi un imperatore per quadro a cavallo – opera di mano di Giulio Romano" (see *The Royal Gallery of Hampton Court*, by Ernest Law, 1898).

22. The late Charles Yriarte in a recent article, "Sabionneta la petite Athènes," published in the *Gazette des Beaux Arts*, March 1898, states that Bernardino Campi of Cremona, Giulio's subordinate at the moment, painted the Twelfth *Cæsar*, but adduces no evidence in support of this departure from the usual assumption.

23. See "The Picture Gallery of Charles I.," *The Portfolio*, October 1897, pp. 98, 99.

24. Nos. 529-540 – Catalogue of 1891 – Provincial Museum of Hanover. The dimensions are 0.19 *c.* by 0.15 *c.*

25. Of all Pordenone's exterior decorations executed in Venice nothing now remains. His only works of importance in the Venetian capital are the altar-piece in S. Giovanni Elemosinario already mentioned; the *San Lorenzo Giustiniani* altar-piece in the Accademia delle Belle Arti; the magnificent though in parts carelessly painted *Madonna del Carmelo* in the same gallery; the vast *St. Martin and St. Christopher* in the church of S. Rocco; the *Annunciation* of S. Maria degli Angeli at Murano.

26. No. 108 in the Winter Exhibition at Burlington House in 1896. By Franceschini is no doubt meant Paolo degli Franceschi, whose portrait Titian is known to have painted. He has been identified among the figures in the foreground of the *Presentation of the Virgin*.

27. See a very interesting article, "Vittore Carpaccio – La Scuola degli Albanesi," by Dr. Gustav Ludwig, in the *Archivio Storico dell' Arte* for November-December 1897.

28. A gigantic canvas of this order is, or rather was, the famous *Storm* of the Venetian Accademia, which has for many years past been dubitatively assigned to Giorgione. Vasari described it as by Palma Vecchio, stating that it was painted for the Scuola di S. Marco in the Piazza SS. Giovanni e Paolo, in rivalry with Gian Bellino(!) and

Mansueti, and referring to it in great detail and with a more fervent enthusiasm than he accords to any other Venetian picture. To the writer, judging from the parts of the original which have survived, it has long appeared that this may indeed be after all the right attribution. The ascription to Giorgione is mainly based on the romantic character of the invention, which certainly does not answer to anything that we know from the hand or brain of Palma. But then the learned men who helped Giorgione and Titian may well have helped him; and the structure of the thick-set figures in the foreground is absolutely his, as is also the sunset light on the horizon.

29. This is an arrangement analogous to that with the aid of which Tintoretto later on, in the *Crucifixion* of San Cassiano at Venice, attains to so sublime an effect. There the spears – not brandished but steadily held aloft in rigid and inflexible regularity – strangely heighten the solemn tragedy of the scene.

30. Crowe and Cavalcaselle, *Life of Titian*, vol. vi. p. 59.

31. The writer is unable to accept as a genuine design by Titian for the picture the well-known sepia drawing in the collection of the Uffizi. The composition is too clumsy in its mechanical repetition of parts, the action of the Virgin too awkward. The design looks more like an adaptation by some Bolognese eclectic.

32. This double portrait has not been preserved. According to Crowe and Cavalcaselle, the full length of Pier Luigi still exists in the Palazzo Reale at Naples (not seen by the writer).

33. The writer, who has studied in the originals all the other Titians mentioned in this monograph, has had as yet no opportunity of examining those in the Hermitage. He knows them only in the reproductions of Messrs. Braun, and in those new and admirable ones recently published by the Berlin Photographic Company.

34. This study from the life would appear to bear some such relation to the finished original as the *Innocent X.* of Velazquez at Apsley House bears to the great portrait of that Pope in the Doria Panfili collection.

35. This portrait-group belongs properly to the time a few years ahead, since it was undertaken during Titian's stay in Rome.

36. The imposing signature runs *Titianus Eques Ces. F. 1543.*

37. The type is not the nobler and more suave one seen in the *Cristo della Moneta* and the *Pilgrims of Emmaus*; it is the much less exalted one which is reproduced in the *Ecce Homo* of Madrid, and in the many repetitions and variations related to that picture, which cannot itself be accepted as an original from the hand of Titian.

38. Vasari saw a *Christ with Cleophas and Luke* by Titian, above the

door in the Salotta d'Oro, which precedes the Sala del Consiglio de' Dieci in the Doges' Palace, and states that it had been acquired by the patrician Alessandro Contarini and by him presented to the Signoria. The evidence of successive historians would appear to prove that it remained there until the close of last century. According to Crowe and Cavalcaselle the Louvre picture was a replica done for Mantua, which with the other Gonzaga pictures found its way into Charles I.'s collection, and thence, through that of Jabach, finally into the gallery of Louis XIV. At the sale of the royal collection by the Commonwealth it was appraised at £600. The picture bears the signature, unusual for this period, "Tician." There is another *Christ with the Pilgrims at Emmaus* in the collection of the Earl of Yarborough, signed "Titianus," in which, alike as to the figures, the scheme of colour, and the landscape, there are important variations. One point is of especial importance. Behind the figure of St. Luke in the Yarborough picture is a second pillar. This is not intended to appear in the Louvre picture; yet underneath the glow of the landscape there is just the shadow of such a pillar, giving evidence of a *pentimento* on the part of the master. This, so far as it goes, is evidence that the Louvre example was a revised version, and the Yarborough picture a repetition or adaptation of the first original seen by Vasari. However this may be, there can be no manner of doubt that the picture in the Long Gallery of the Louvre is an original entirely from the hand of Titian, while Lord Yarborough's picture shows nothing of his touch and little even of the manner of his studio at the time.

39. Purchased at the sale of Charles I.'s collection by Alonso de Cardenas for Philip IV. at the price of £165.

40. Crowe and Cavalcaselle, *Life of Titian*, vol. ii., Appendix (p. 502).

41. Moritz Thausing has striven in his *Wiener Kunstbriefe* to show that the coat of arms on the marble bas-relief in the *Sacred and Profane Love* is that of the well-known Nuremberg house of Imhof. This interpretation has, however, been controverted by Herz Franz Wickhoff.

42. Cesare Vecellio must have been very young at this time. The costume-book, *Degli abiti antichi e moderni*, to which he owes his chief fame, was published at Venice in 1590.

43. "Das Tizianbildniss der königlichen Galerie zu Cassel," *Jahrbuch der königlich-preussischen Kunstsammlungen*, Funfzehnter Band, III. Heft.

44. See the *Francesco Maria, Duke of Urbino* at the Uffizi; also, for the modish headpiece, the *Ippolito de' Medici* at the Pitti.

45. A number of fine portraits must of necessity be passed over in these remarks. The superb if not very well-preserved *Antonio Portia*, within the last few years added to the Brera, dates back a good many years from this time. Then we have, among other things, the *Benedetto*

*Varchi* and the *Fabrizio Salvaresio* of the Imperial Museum at Vienna – the latter bearing the date 1558. The writer is unable to accept as a genuine Titian the interesting but rather matter-of-fact *Portrait of a Lady in Mourning*, No. 174 in the Dresden Gallery. The master never painted with such a lack of charm and distinction. Very doubtful, but difficult to judge in its present state, is the *Portrait of a Lady with a Vase*, No. 173 in the same collection. Morelli accepts as a genuine example of the master the *Portrait of a Lady in a Red Dress* also in the Dresden Gallery, where it bears the number 176. If the picture is his, as the technical execution would lead the observer to believe, it constitutes in its stiffness and unambitious *naïveté* a curious exception in his long series of portraits.

46. It is impossible to discuss here the atelier repetitions in the collections of the National Gallery and Lord Wemyss respectively, or the numerous copies to be found in other places.

47. For the full text of the marriage contract see Giovanni Morelli, *Die Galerien zu München und Dresden*, pp. 300-302.

48. Joshua Reynolds, who saw it during his tour in Italy, says: "It is so dark a picture that, at first casting my eyes on it, I thought there was a black curtain before it."

49. Crowe and Cavalcaselle, vol. ii. p. 272.

50. They were, with the *Rape of Europa*, among the so-called "light pieces" presented to Prince Charles by Philip IV., and packed for transmission to England. On the collapse of the marriage negotiations they were, however, kept back. Later on Philip V. presented them to the Marquis de Grammont. They subsequently formed part of the Orleans Gallery, and were acquired at the great sale in London by the Duke of Bridgewater for £2500 apiece.

51. This great piece is painted on a canvas of peculiarly coarse grain, with a well-defined lozenge pattern. It was once owned by Van Dyck, at the sale of whose possessions, in 1556, a good number of years after his death, it was acquired by Algernon Percy, Earl of Northumberland. In 1873 it was in the exhibition of Old Masters at the Royal Academy.

52. The best repetition of this Hermitage *Magdalen* is that in the Naples Museum; another was formerly in the Ashburton Collection, and yet another is in the Durazzo Gallery at Genoa. The similar, but not identical, picture in the Yarborough Collection is anything but "cold in tone," as Crowe and Cavalcaselle call it. It is, on the contrary, rich in colour, but as to the head of the saint, much less attractive than the original.

53. This picture was presented by Philip IV. to Prince Charles of England, and was, at the sale of his collection, acquired by Jabach for

£600, and from him bought by Cardinal Mazarin, whose heirs sold it to Louis XIV. The Cardinal thus possessed the two finest representations of the *Jupiter and Antiope* legend – that by Correggio (also now in the Louvre) and the Titian. It was to these pictures especially that his touching farewell was addressed a few hours before his death.

54. See Crowe and Cavalcaselle, vol. ii., Appendix, p. 340.

55. See as to the vicissitudes through which the picture has passed an article, "Les Restaurations du tableau du Titien, *Jupiter et Antiope*" by Fernand Engerand, in the *Chronique des Arts* of 7th May 1898.

56. This picture came to England with the Orleans Gallery, and was until lately at Cobham Hall in the collection of the Earl of Darnley. It has now passed into that of Mrs J.L. Gardner of Boston, U.S. It is represented in the Prado Gallery by Rubens's superb copy. A Venetian copy on a very small scale exists in the Wallace Collection.

57. A very clever adaptation of this work is No. 490 in the Prado Gallery under the name of the master. It is remarkable for the contrast between the moonlight which irradiates the Christ and the artificial light supplied by the lantern carried by one of the soldiers.

58. This picture is mentioned in the list of 1574 furnished by Titian to Secretary Antonio Perez. A *Perseus and Andromeda* by, or attributed to, Titian was in the Orleans Gallery. Is this the canvas now in the Wallace Collection, but not as yet publicly exhibited there? This last piece was undoubtedly produced in the *entourage* and with the assistance of Titian, and it corresponds perfectly to Vasari's description of the *Deliverance of Andromeda*. It has the loose easy touch of the late time, but obscured as it at present is by dirt and successive coats of now discoloured varnish, no more definite opinion with regard to its merits can be given. No. 135 in the Hermitage is a canvas identical in subject and dimensions with this last-named picture. It was once attributed to Tintoretto, but is now put down to the school of Titian.

59. Somewhat earlier in the order of the late works should come in, if we may venture to judge from the technique of a work that is practically a ruin, the *Adam and Eve* of the Prado, in which, for the usual serpent with the human head of the feminine type, Titian has substituted as tempter an insignificant *amorino*. Far more enjoyable than this original in its present state is the magnificent copy, with slight yet marked variations, left behind by Rubens. This is also to be found in the Prado. A drawing by the great Antwerper from Titian's picture is in the Louvre. This is more markedly Flemish in aspect than the painted canvas, and lacks the foolish little Love.

60. Formerly in the collection of the Earl of Dudley, upon the sale of

which it was acquired by Mr. Ludwig Mond. It was in the Venetian exhibition at the New Gallery. There is an engraving of it by Pieter de Jode, jun.

61. This is No. 186 in the catalogue of 1895. An etching of the picture appeared with an article "Les Écoles d'Italie au Musée de Vienne," from the pen of Herr Franz Wickhoff, in the *Gazette des Beaux Arts* for February 1893. It was badly engraved for the Teniers Gallery by Lissebetius.

62. Now in the Accademia delle Belle Arti of Venice.

63. It was the intention of the writer to add to this monograph a short chapter on the drawings of Titian. The subject is, however, far too vast for such summary treatment, and its discussion must therefore be postponed. Leaving out of the question the very numerous drawings by Domenico Campagnola which Morelli has once for all separated from those of the greater master, and those also which, while belonging to the same class and period, are neither Titian's nor even Campagnola's, a few of the genuine landscapes may be just lightly touched upon. The beautiful early landscape with a battlemented castle, now or lately in the possession of Mr. T.W. Russell (reproduction in the British Museum marked 1879-5-10-224) is in the opinion of the writer a genuine Titian. *The Vision of St. Eustace*, reproduced in the first section of this monograph ("The Earlier Work of Titian") from the original in the British Museum, is a noble and pathetic example of the earlier manner. Perhaps the most beautiful of the landscape drawings still preserving something of the Giorgionesque aroma is that with the enigmatic female figure, entirely nude but with the head veiled, and the shepherds sheltering from the noonday sun, which is in the great collection at Chatsworth (No. 318 in Venetian Exhibition at New Gallery). Later than this is the fine landscape in the same collection with a riderless horse crossing a stream (No. 867 in Venetian Exhibition at New Gallery). The well-known *St. Jerome* here given (British Museum) is ascribed by no less an authority than Giovanni Morelli to the master, but the poor quality of the little round trees, and of the background generally, is calculated to give pause to the student. A good example of the later style, in which the technique is more that of the painter and less that of the draughtsman, is the so-called *Landscape with the Pedlar* at Chatsworth. But, faded though it is, the finest extant drawing of the later period is that here (p. 78) for the first time reproduced by the kind permission of the owner, Professor Legros, who had the great good fortune and good taste to discover it in a London bookshop. There can be no doubt that this ought to be in the Print Room at the British Museum. A good instance, on the other hand, of a drawing which cannot without demur be left to Titian, though it is a good deal too late in style for Domenico

Campagnola, and moreover, much too fine and sincere for that clever, facile adapter of other people's work, is the beautiful pastoral in the Albertina at Vienna (B. 283), with the shepherd piping as he leads his flock homewards.

# CRESCENT MOON PUBLISHING

web: www.crmoon.com e-mail: cresmopub@yahoo.co.uk

## ARTS, PAINTING, SCULPTURE

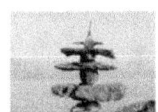
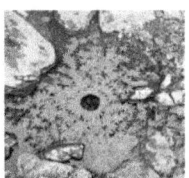
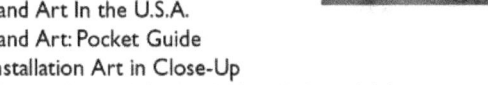
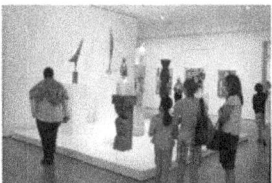
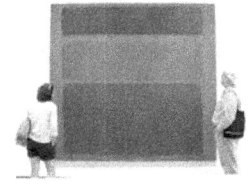

The Art of Andy Goldsworthy
Andy Goldsworthy: Touching Nature
Andy Goldsworthy in Close-Up
Andy Goldsworthy: Pocket Guide
Andy Goldsworthy In America
Land Art: A Complete Guide
The Art of Richard Long
Richard Long: Pocket Guide
Land Art In the UK
Land Art in Close-Up
Land Art In the U.S.A.
Land Art: Pocket Guide
Installation Art in Close-Up
Minimal Art and Artists In the 1960s and After
Colourfield Painting
Land Art DVD, TV documentary
Andy Goldsworthy DVD, TV documentary
The Erotic Object: Sexuality in Sculpture From Prehistory to the Present Day
Sex in Art: Pornography and Pleasure in Painting and Sculpture
Postwar Art
Sacred Gardens: The Garden in Myth, Religion and Art
Glorification: Religious Abstraction in Renaissance and 20th Century Art
Early Netherlandish Painting

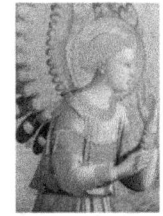

Leonardo da Vinci
Piero della Francesca
Giovanni Bellini
Fra Angelico: Art and Religion in the Renaissance
Mark Rothko: The Art of Transcendence
Frank Stella: American Abstract Artist
Jasper Johns
Brice Marden
Alison Wilding: The Embrace of Sculpture
Vincent van Gogh: Visionary Landscapes
Eric Gill: Nuptials of God
Constantin Brancusi: Sculpting the Essence of Things
Max Beckmann
Caravaggio
Gustave Moreau
Egon Schiele: Sex and Death In Purple Stockings
Delizioso Fotografico Fervore: Works In Process 1
Sacro Cuore: Works In Process 2
The Light Eternal: J.M.W. Turner
The Madonna Glorified: Karen Arthurs

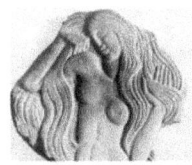
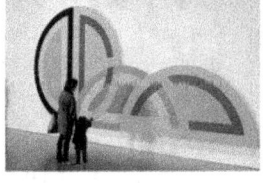
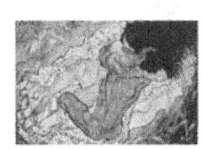
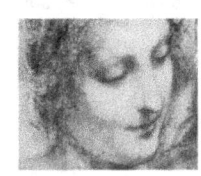
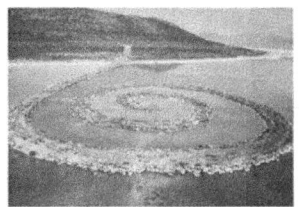

# LITERATURE

J.R.R. Tolkien: The Books, The Films, The Whole Cultural Phenomenon
J.R.R. Tolkien: Pocket Guide
Tolkien's Heroic Quest
The *Earthsea* Books of Ursula Le Guin
Beauties, Beasts and Enchantment: Classic French Fairy Tales
German Popular Stories by the Brothers Grimm
Philip Pullman and *His Dark Materials*
Sexing Hardy: Thomas Hardy and Feminism
Thomas Hardy's *Tess of the d'Urbervilles*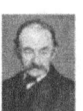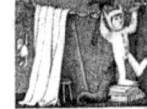
Thomas Hardy's *Jude the Obscure*
Thomas Hardy: The Tragic Novels
Love and Tragedy: Thomas Hardy
The Poetry of Landscape in Hardy
Wessex Revisited: Thomas Hardy and John Cowper Powys
Wolfgang Iser: Essays and Interviews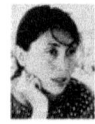
Petrarch, Dante and the Troubadours
Maurice Sendak and the Art of Children's Book Illustration
Andrea Dworkin
Cixous, Irigaray, Kristeva: The *Jouissance* of French Feminism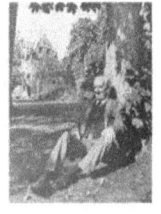
Julia Kristeva: Art, Love, Melancholy, Philosophy, Semiotics and Psychoanalysis
Hélène Cixous I Love You: The *Jouissance* of Writing
Luce Irigaray: Lips, Kissing, and the Politics of Sexual Difference
Peter Redgrove: Here Comes the Flood
Peter Redgrove: Sex-Magic-Poetry-Cornwall
Lawrence Durrell: Between Love and Death, East and West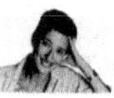
Love, Culture & Poetry: Lawrence Durrell
Cavafy: Anatomy of a Soul
German Romantic Poetry: Goethe, Novalis, Heine, Hölderlin
Feminism and Shakespeare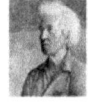
Shakespeare: Love, Poetry & Magic
The Passion of D.H. Lawrence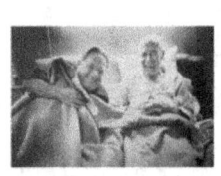
D.H. Lawrence: Symbolic Landscapes
D.H. Lawrence: Infinite Sensual Violence
Rimbaud: Arthur Rimbaud and the Magic of Poetry
The Ecstasies of John Cowper Powys
Sensualism and Mythology: The Wessex Novels of John Cowper Powys
Amorous Life: John Cowper Powys and the Manifestation of Affectivity  (H.W. Fawkner)
Postmodern Powys: New Essays on John Cowper Powys (Joe Boulter)
Rethinking Powys: Critical Essays on John Cowper Powys
Paul Bowles & Bernardo Bertolucci
Rainer Maria Rilke
Joseph Conrad: *Heart of Darkness*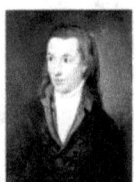
In the Dim Void: Samuel Beckett
Samuel Beckett Goes into the Silence
André Gide: Fiction and Fervour
Jackie Collins and the Blockbuster Novel
Blinded By Her Light: The Love-Poetry of Robert Graves
The Passion of Colours: Travels In Mediterranean Lands
Poetic Forms

## POETRY

Ursula Le Guin: Walking In Cornwall
Peter Redgrove: Here Comes The Flood
Peter Redgrove: Sex-Magic-Poetry-Cornwall
Dante: Selections From the Vita Nuova
Petrarch, Dante and the Troubadours
William Shakespeare: Sonnets
William Shakespeare: Complete Poems
Blinded By Her Light: The Love-Poetry of Robert Graves
Emily Dickinson: Selected Poems
Emily Brontë: Poems
Thomas Hardy: Selected Poems
Percy Bysshe Shelley: Poems
John Keats: Selected Poems
Joh n Keats: Poems of 1820
D.H. Lawrence: Selected Poems
Edmund Spenser: Poems
Edmund Spenser: Amoretti
John Donne: Poems
Henry Vaughan: Poems
Sir Thomas Wyatt: Poems
Robert Herrick: Selected Poems
Rilke: Space, Essence and Angels in the Poetry of Rainer Maria Rilke
Rainer Maria Rilke: Selected Poems
Friedrich Hölderlin: Selected Poems
Arseny Tarkovsky: Selected Poems
Arthur Rimbaud: Selected Poems
Arthur Rimbaud: A Season in Hell
Arthur Rimbaud and the Magic of Poetry
Novalis: Hymns To the Night
German Romantic Poetry
Paul Verlaine: Selected Poems
Elizaethan Sonnet Cycles
D.J. Enright: By-Blows
Jeremy Reed: Brigitte's Blue Heart
Jeremy Reed: Claudia Schiffer's Red Shoes
Gorgeous Little Orpheus
Radiance: New Poems
Crescent Moon Book of Nature Poetry
Crescent Moon Book of Love Poetry
Crescent Moon Book of Mystical Poetry
Crescent Moon Book of Elizabethan Love Poetry
Crescent Moon Book of Metaphysical Poetry
Crescent Moon Book of Romantic Poetry
Pagan America: New American Poetry

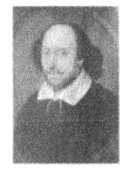
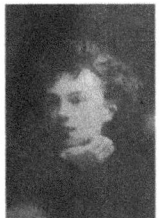
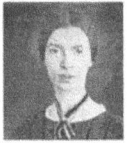
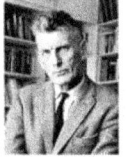
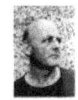
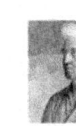
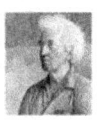
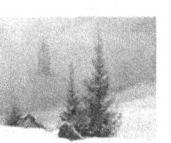
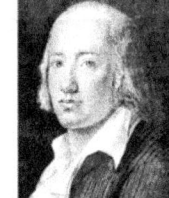
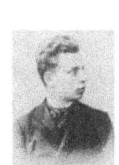
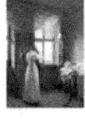
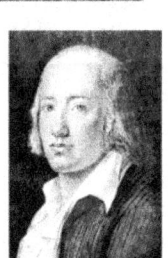

## MEDIA, CINEMA, FEMINISM and CULTURAL STUDIES

J.R.R. Tolkien: The Books, The Films, The Whole Cultural Phenomenon
J.R.R. Tolkien: Pocket Guide
The *Lord of the Rings* Movies: Pocket Guide
The Cinema of Hayao Miyazaki
Hayao Miyazaki: *Princess Mononoke*: Pocket Movie Guide
Hayao Miyazaki: *Spirited Away*: Pocket Movie Guide
Tim Burton : Hallowe'en For Hollywood
Ken Russell
Ken Russell: *Tommy*: Pocket Movie Guide
The Ghost Dance: The Origins of Religion
The Peyote Cult
Cixous, Irigaray, Kristeva: The *Jouissance* of French Feminism
Julia Kristeva: Art, Love, Melancholy, Philosophy, Semiotics and Psychoanalysis
Luce Irigaray: Lips, Kissing, and the Politics of Sexual Difference
Hélène Cixous I Love You: The *Jouissance* of Writing
Andrea Dworkin
'Cosmo Woman': The World of Women's Magazines
Women in Pop Music
HomeGround: The Kate Bush Anthology
Discovering the Goddess (Geoffrey Ashe)
The Poetry of Cinema
The Sacred Cinema of Andrei Tarkovsky
Andrei Tarkovsky: Pocket Guide
Andrei Tarkovsky: *Mirror*: Pocket Movie Guide
Andrei Tarkovsky: *The Sacrifice*: Pocket Movie Guide
Walerian Borowczyk: Cinema of Erotic Dreams
Jean-Luc Godard: The Passion of Cinema
Jean-Luc Godard: *Hail Mary*: Pocket Movie Guide
Jean-Luc Godard: *Contempt*: Pocket Movie Guide
Jean-Luc Godard: *Pierrot le Fou*: Pocket Movie Guide
John Hughes and Eighties Cinema
*Ferris Bueller's Day Off*: Pocket Movie Guide
Jean-Luc Godard: Pocket Guide
The Cinema of Richard Linklater
Liv Tyler: Star In Ascendance
*Blade Runner* and the Films of Philip K. Dick
Paul Bowles and Bernardo Bertolucci
Media Hell: Radio, TV and the Press
An Open Letter to the BBC
Detonation Britain: Nuclear War in the UK
Feminism and Shakespeare
Wild Zones: Pornography, Art and Feminism
Sex in Art: Pornography and Pleasure in Painting and Sculpture
Sexing Hardy: Thomas Hardy and Feminism

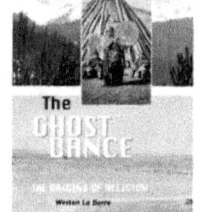
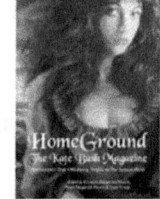
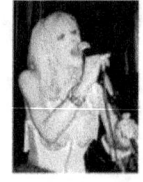
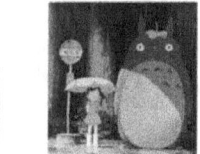
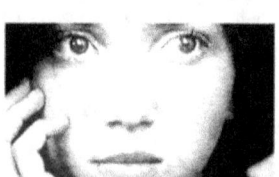

*The Light Eternal* is a model monograph, an exemplary job. The subject matter of the book is beautifully
organised and dead on beam. (Lawrence Durrell)
It is amazing for me to see my work treated with such passion and respect. (Andrea Dworkin)

CRESCENT MOON PUBLISHING
P.O. Box 1312, Maidstone, Kent, ME14 5XU, Great Britain. www.crmoon.com

cresmopub@yahoo.co.uk   www.crescentmoon.org.uk

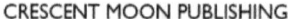

www.ingramcontent.com/pod-product-compliance
Lightning Source LLC
Chambersburg PA
CBHW051306220526
45468CB00004B/1227